Voices of America

Brattleboro Remembers

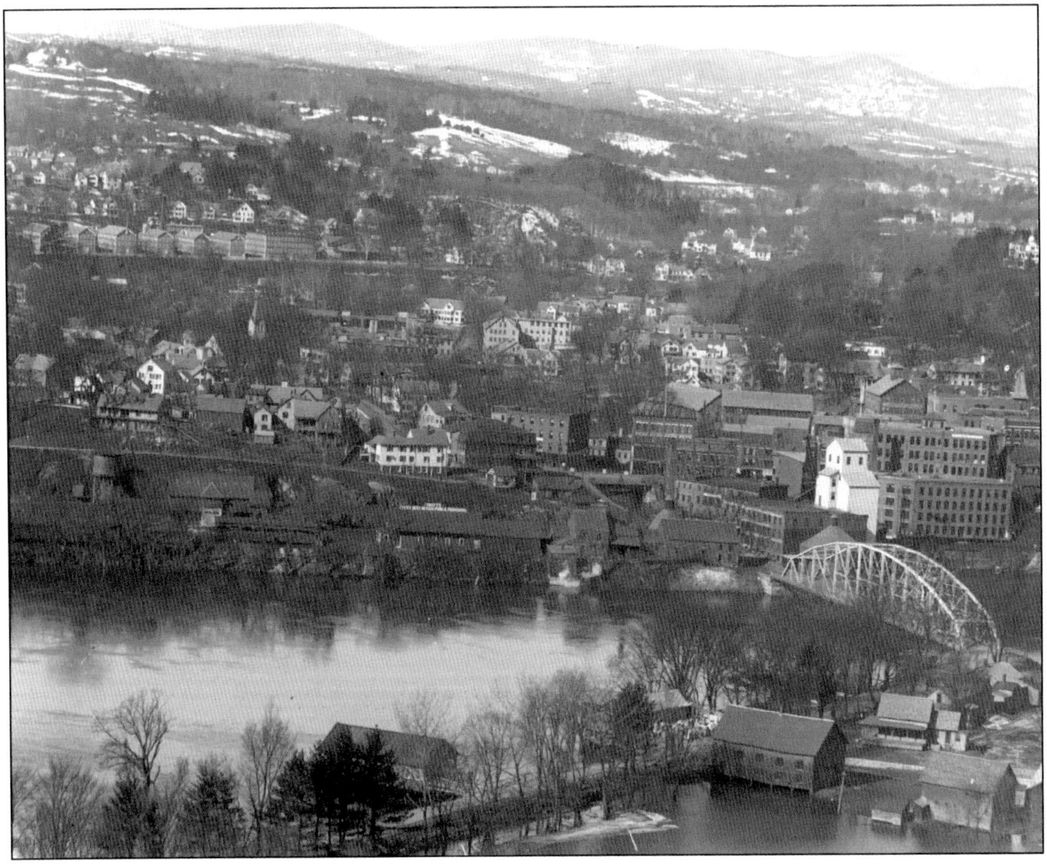

Through the years, many photographs of Brattleboro have been taken from Wantastiquet Mountain, across the Connecticut River in New Hampshire. This view, dating from the period from 1903 to 1911, features some of the same landmarks that would appear in a 2001 photograph. The railroad tracks still parallel the river through town. The gasworks building remains on the left as one crosses the bridge from the island. The prominent Estey Organ Company buildings stand in a row along Birge Street. At the far right, the former Methodist church has been adapted for commercial use. Although high water does not pose the severe threat it once did, the effects of spring runoff, as shown in this early photograph, still command caution and respect as the river approaches flood stage and the current flows more strongly toward the sea.

On the cover: *Having some winter fun on the Connecticut River are Harriet Melton (right), Marguerite (White) Stockwell (second from right), and three of their friends.*

Voices of America

Brattleboro Remembers

Compiled by

Brattleboro Historical Society

ARCADIA
PUBLISHING

ISBN 978-0-7385-0872-6

Published by Arcadia Publishing
Charleston, South Carolina

Printed in the United States of America

Library of Congress Catalog Card Number: 2001093678

For all general information contact Arcadia Publishing at:
Telephone 843-853-2070
Fax 843-853-0044
E-Mail sales@arcadiapublishing.com
For customer service and orders:
Toll-Free 1-888-313-2665

Visit us on the Internet at www.arcadiapublishing.com

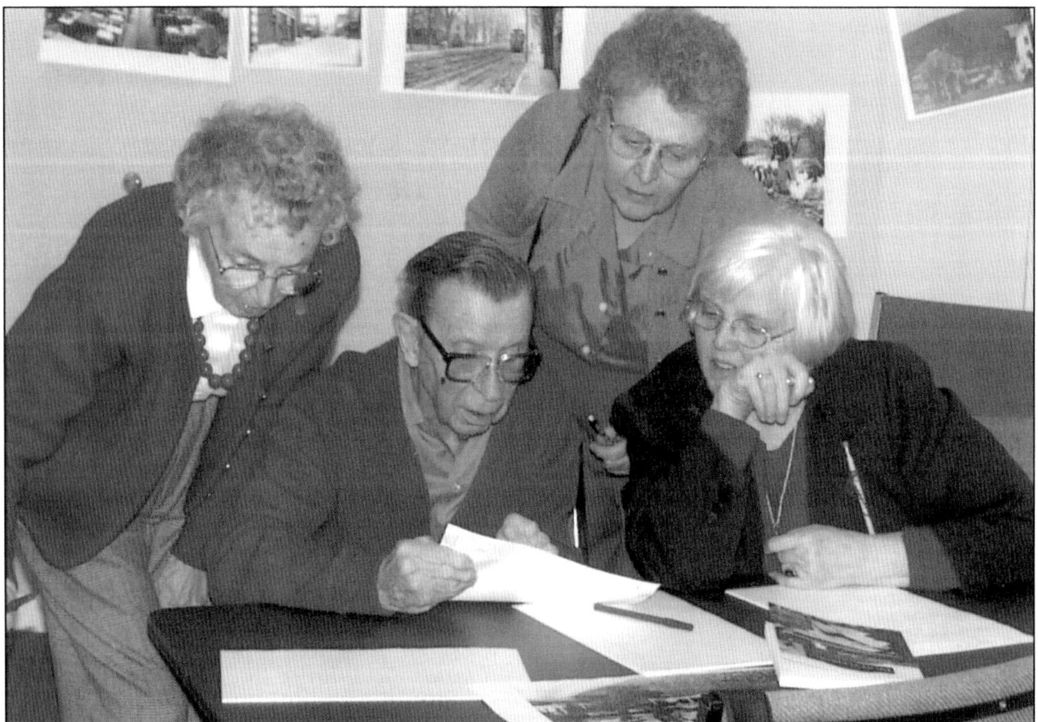

Let the memories return. Dot Milkey and Hazel Anderson look on as Ed Milkey points out a detail he recalls in a historical photograph. Gloria Klein, serving as a writing workshop scribe, listens intently to Milkey's comments before noting them down.

CONTENTS

ACKNOWLEDGMENTS

Appreciation is given to the Council on Aging for Southeastern Vermont for the grant that made this project possible.

Other contributors include Brattleboro Savings and Loan, PhotoArk Digital Archiving, and Boardrush Media.

Credit is also given to the following photographers: Hayes Bigelow, Benjamin Crown, Lewis Brown, Robert George, Jeff Barry, Mary Lou Buchanan, C.L. Howe, and George Clapp, whose photographs served as the writing prompts.

Photographs from the Anderson family, Brattleboro Reformer, Brattleboro High School-Brattleboro Union High School Alumni Association, Constantine M. Broutsas, Marguerite Douglas, and Richard Michelman were included.

Gratitude is extended to the following scribes: c.j. king, Robert Tortolani, Joann Nichols, Gloria Klein, Cheryl Wilfong, Verandah Porche, Jeff Nugent, Sarah Edwards, Wayne Carhart, and Cynthia Shelton.

Special recognition goes to the editors: Hazel Anderson, Mary Lou Buchanan, Wayne Carhart, and Douglas Goertzen.

Introduction

Much of a community's history is held in the minds of its citizens. Yes, there is the "official" history documented by land deeds, birth, marriage, and death records, and other documents with official seals, but the personal memories of the day-to-day happenings give the community its character. Such is the case with Brattleboro.

The Brattleboro Historical Society is fortunate to have a large and high-quality historical photograph collection, owing to the fact that in the early days of photography, during the last half of the 1800s, there were many photographic studios operating in Brattleboro. Many of these images have remained in the area and have found their way to the historical society thanks to the efforts of contemporary photographers and local historians.

When these photographs are displayed by the historical society in the newspaper or at events, they ignite memories followed by conversation. Such an event occurred in the summer of 2000, when the Vermont Council on Aging asked the Brattleboro Historical Society to conduct a walking tour of Brattleboro's downtown buildings. The group met at the historical society's offices and was given a chance to look at some of the historical photos of the buildings that the group was to see on the tour. The group never left the offices because everyone became so caught up in relating stories to each other about a memory that a photographic image brought to mind. The idea for this book was conceived at that gathering.

Fact-checking services were provided by the Brattleboro Historical Society to insure accuracy of information. Professional copyediting services were used for grammar and spelling; however, the stories told are those of the authors, in their own voices. More than 100 photographs were used for this project, and this book is the result of the storytellers looking at the historical photos of their community and sharing their reminiscences.

Chapter One
Downtown Ventures

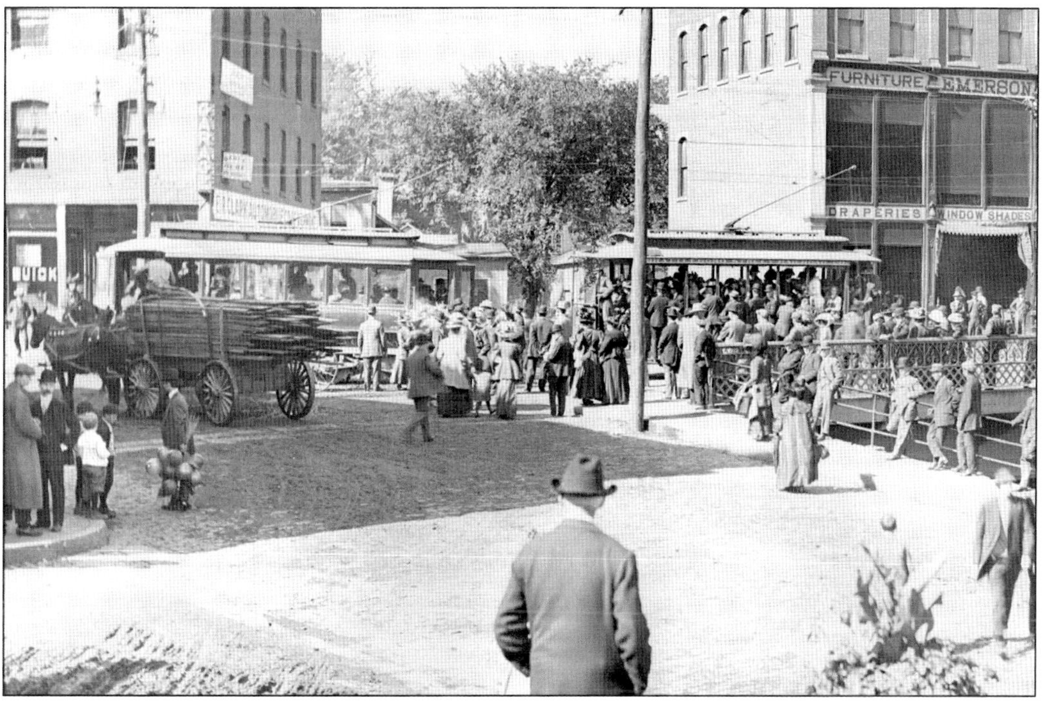

Lower Main Street has always presented traffic challenges. In this early-20th-century photograph, a crowd of people boarding the trolley occupies the entire street. Some of them may have come from the nearby railroad station or the Brattleboro House and are on their way to the Valley Fair at the southern end of town. The team of horses pulling the lumber wagon foreshadows a traffic problem of later years: the maneuvering of lengthy trailer trucks through the intersection. Automobiles were soon to be added to the transportation mix, as indicated by the Buick dealership next to the bridge. Although Emerson Furniture moved from Main Street, it is still doing business today at its Elliot Street location.

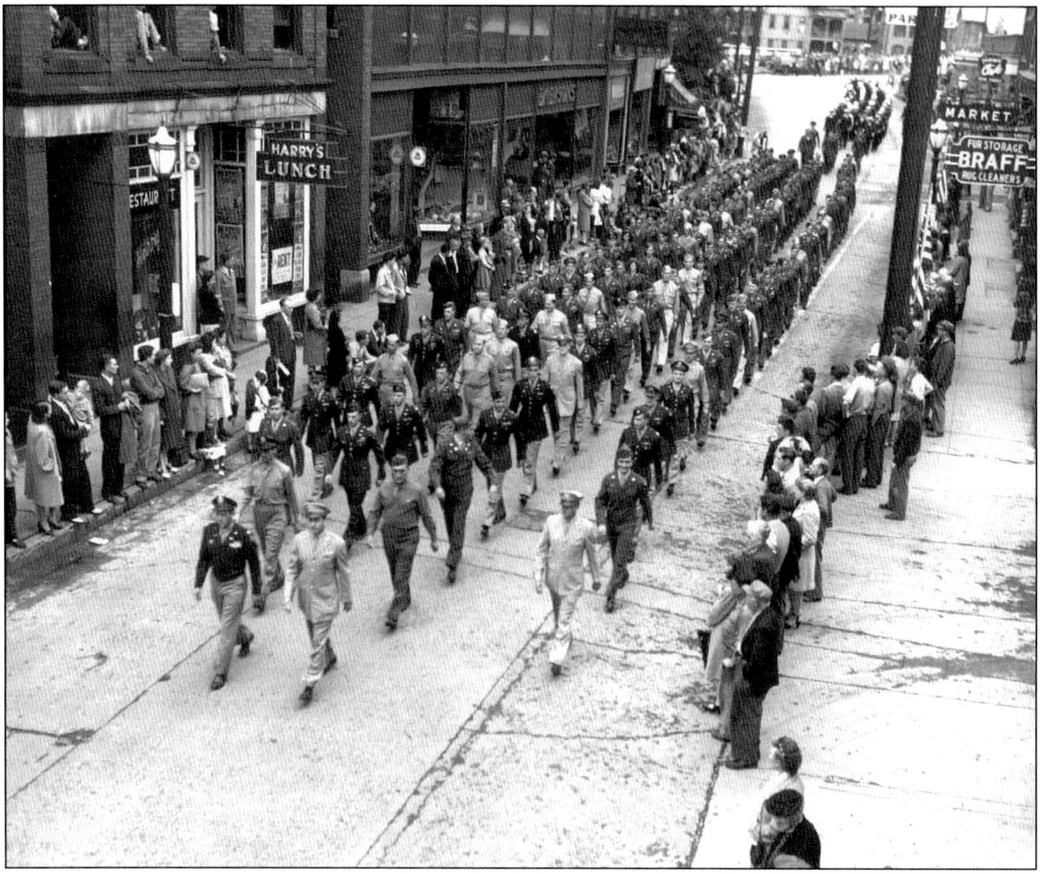

This August 14, 1946 photograph shows the first anniversary parade of VJ Day on Elliot Street.

Returning World War II Veterans

I marched. I know I'm in here. I was the shortest.

I got out June 30, 1945, because I had 91 points. I had flown 40 missions in the Pacific against the Japanese. I was the second guy in Brattleboro to get discharged. I flew in the B-24 as a gunner, a top-turret gunner in the Bat out of Hell Squadron, 7th Air Force. Seventeen of those missions were at Iwo Jima. I was there the day of the invasion, February 19, 1945. The rest of my mission were islands held by the Japanese, such as Truk and Haha Jima atolls and Chichi Jima, where President Bush was shot down. He was a pilot for the navy. I think he flew off a carrier.

This was taken right after World War II. There's Emerson's. These are all navy in the back. In the front is army and marines. Veterans. This is, I think, sort of a Victory March after the war ended.

—*Wallace Briggs*

Library Revelations

As a young child having just started school and learning to read, an anticipated event was to borrow books from the Brooks Library. I remember descending several steps on the south side of the main stairs to a dark entryway with a heavy door. The children's room was partly below ground level, but it always seemed a light and pleasant place to me. The large windows that were located in the upper half of the walls provided abundant natural light.

The children's librarian during my early school years was Miss Sarah Taft. Her desk was directly in front of the door, so she saw everyone who entered, and she could supervise both sections of the children's room.

At the time I started signing out books, the greatest challenge was to write my name small enough to fit on the narrow filing card that was inside the back cover. For several years I enjoyed taking books home from the children's section but always anticipated advancing to the upper level. Finally, I was old enough to move upstairs.

There were two reading rooms on the second floor, one on each side of the front of the building, that were furnished with long tables and straight-backed chairs, as I recall. There were encyclopedias and other reference materials for research in these rooms. Off the center aisle that extended the length of the building were alcoves for the books grouped by subject and the Dewey Decimal System. Connecting the basement level and the second floor was a narrow spiral staircase that was primarily for the use of library employees, but I remember climbing up and down a few times with permission.

The library also served as a museum with historical artifacts and paintings displayed in the gallery on the third floor. I do

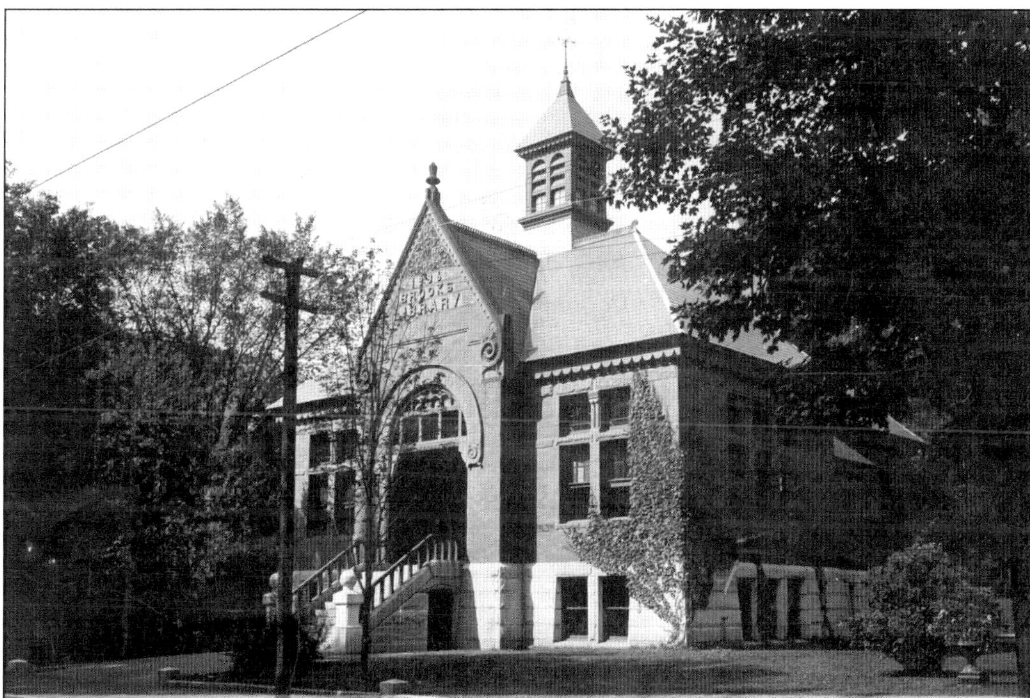

The original Brooks Library was erected in 1886 on Main Street. It was demolished in 1971.

not remember the specific items other than "Thunderbolt" memorabilia and the painting of the Prodigal Son in its impressive location on the back wall.

It was a sad day when the old library succumbed to the demands of "progress," the need for a larger, modern facility, and for increased parking for the adjacent post office. The wreckers made short work of the beautiful building in 1971. Many residents salvaged bricks, parts of the steps, and other pieces of the structure. In recent years, part of the stone slab identifying the building has resurfaced. The word "LIBRARY" and the year "1886" have been attached to the north side of the present library. It has been said that the word "BROOKS" lies in the West River near the Putney Road bridge. Even though the old site was leveled for a parking lot, bits and pieces of this historic building still survive around town.

—*Hazel J. Anderson*

An Unexpected Gift

Over the years I've had many opportunities to look at the Brattleboro Historical Society collection of old photographs. I consistently find these pictures mesmerizing, not so much for their historical record but for their ability to instantly capture specific people's "slices of life." You can see the obvious—what people wore, how they got around, and what the Brattleboro physical surrounding looked like. But, more important to me, you also get to peek into and conjecture about the personal lives of the people captured visually at a specific moment in time. They tell a story.

My favorite set of photographs are those that depict downtown. One of the things that impresses me about this part of town is that, with few exceptions, you can remove today's vehicles and modern dress and see Brattleboro a hundred or more years ago.

One picture in particular comes to mind. It is a view looking north up Main Street from Plaza Park. Directly in the foreground, taking up most of the space in the picture, is one of Brattleboro's trolley cars in the process of letting off and picking up passengers. There is a crowd literally surrounding the trolley. The people are ready to push their way on board—clearly there's enough room for all of them. A little girl in her Sunday best just got on board. A matronly woman farther back toward the middle of the car looks determined to find a place in the car. Where are they going and what's the occasion? A young couple are also in the crowd, the gentleman's hand protectively and lovingly around the waist of his partner in a demonstration of their personal feeling and relationship.

Others of these pictures show circuses, soldiers going off to war, religious groups, and good old Fourth of July parades. What interests me most, however, are the people on the sidelines watching these events. To me it's like they're alive, each one more interesting than the other.

My own Main Street story involves my daughter and myself. We were out for a walk one day near Christmas about 15 years ago. We had been living in a third-floor apartment on Chapin Street and had been in town about three or four years. At the time, our economic situation was not good. These walks we took always served several purposes, and in this case, not only were we out to enjoy each other's company, but to get some fresh air and inexpensive distraction as well. We were walking past what was the Rite Aid building, now the River Garden Walk, when I happened to look down. Right in front of me was a small wad of money folded up. I reached down, picked it up, and looked around for the person who dropped it. No one claimed it, or even seemed to notice that I picked it up. It was a busy time of day and people were walking past us right and left. The conflict of whether or not to pocket the money or to make more of an effort to find its owner was resolved for me as minutes passed with no one claiming the money.

So, still feeling guilty, we went home with our story and with what I still believe today to be a gift meant just for us.

—*Gerry Gatz*

Shopping at Goodnow, Pearson, and Hunt

One of my early memories of shopping in downtown Brattleboro was an excursion to Goodnow, Pearson, and Hunt. The store occupied the entire ground floor of the American Building, with the women's departments at the northernmost end, and the men's department down the hill. The goal of my shopping trip was to purchase a Christmas tie for my father. The ties were displayed on a long wire above the counter. The selection ranged from plain colors to a variety of stripes to colorful designs. After considerable deliberation, my choice was a conservative stripe or subdued pattern tie that was appropriate for business wear. An added treat when shopping at Goodnow's was to watch the money container that snapped onto a wiring system and sped on its way from the counter to the cashier's office and back.

—*Hazel J. Anderson*

Goodnow, Pearson, and Hunt

I remember being downtown at Goodnow, Pearson, and Hunt. It's now a thrift store. We went up onto the balcony, where the boys' clothes were. The bills were clipped to a set of parallel wires and were sent that way to the office and back.

—*Elisha Prouty*

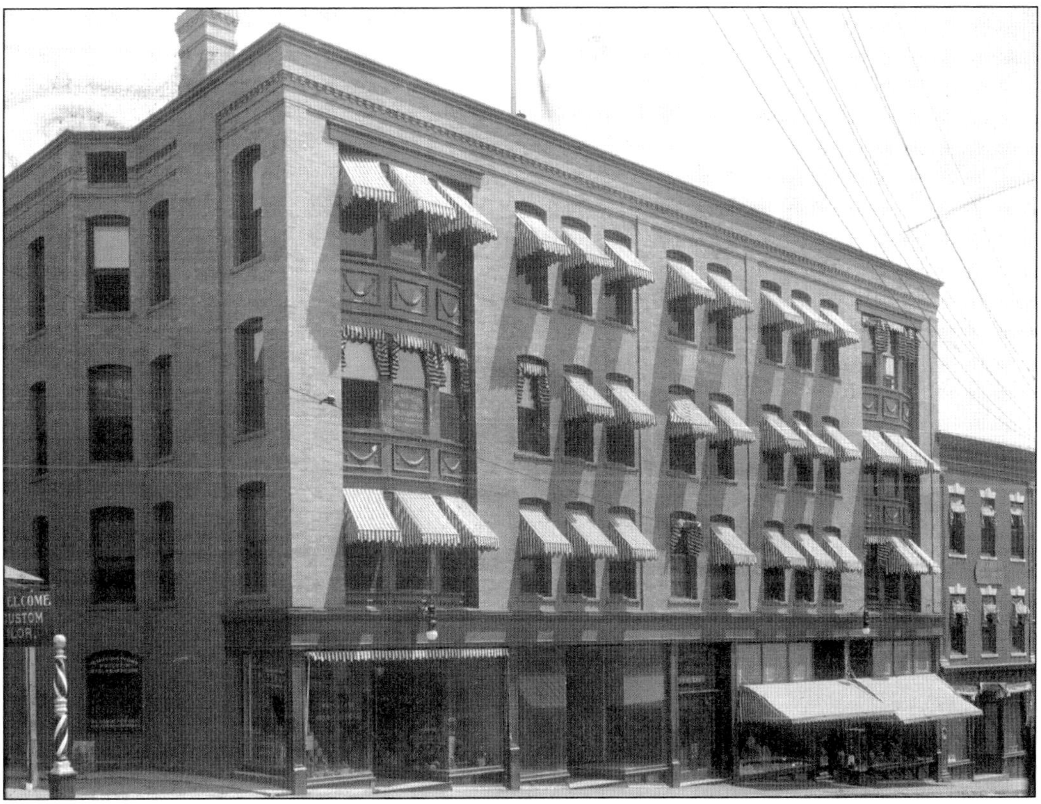

This c. *1912 view shows the American Building, located on lower Main Street.*

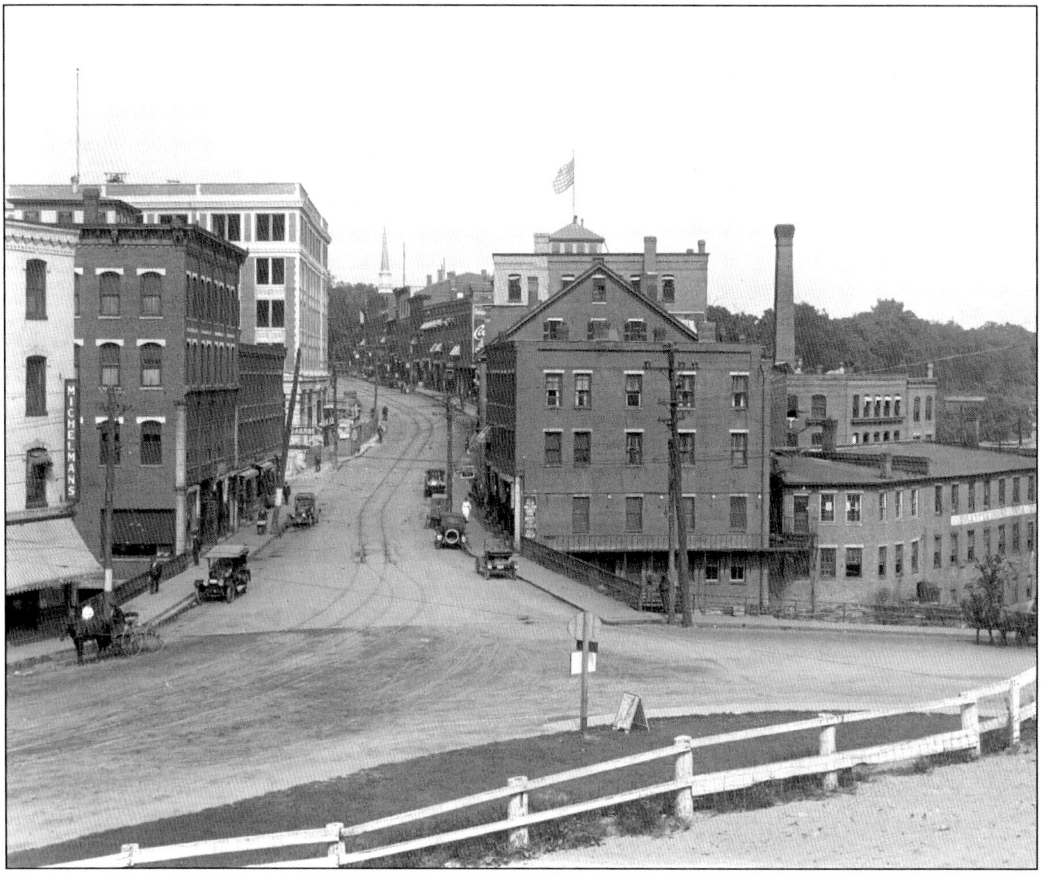

This view of Lower Main Street was taken looking north, c. *1918.*

Living Downtown

In the fall of 1964, I moved from 19 Harris Place (which no longer exists) to 39 Main Street into the Barrows Block. My apartment was on the second floor above the All States Restaurant. It was a very warm apartment, as the heating pipes to the rest of the building ran up through the rooms. I remember the first night that I lived there I had the window partway open and all night long heard the traffic going up and down Main Street hill. I wondered what I had got myself into by moving there! But that was the only time it bothered me. In 1965, I moved from this apartment to a house on Western Avenue, which a friend and I had purchased. In January of 1977, there was a fire in the Barrows Block, destroying the three stories of the building. The only part left was the Barrows Coal Company office.

Another thing I remember about this block is the All States Restaurant. When I first came to Brattleboro in 1948 to work at the Holstein Friesian Association of America, I stopped for breakfast at the All States. I guess when I told people where I ate, they must have discouraged me from eating there, as always after I'd have breakfast at the Latchis Coffee Shop across the street.

—Joann H. Nichols

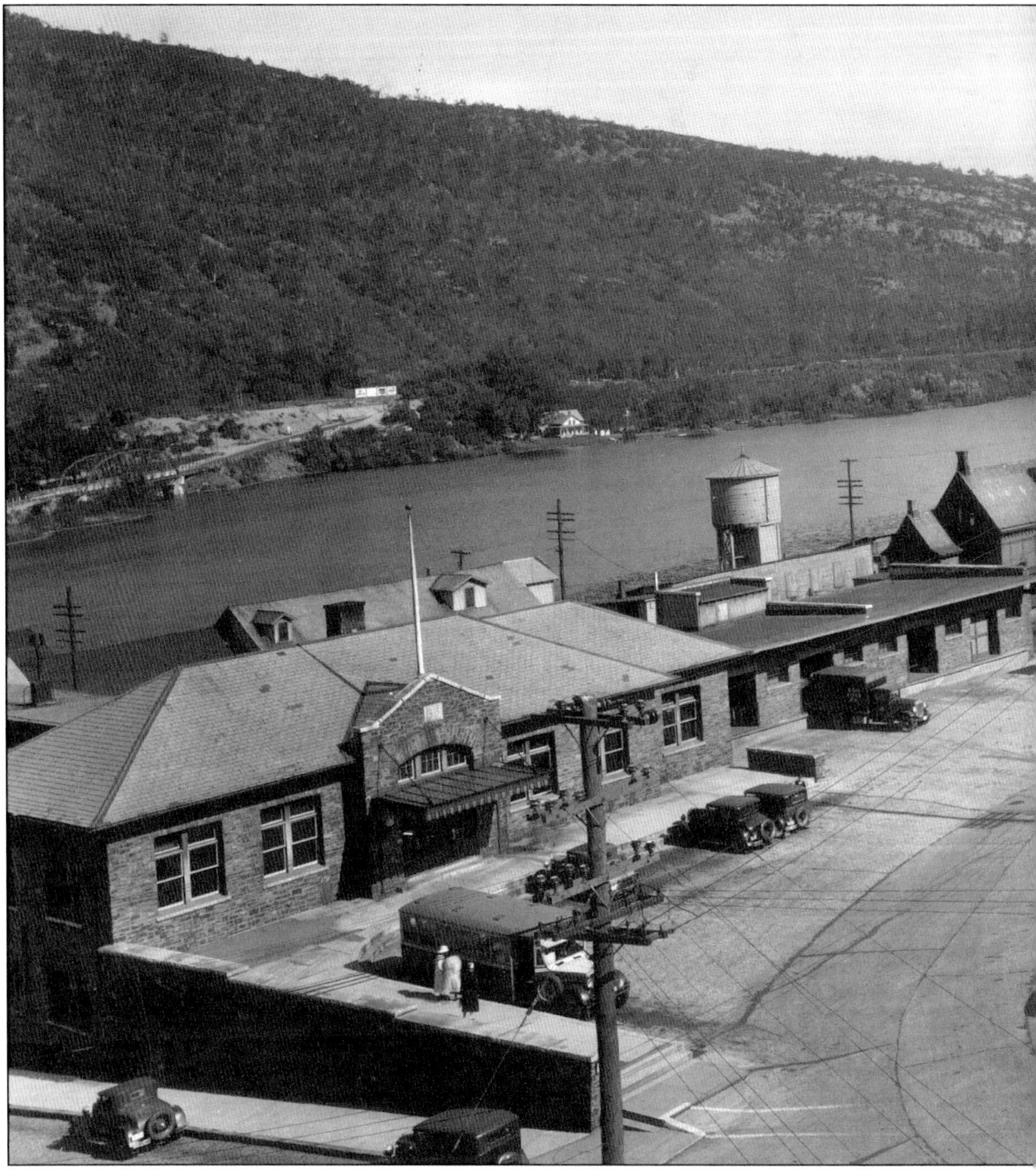

This c. *1930 view shows the present railroad station, with Plaza Park and the sculpture*

A NIGHT ON THE TOWN

I became a resident of Putney in 1939 when I was 12 years old. My friends and I got down to "Bratt" (or "Bustleburg," as we called it) about once a month, so it was a big event. A group of us actually walked to Bratt one Sunday morning, lured by a place out on Putney Road that offered "All the Pancakes you can eat for 50 cents." It took us about three hours to get there, and I can remember I had room for about 30 pancakes, with butter and syrup.

Brattleboro was a gourmand's delight for a teenager. If you had the money to buy a Boston cream pie at the Dutch Bakery [windmill in its window] and could get it

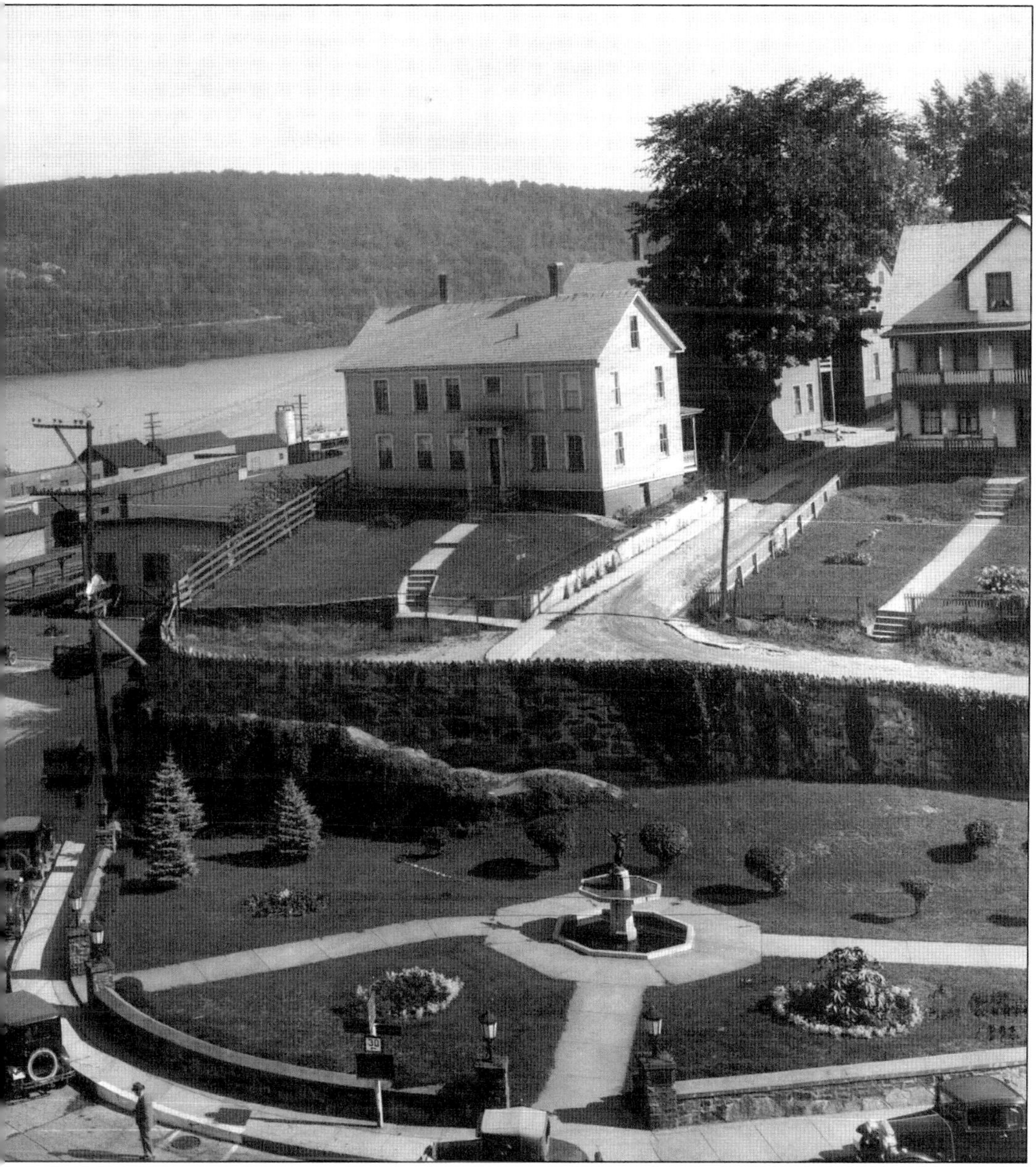

Spirit of Life *on the right.*

back to Putney before you ate it, you were the most popular person in the dorm.

Brattleboro was glamorous, exotic, and busy compared to Putney. It had two movie theaters and a railroad station! I saw *Gone with the Wind* and *The Great Dictator* at the Latchis Theatre. So did everyone else. When the train from New York came in, there were more local spectators than disembarking passengers. During the war, freight trains with over 100 flatcars, each loaded with new army tanks headed for Halifax, Nova Scotia, would be pulled through town by three or four locomotives.

Behind this picture of the station is the

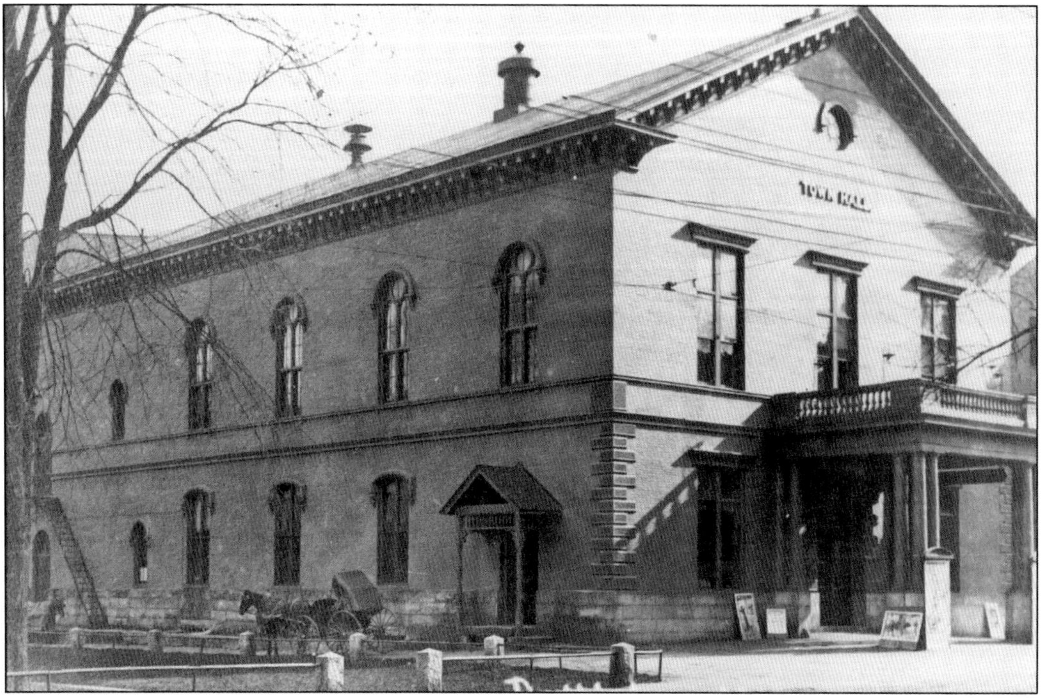

Town Hall was built in 1855 as a municipal building. It was also used as a convention center and concert hall.

forested hillside of Mount Wantastiquet in New Hampshire. None of the trees you see there survive today because in 1944 the whole mountain burned for a week. I remember watching it burn from a vantage point on West Hill in Putney. It burned for so long because there weren't many able-bodied men around to fight it owing to the war. We joked about "the hot time" we could have in Brattleboro.

Inside the station there were long, high-backed wooden benches. One night, pretending to be a hobo, I slept on one of them, using newspapers for a blanket. I was hitchhiking down to Longmeadow, Massachusetts, to visit my girlfriend. The bench was hard, but the room was warm, so I did finally sleep. About 5:00 a.m. I felt someone shaking my feet, and awoke to hear a Brattleboro policeman, gently but firmly, tell me I had to move on. I felt very grown up that day.

—David Clarkson

The Town Hall and Auditorium

I cried when they tore the town hall down! There was a beautiful theater in there with two balconies and there was also the police department and town offices located there.

Stock companies which traveled from town to town, putting on entertainment, used to come there.

We school kids used to perform on the stage and sang in our little white dresses "We're Forever Blowing Bubbles." What a thrill when that curtain came up!

I almost ran over a movie star who came to Brattleboro to entertain at the theater!

—Mary Brackett

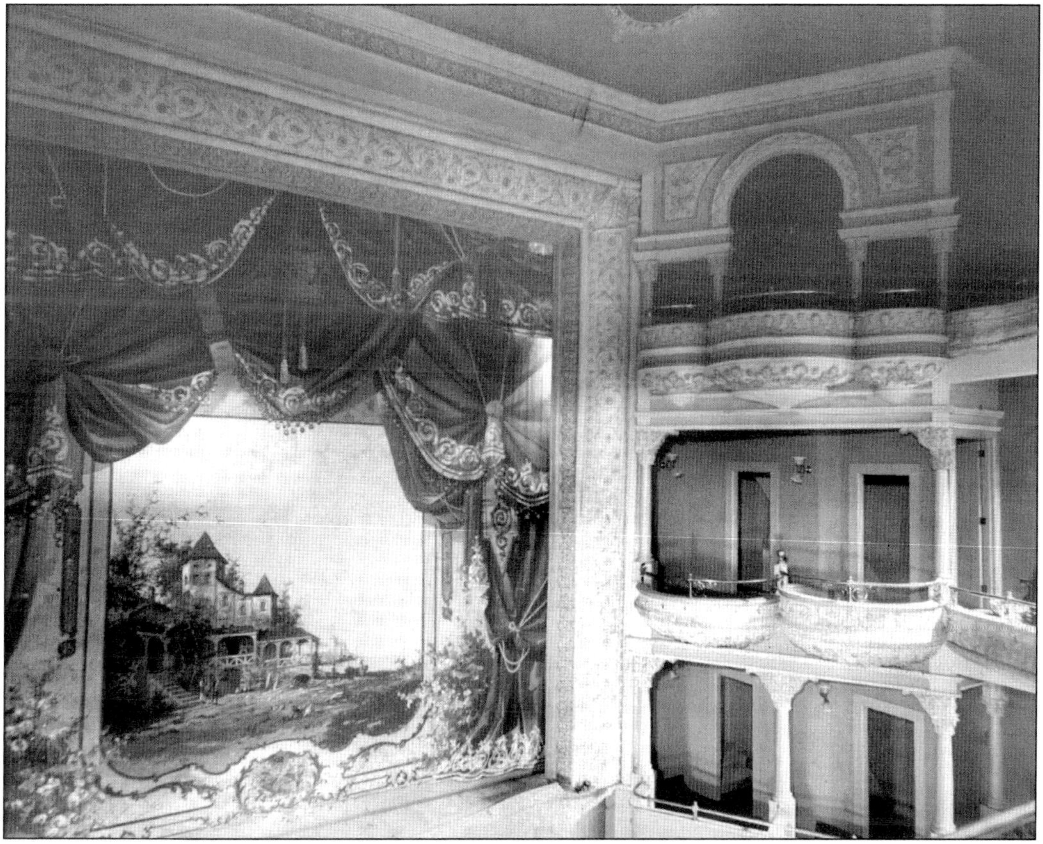

This is a view of the interior of the auditorium that was added to town hall in 1896. Both town hall and the auditorium were later razed.

SHOWS AT THE AUDITORIUM

I was born in West Brattleboro, and when I was six years old, about 1933, my father died. This memory was before that, but while I could still remember, so it must've been the year before, 1932, when I was five. My aunt Mary Prouty was a singer, and she lived in the Prouty Homestead on Bonnyvale Road in West Brattleboro, and she sang in the church choir. A minstrel show was put on by her singing group in the auditorium. The auditorium was also the opera house. The scenery for the shows came up the Connecticut River on barges. The theater was very attractive, with three seating areas: the orchestra seating, the balcony, and seating above the balcony. I remember velvet curtains in the auditorium. Aunt Mary and the other singers were all in blackface. My father, mother, and I went from West Brattleboro in horse and wagon to see the show. Obviously, I was very impressed. I probably slept all the way home, but I don't remember that.

The auditorium had a lot of meaning for me. It was the site of graduations (I graduated in 1945) and of Fourth of July celebrations—someone always said the Gettysburg Address. It became the movie house. And while I was in high school, around 1943 or 1944, we put on musicals there. It was a local theater group that did it, not a high school production, and different small groups did vaudeville-type songs. I did dancing; I wasn't a very good singer. We danced the rumba. The boys wore white shirts and white trousers. I

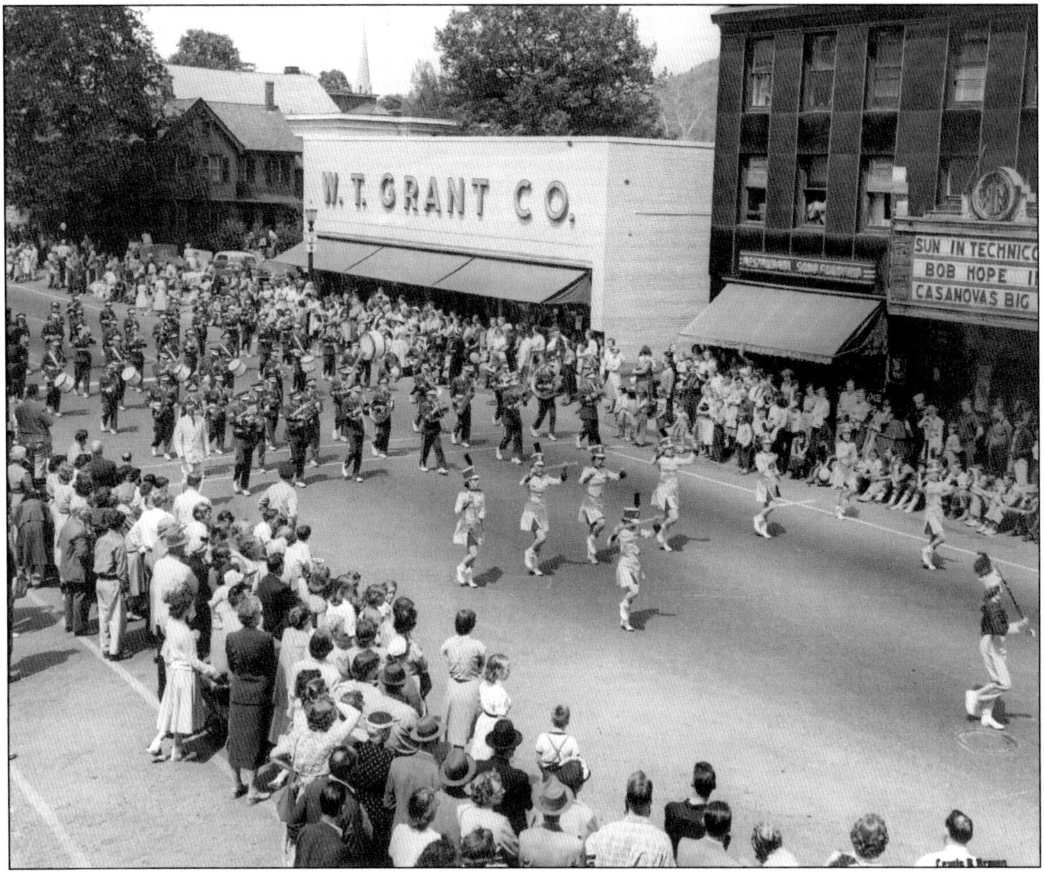

This Brattleboro High School alumni parade c. *1950 includes the Bellows Falls High School band under the direction of Burton Martin, music instructor.*

think I had a white silk shirt. The girls had costumes with lots of hot pink.

Winchester Warnicke, of Bakers Music Shop, was very theatrical, and he was the producer of these shows. Some very good musicians went through there. Sonny Williams, the pianist, played with us, and later he went on to play with some of the big bands.

We saw some famous actors there, such as the Straw Circuit Group, with Edward Everett Horton and others whose names I can't remember. They did summer theater there when I was in high school.

—*Elisha Prouty*

Going Downtown

Starting in 1955, at age 14, I spent summers with the Schwan family. They were building a summer home in Westminster West, a small town about 20 miles north of Brattleboro. My father had recently been killed in an auto accident, and Mr. and Mrs. Schwan, my friend's parents, had suggested that I join them in Vermont. I guess they felt such an invitation would give my mother a chance to get her life in order. We were all neighbors on Long Island.

The opportunity to spend my summer living in the woods while we built a house was exciting. The Schwans were

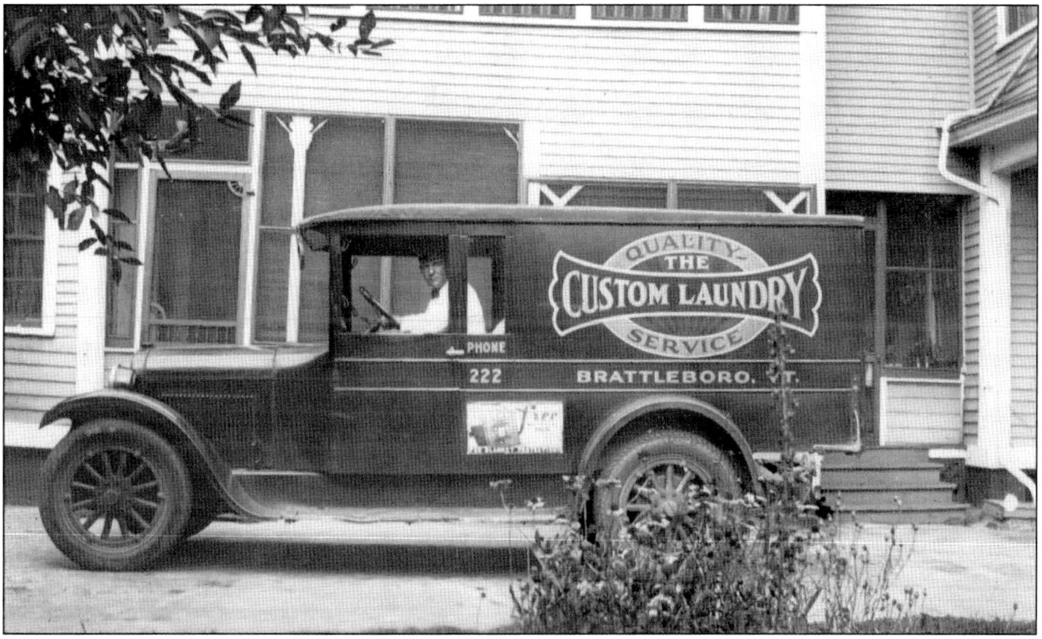

Custom Laundry owner Ralph Yeaw drives his truck in Brattleboro.

particularly adept at understanding the needs of adolescents. Every day at 3:00 p.m. we went to a swimming hole, and on Saturdays we went to Brattleboro, first for some shopping and later a movie at either the Latchis or the Paramount Theaters.

W.T. Grant was the store that seemed to have most of the things we needed: socks, some extra underwear, a cooking pot, and some postcards to send to friends back on Long Island.

There were several great soda fountains where you could get a black-and-white ice-cream soda for 35 cents. These trips to Brattleboro, on Saturday afternoons, were something we looked forward to.

—*Wayne Carhart*

A Kid's Time in Town

We had no car, so I lived in town. Often, people took in kids who lived far out like that so they could go to school regularly. The first year, I got a ride with a farmer nearby who could get tires and gas during the war. Then I lived with the Agnews. They ran the Custom Laundry (still there, up on Elliot Street, near the firehouse). I worked in the laundry after school. It was a big help toward my room and board. Lots of kids had jobs, and they didn't think anything about it. There were no men left in town, so kids and women did their jobs. We would get out of school at something like 1:20, then have to grab something to eat, like a cream cheese and olive sandwich at the drugstore lunch counter, and be at work at 1:30.

—*Elisha Prouty*

The Alumni Parade is held once a year in June. It starts at the end of Canal Street by the high school. I went to almost every parade they ever had. Exactly what year this photo is, I couldn't tell you. There's a float and that means an alumni parade.

Every fifth year the class builds a float. My class is 1943. So the next time we build a float is '48, I think. Then they're judged and given a cup.

This is at the foot of Main Street. This is way back. Let me see if I can distinguish the cars: 1932 or 1933. The building on the left is where the parking lot is now. The Whetstone Brook goes between the two buildings [on the left]. There was a hotel there called the Billings Hotel. It took up most of the space. Behind the hotel was a big area. They flooded it in the winter and made a skating rink. They did that back in the late 1930s, early 1940s.

And, of course, up here in this building is where Sam's is. His father started Sam's Army-Navy. Right in that same building before Sam's was the Crystal Restaurant. Marble floors, they had marble countertops and chandeliers. It was a fabulous place.

That's when I used to deliver papers for Baker's. In the same locale, across the street where it is now, but it was a very small store.

On Sundays I would go down and stuff all the circulars into one section of the paper. Jimmy Baker's father worked with me stuffing papers. And then we would load a certain amount of all the different papers, like the *Springfield Union,* all the Boston papers, the *Boston Herald,* the *Boston Globe,* all the New York papers. We'd load them into various automobiles, usually station wagons. The cars had running boards on them. We young deliverers would stand on the running boards of the car with our arms inside the window and go from house to house delivering papers. All over Brattleboro. Every street in Brattleboro.

A number of different men drove. Phil Hallgren. He's the one I rode with all the time.

As a stuffer and a deliverer, I would usually start work about five o'clock Sunday

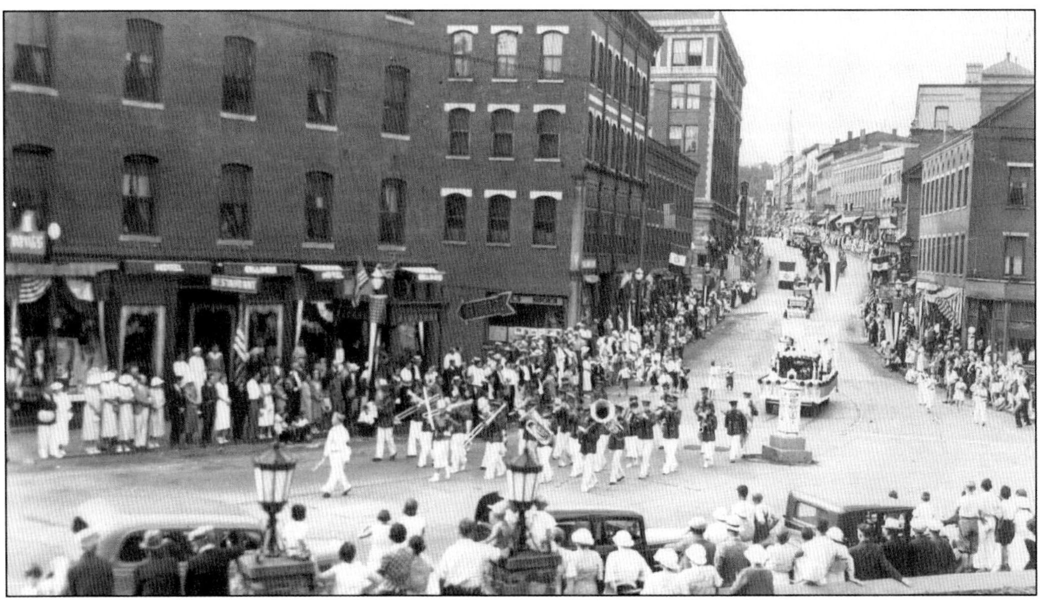

The Brattleboro High School alumni parade proceeds along Main Street in 1930.

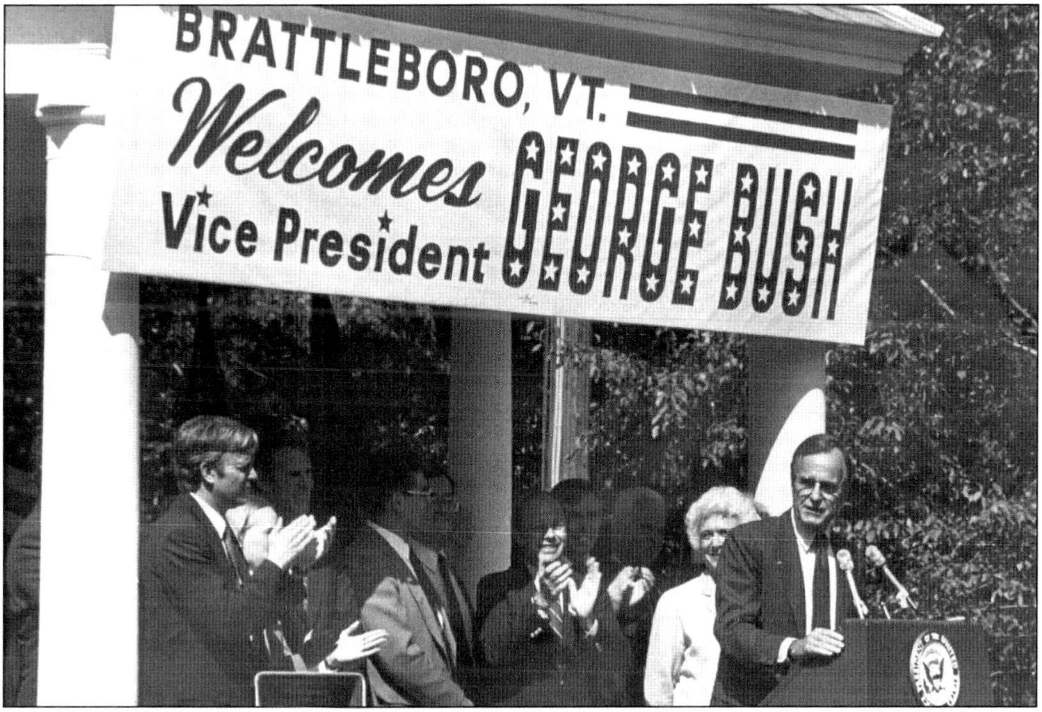

Vice Pres. George Bush (right) and Barbara Bush visit Brattleboro. Pictured with them in this 1980 photograph, are, from left to right, Peter Smith, two unidentified persons, Dart Everett, unidentified, Steve Morse, and Bob Gannett.

morning and get done about one o'clock. For all that, I got paid 25 cents plus my tips.

That's the only place you could go to buy papers between 1930 and 1940.

One day I came down to go to work and the Princess Theater had burned down on a Saturday night. It was where Lawton's Dry Cleaners is now. It was a big hotel as well as a theater. A fire started in one of the hotel rooms after the Saturday night showing of the movies. After midnight. It burned right down to the ground. Three men died in that hotel fire. The fire department was down farther on Elliot Street, just to the right of where the entrance to the Harmony Parking Lot is now. On Sunday afternoon, practically all of Brattleboro was surrounding the area, watching the fire department picking up parts of humans and everything else.

—*Wallace Briggs*

FOUR MORE YEARS

It was probably in 1987; George Bush was running for president. He had come to Brattleboro to give a speech on the [Brattleboro] Common. Many people attended this event. I recognize some people in this picture in addition to Mr. and Mrs. Bush. There's Bob Gannett and Dart Everett. Someone I don't see whom I know was there was Al Moulton. He gave a speech and led a rousing cheer of "four more years, four more years!" I didn't go to this affair, probably because I'm not of the Republican persuasion, but the office I worked at was on Main Street, close enough to the common to hear the noise, and it was broadcast on the radio.

—*Joann H. Nichols*

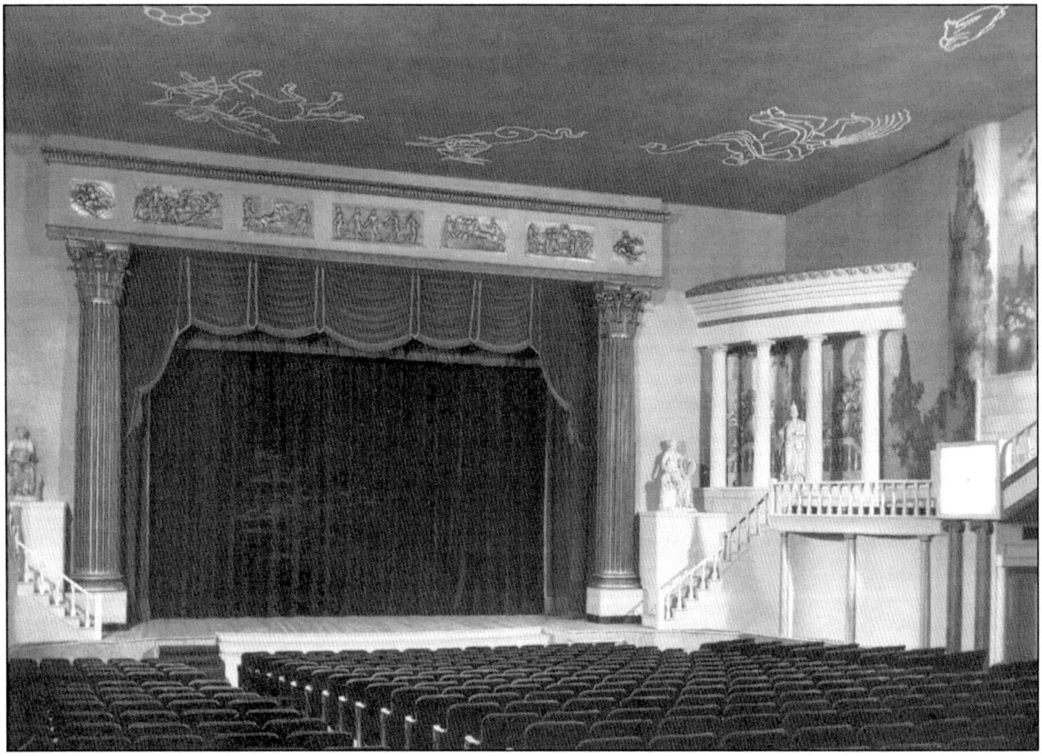

This 1938 view shows the interior of the Latchis Theater.

THE LATCHIS THEATER

I remember when the Latchis first opened. All of the Greek designs were so impressive. We saw the von Trapp singers there. They wore heavy Austrian costumes—they must've melted! This was summer. They all had recorders. They hadn't settled anywhere yet. They had just arrived in America. Maybe they were living in Connecticut? The whole block with the Latchis in it was built as a hotel. The Estey and Green factory was next door.

—Elisha Prouty

EVENTS AT THE LATCHIS THEATER

Among my childhood memories are those of the Latchis Theater. Being from a town in central Vermont, the size of the local theater was very small. Moving to Brattleboro in 1938, my father was anxious to show me the new theater in town. Because the only movie I had ever seen was Shirley Temple in *The Little Colonel,* in black-and-white, my father was so proud to take me to see the *Wizard of Oz* showing in Technicolor, something new to us.

Imagine the amazement I felt when I walked through the doors and onto the beautiful marble floor and to see the Greek architecture that I did not understand, then to see twinkling lights in the ceiling when the lights were dimmed. When in junior high school, our science teacher, Miss Fiske, taught us about the signs of the zodiac that were in the night sky. This was very interesting, as then I knew the meaning of the twinkling lights and the drawing on the ceiling. Now, with the invention of television, I'm learning about Greek history.

Saturday matinees were so interesting with the vaudeville act with acrobats, dancers,

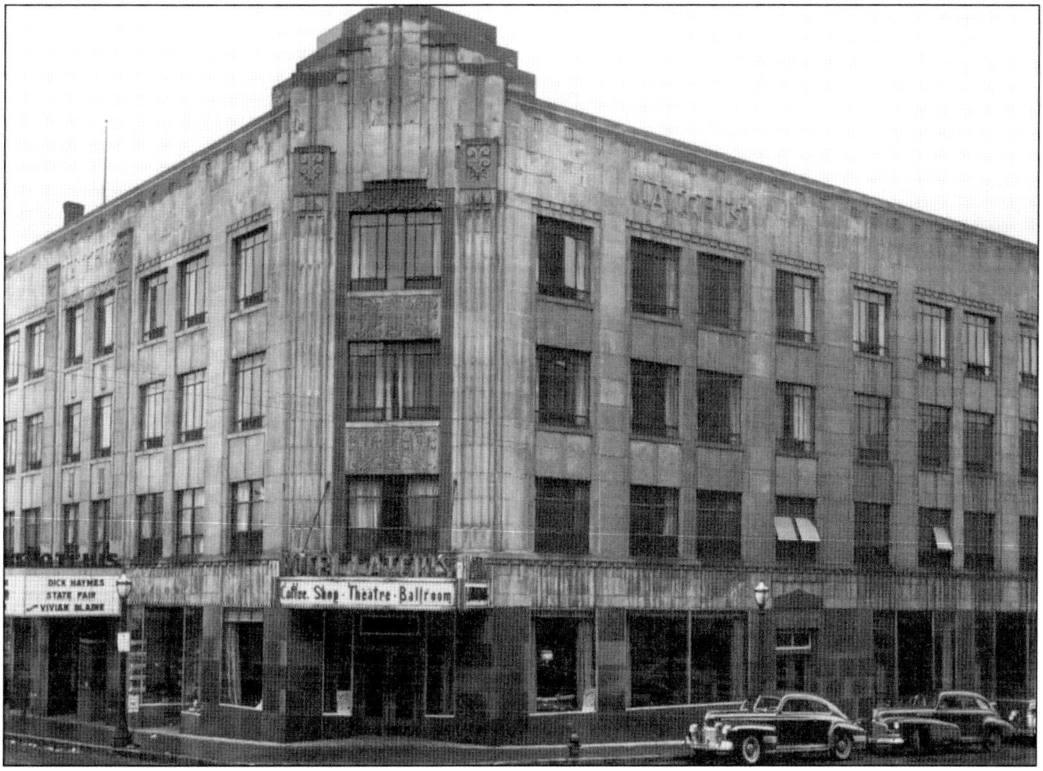

This 1940 view shows the Latchis Hotel, 50 Main Street.

and musical artists. Live entertainment is so much fun to watch, even today. Then there were special concerts, including Rudolf Serkin, renowned pianist. In 1944, the Community Concert Association had a series of programs in which artists from the Metropolitan Opera Association performed. By selling tickets, I could attend for free; that helped add to my interest in classical music.

In the fall, Saturdays always meant that there would be cartoons and sometimes westerns. At Thanksgiving time we would bring food to be distributed to the needy. Also, at the Saturday before Christmas, the children of the town would congregate to see another show. Waiting in long lines for the doors to open, it would be cold with snow coming down, making our feet and hands quite cold. We would stamp our feet and clap hands to keep warm. The hum of the voices and the giggles of the children are pleasant memories. Mr. Latchis, usually with his family, would pass out little boxes, with a string for a handle, filled with Christmas candy. I'd carry mine home oh so carefully, as it was a special prize.

New Year's was also a special time. In 1948, I was dating my future husband, and as I look in my scrapbook, I find the following: "Latchis Gala New Years Eve Dec 31, 3 complete shows, 7:30, 9:30 and 11:40. Start the New Year right—Best show for miles around, You may look everywhere! But none can compare with Dennis Morgan in 'my wild irish rose' in magnificent Technicolor 60 cents! What better way to celebrate the New Year."

It has been a pleasure to know the Latchis family, and I used to walk to school with some of them. The Latchis Building is a great landmark for our area, and I know many of you have many memories and hope I have related them correctly.

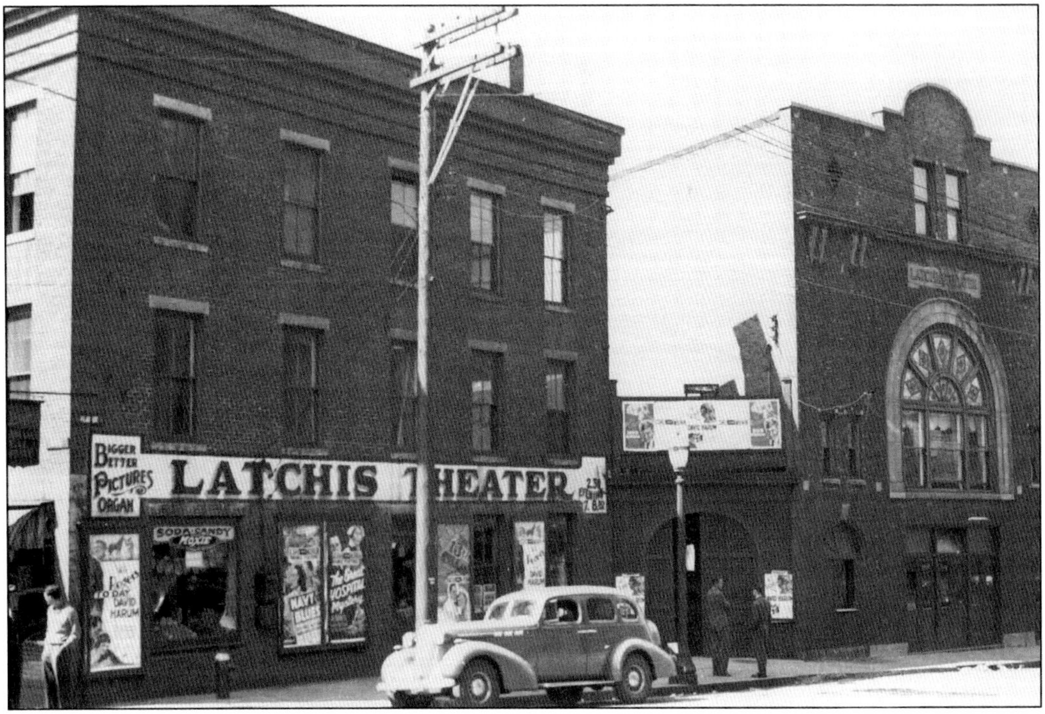

Pictured are the Latchis Block and Theater, on Flat Street, c. *1940.*

The saddest scene was when we watched the Vermont 43rd Division of the Armed Services men marching down Main Street on their way to board the train to go to war. I was standing in front of the Latchis Theater along with many others that day.

The coffee shop and restaurant were also among the memories of the Latchis business ventures, which are still enduring today.

As you can see, the Latchis name is very special to many of us here in the Brattleboro area. The size of the theater appears much smaller than it did at the tender age of 11, but it could be that our perception changes from child to adult. The theater and associated ventures have given this town a name to be proud of. Remember when there were special movies, there were long lines of patrons up and down Main Street. Television has sure changed our entertainment habits. The arts are very special to our area, and a lot of us cannot travel to nearby areas and wish to see them return to the theater soon. I am glad that I can share the memories with all who read this.

—Elfleda Pike

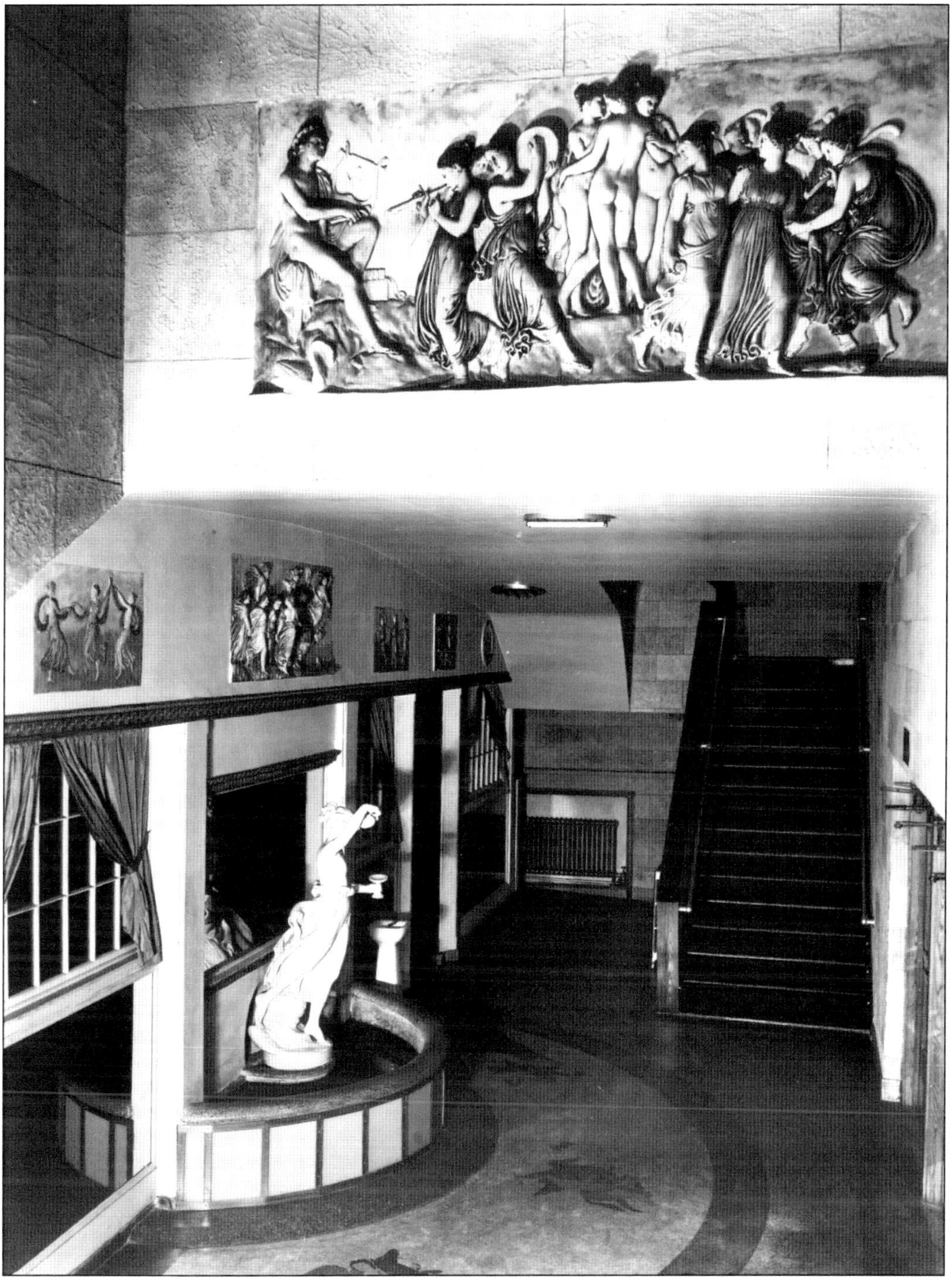

A bas-relief of Greek muses adorns the rear lobby of the Latchis Theater.

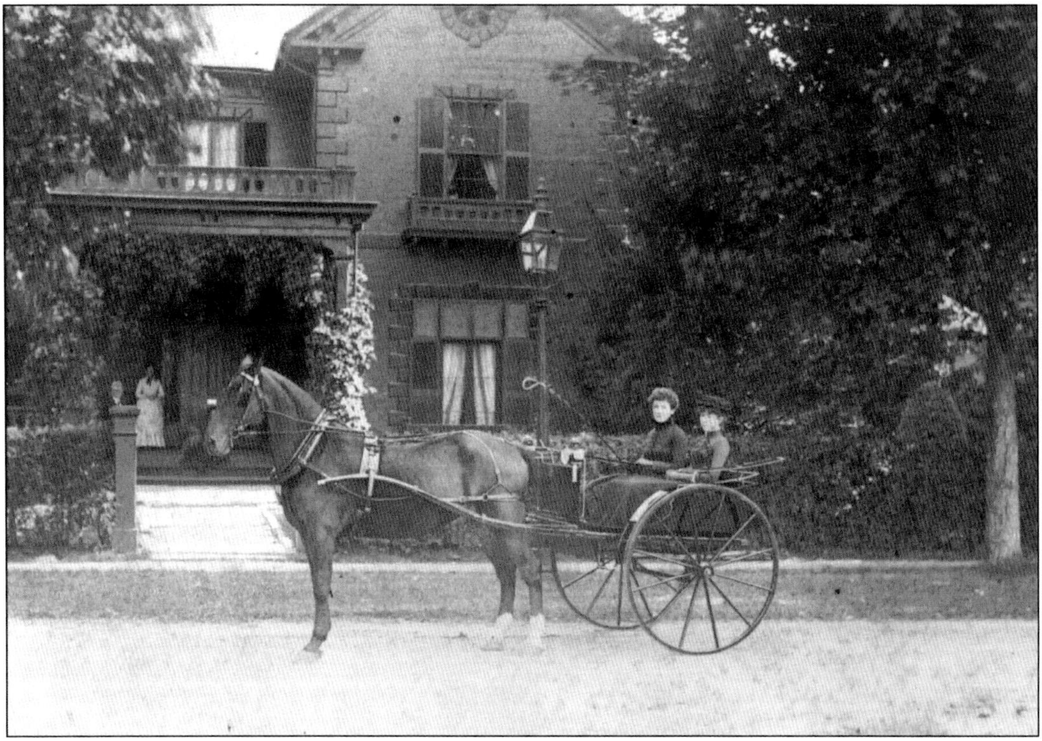

As the town expanded north on Linden Street and Putney Road, Park Place evolved as a connecting street with gracious homes across the way from the Brattleboro Common. Historical records list names of influential local residents as owners of the properties. Until recent years, most of the homes had beautiful flowers and colorful bushes that passersby could enjoy. Perhaps the two women, identified as members of the Brooks family, were out for a ride in their one-horse shay to see how their neighbors' gardens grew.

Chapter Two
Bygone Grandeur

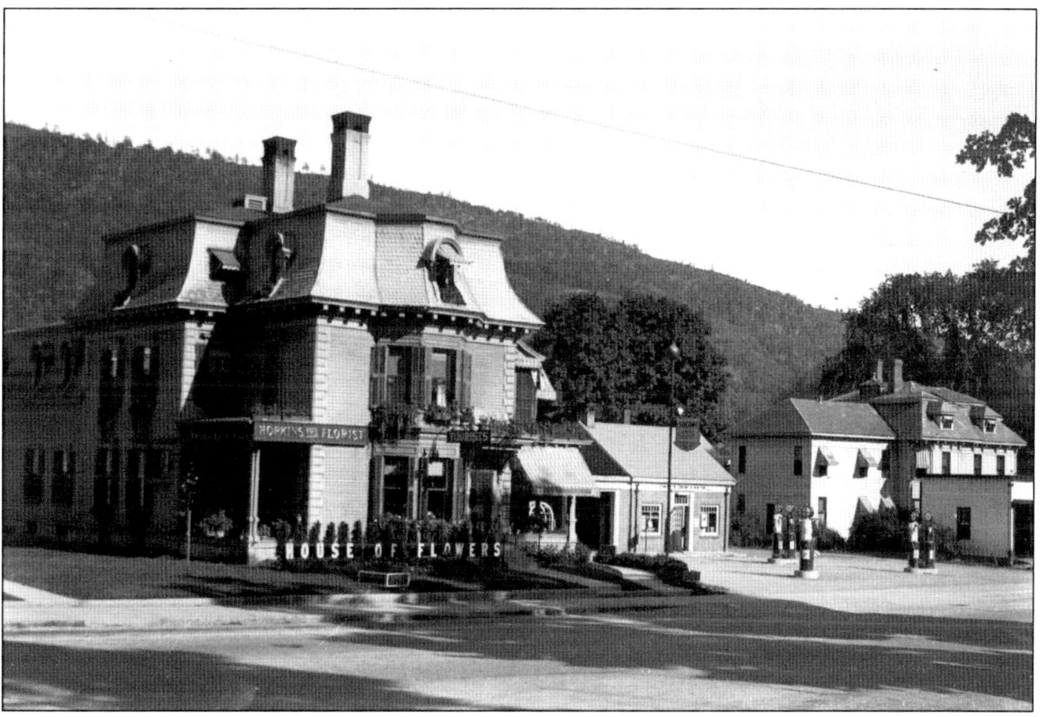

A surviving structure identified as the Dowley home and later as the House of Flowers is now partially obscured by a single-story commercial addition across the front of the building. Looking above street level, the architectural features of this former private dwelling are clearly evident. The photograph depicts the building as a tourist home and florist shop. Eventually, it was converted into apartments. The adjacent properties on Main Street are currently occupied by banking institutions.

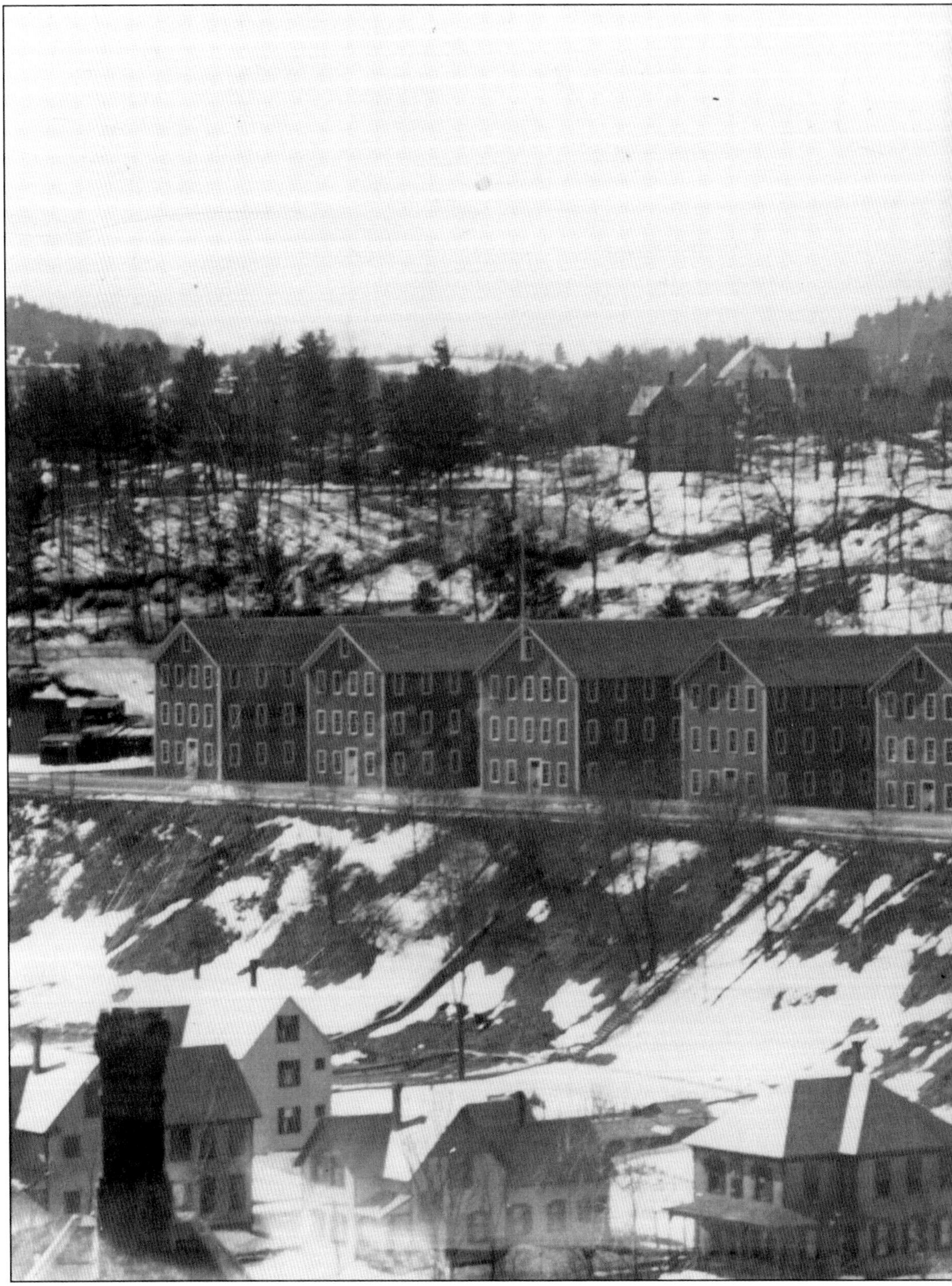

The Estey Organ buildings were located on Birge Street. This view dates from c. 1900. High on the hill is Esteyville, a local neighborhood that provided many homes for Estey

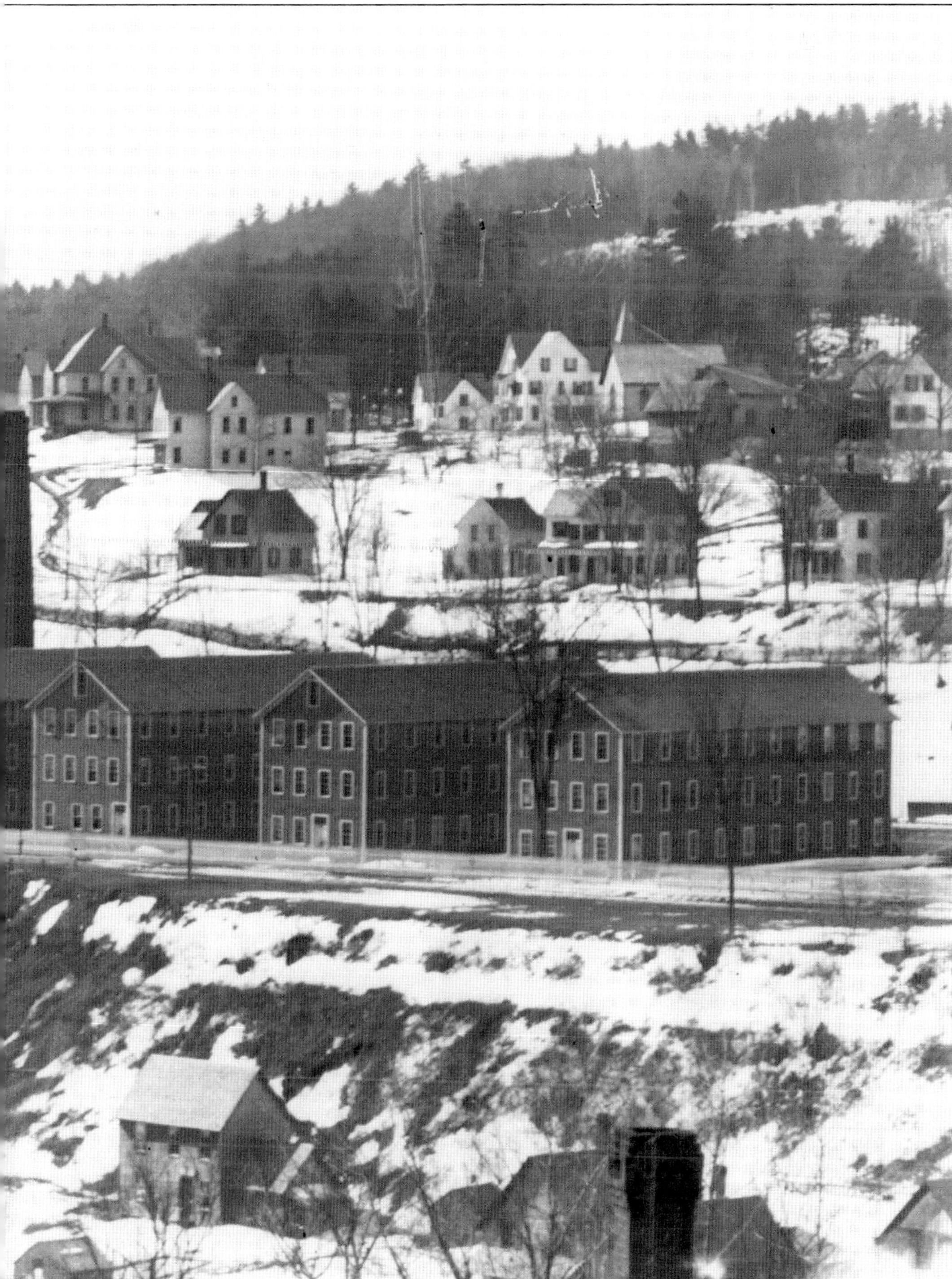

employees during the company's flourishing years.

THE ESTEY BUILDINGS

The Estey buildings are my immediate neighbors to the south. We are parallel to one another, and all my southern views are of the Estey buildings. They are wonderful neighbors—the dignity, practicality, and usefulness offer a sense of security, pattern, and rhythm, and an enduring industry to my days and nights.

In summer, I cannot see them at all during the day; they are hidden by a bank of trees. At night, their lights shimmer through the moving leaves. At the end of summer, as the leaves thin, the buildings slowly reemerge. When all the leaves have fallen, they stand like a row of sentinels, steadfast, full of the memories of work and creativity. They represent a time and spirit of industry that made music and beauty.

They commemorate a time in our history of family business, of making something beautiful and useful, and touching the whole world from a unique place of human experience.

"Memory encompasses a welter of human endeavor; at one end of the spectrum we encounter personal recollection, at the other, history. To remember is at once to recognize the value of life and to confer it through the act of commemoration" (Richard McDougall).

—Helene Henry

THE BROOKS HOTEL

I remember that Eleanor Roosevelt and her entourage used to stop and eat lunch in the Brooks House dining room on her way to Maine. She was so lovely and so nice. Everyone talked about how she would smile and stop to greet people. That was a very fine place, with white linen over everything.

—Elisha Prouty

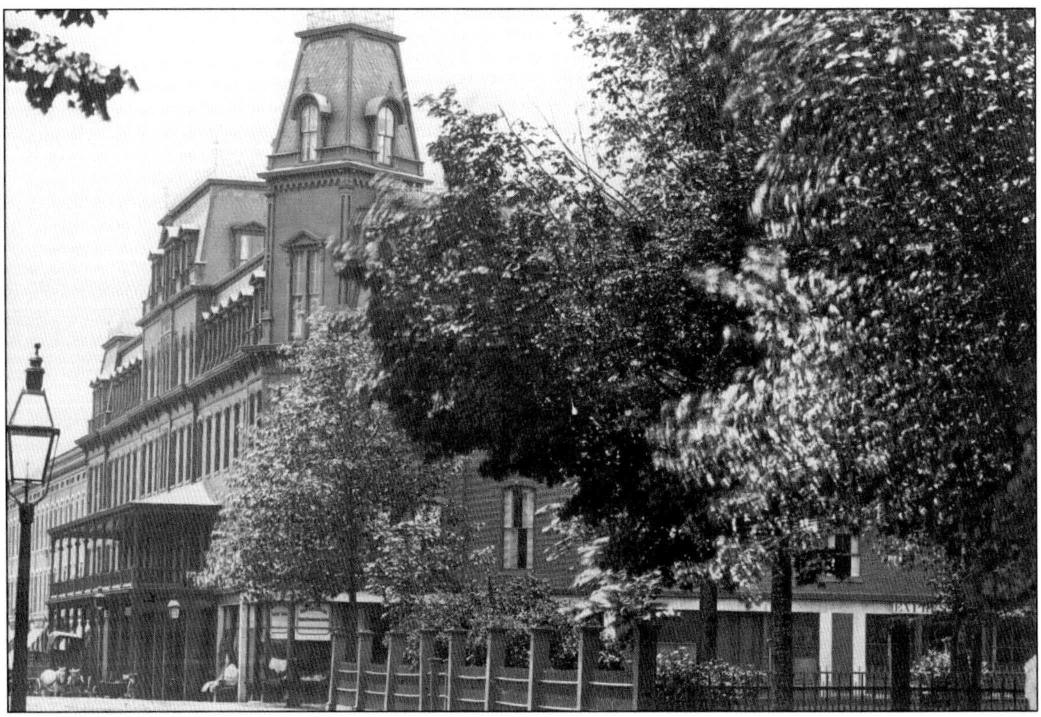

This is the Brooks Hotel, on Main Street, as it appeared c. *1880.*

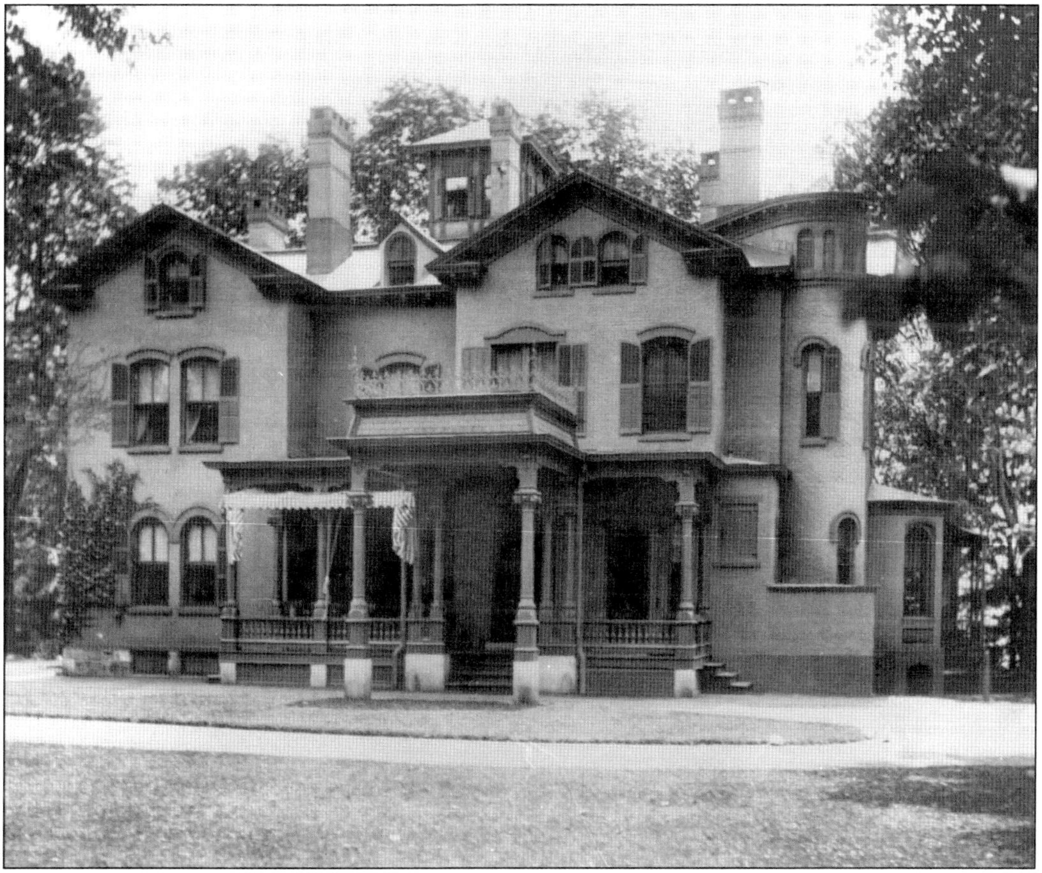

This c. *1910 photograph shows Florence Terrace, on School Street, the home of Julius and Florence Gray Estey.*

THE HAUNTED HOUSE

I went to elementary school at the Green Street School in Brattleboro, more years ago than I'll admit. The school building is still, today, an unpretentious square edifice of stone and ivy, a safe haven in which the children of the neighborhood learn reading, writing, and arithmetic.

But back then, behind the teachers' parking lot, beyond the dodge-ball ring and the jungle gym, was a place of pleasure and fear, of forbidden delight and unspeakable terror. Behind the school was the Haunted House.

In its heyday, it had been the Estey House, manor to some of that great organ-building family whose business helped put Brattleboro on the map by the end of the 1800s. But, by the time I knew it, in the 1950s, it was an abandoned, rat-infested shell of its former glory. Some kids said the last owner had hanged himself in the attic, and some said he'd been murdered and you could see blood on the floors. I never learned what the truth was; all I knew was that it had been abandoned and left to decay at its own pace.

The school playground was bordered at the back by a broken fence, beyond which was the Haunted House, hidden in warm weather by a field of wild black raspberries. We were expressly forbidden to leave the playground during recess, but the lure of berries in the early fall was too great and

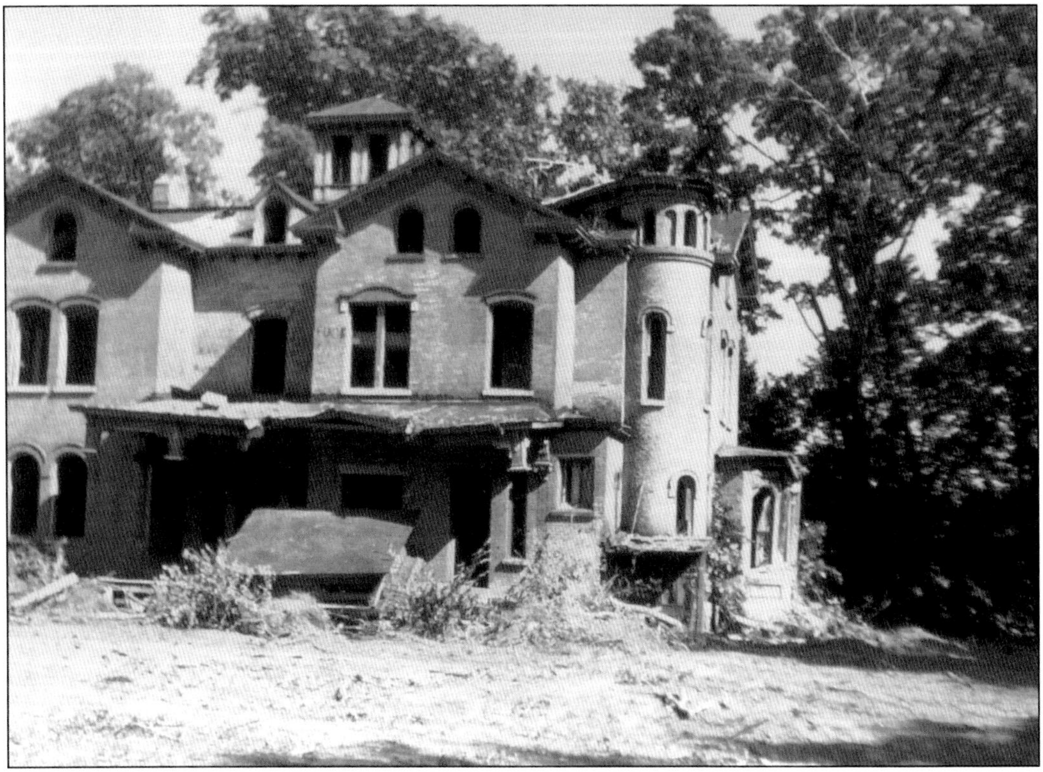

This c. 1965 photograph shows the remains of Florence Terrace, once the home of Julius and Florence Gray Estey.

the teachers generally too busy. So, on rare occasions, one or two of us would go into the bushes to fill our faces with the sweet fruit.

What had once been open lawn had quickly been covered by the persistent berry bushes, which spread by growing long, straight, thorn-covered branches, which would arch into the air five or six feet and then bend down to root in the ground. For small children, this made an impressive tangle, which towered over our heads and hid us from adult view just a few feet away. Years of incursions by grade-schoolers had left a network of paths, which wound in loops along the edge of the playground and led, if one were brave enough to follow, toward the house itself.
Being a generally timid kid, I usually snuck into the field far enough to satisfy myself with a few berries and then would bolt back to the safety of the playground at the first sound of some mysterious noise in the bushes. But, on one occasion, it was a particularly warm day, and I was enjoying myself so much that I ran along the paths farther than I ever had before. I found myself suddenly standing at the broken steps to the front porch of the house.

My first instinct was to turn and run back the way I'd come, but I could hear quite clearly the kids on the playground, so I decided I couldn't be in that much danger. The first thing I noticed was that every single window was broken, with a few bits of curtain hanging in tatters. The house was in a pretty sorry state, the porch was falling apart, and the front doors were wide open. I tried the first step, but it wobbled and creaked so loudly, I succumbed to my fear and bolted for the sanctuary of the schoolyard.

They tore the house down sometime after

I'd grown up and gone on to high school. My mother said it was a firetrap and attracted vagrants, and the neighborhood was a lot better off with the apartments they built.

But I can't help remembering my one glimpse into the front hall, just a momentary vision of a wide entry and a sweeping staircase, strewn with broken beer bottles and trash. And running down the stairs was a stream of water, slowly dripping off the edge of each step. Drip. Drip. Drip.

My sister said it was the rain that had leaked through the holes in the roof.

Me, I still think the house was crying. Alone, abandoned, it shed tears for the past.

—Jane Douglas

LINDENHURST

Lindenhurst was built in 1859. It was the Crowell mansion when I went by the house to elementary school every day. No one lived there then. It was gradually deteriorating. There were terraces on the south side of the house that went all the way down to Beech Street. I think there were gardens on the terraces. I can remember going into the house with a friend to see what it was like. The woodwork was beautiful. The mantles and woodwork were chestnut.

The Crowell mansion was razed in 1936. The land was once considered for a high school.

—Ed Milkey

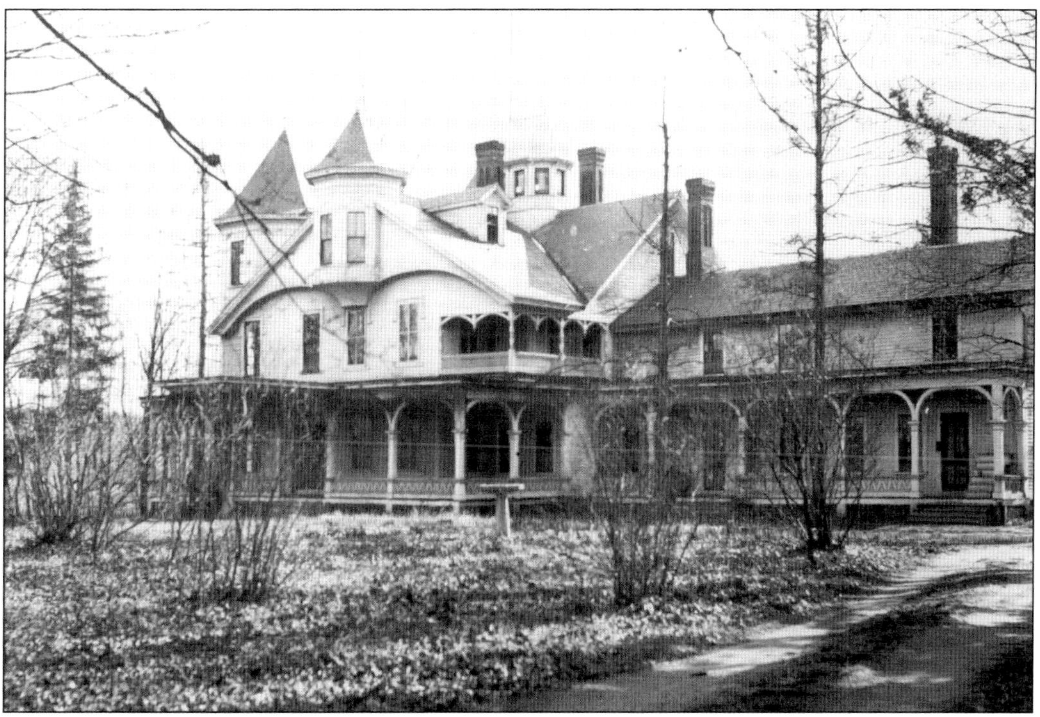

Crowell House, also called Lindenhurst, is shown c. *1888. Its site, at the intersection of High Street, Green Street, and Western Avenue, is now Crowell Lot, which is a neighborhood playground.*

SHERRI'S CASTLE

On the thick blue paper of Antoinette Sherri's architectural drawings, "The Castle" stands out in the lower right-hand corner. All of us play with the idea of planting a tree within our home: she actually did it. By the time I saw it, it stood in the enclosed porch, rising through the upper balcony on up to the sky—a beautiful maple.

In a cove near the front door, another maple, given space for its expanding trunk. The unusual curved stone stairs are still there after 70 years, suffering from frost heaves.

It is a castle. It is Madame Sherri's castle. In the middle of the woods in West Chesterfield, New Hampshire. It was her design, her dream. Even now, in what's left of the ruins, which is its entire foundation of stone with inlaid mortar, it carries excitement and mystery: fantasies on every level of grandeur begin instantly to sprout from our imaginations.

People marry there, picnic, photograph. Last year I happened to arrive on an afternoon, where four young women—absorbing Madame Sherri herself?—were dressed to the nines: sophisticated, literary, so modern in their old-fashioned dresses. Oh if ever four feminine youths were lost in fantasy . . .

—Ann R. Stokes

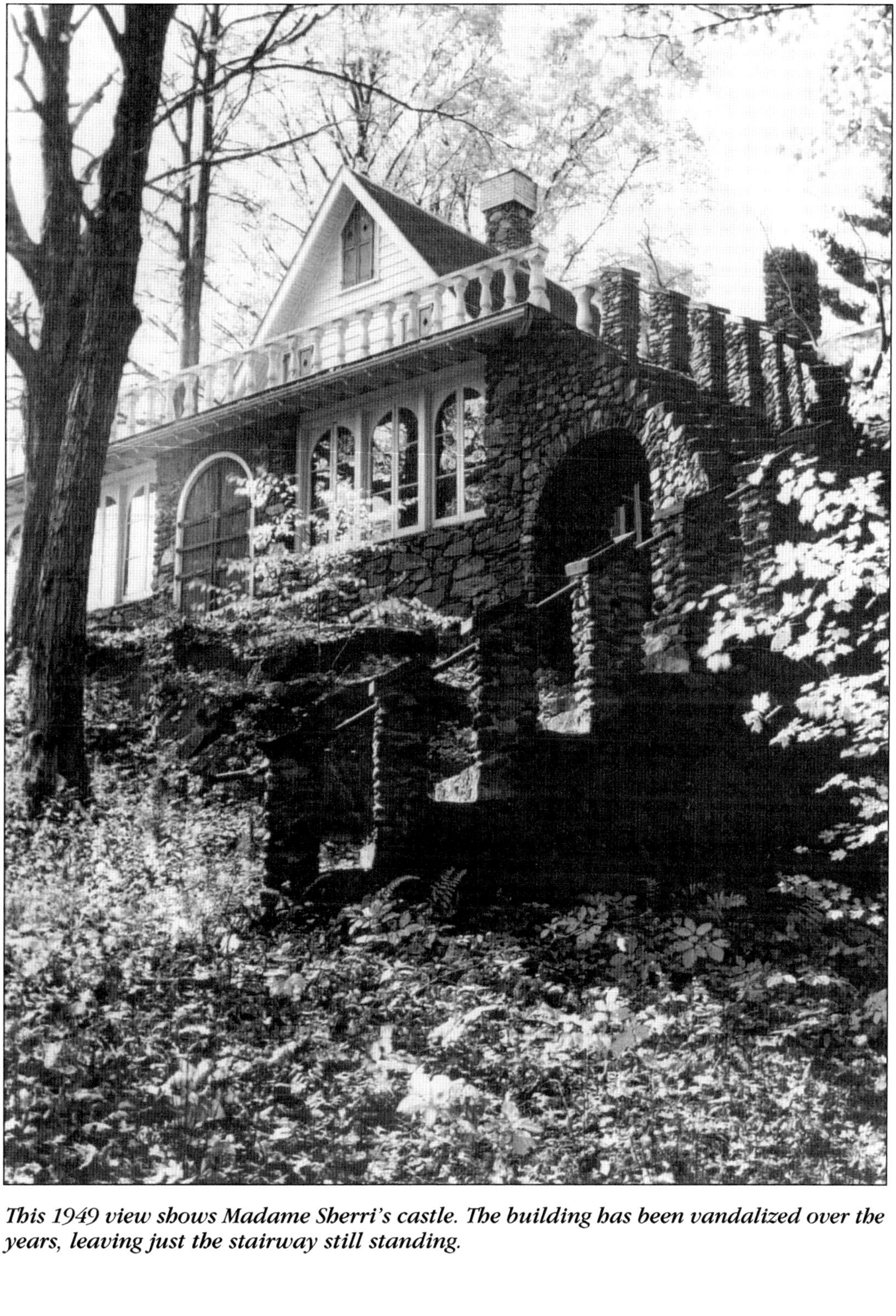

This 1949 view shows Madame Sherri's castle. The building has been vandalized over the years, leaving just the stairway still standing.

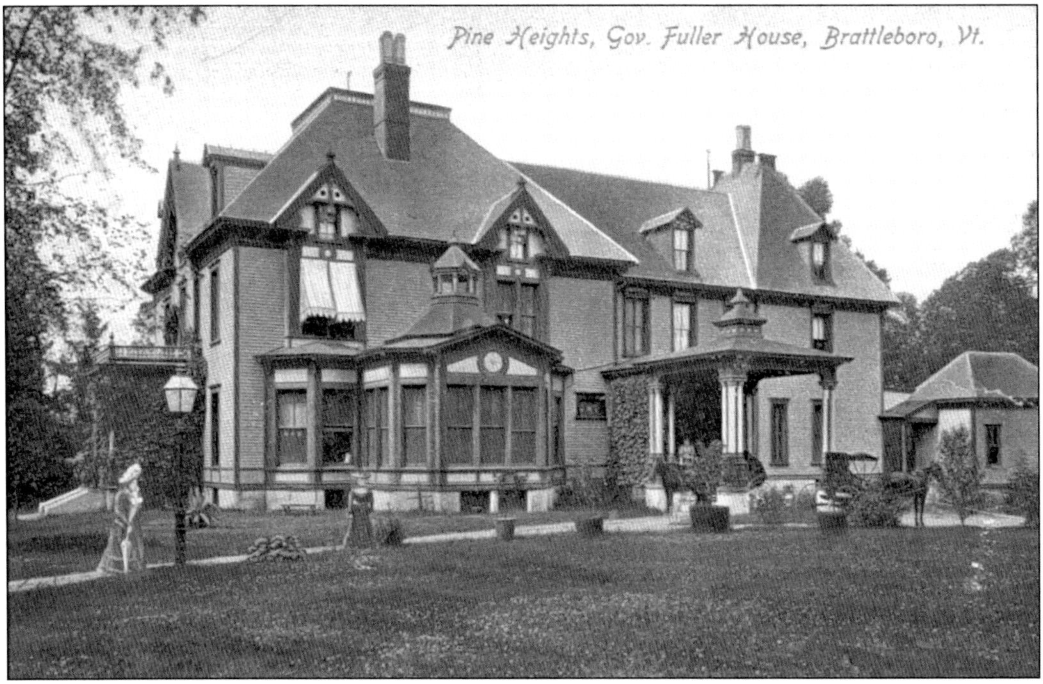

Shown c. *1900 is Pine Heights, the home of Gov. Levi Fuller and his wife, Abby Estey Fuller. Today, it is the site of Eden Park Nursing Home.*

PINE HEIGHTS

The old Fuller Estate at Pine Heights was a splendid Victorian mansion where my sisters Gloria and Joyce and I spent many play hours in our childhood. We knew every inch of the estate, from the large library to the observatory; we romped through the huge barn, and the beautiful pine groves, the pet cemetery, and the long walkway from Canal Street.

I met Everett Gorton there in the early 1940s while playing with Ann Batton, the daughter of the Fenton Battons. We later married and lived in the same estate, which was made into apartments before being demolished in the 1960s.

In the winter we would slide down the hill beside the estate, which is now Fuller Drive. Our dad would sew leather on the seat of our pants and the knees to make our snowsuits last longer. At first this was an embarrassment to us, until other parents called and asked if he could do the same for their children. Those were tough times, and you could not just go out and purchase new snowsuits without considerable expense. This was in the 1930s, and times were tough.

Levi Fuller, who built the estate, studied electronics in Boston. He was a progressive man for the 1800s. He had one of the finest telescopes in the eastern United States. He patented 100 items, donated buildings to Vermont Academy, contributed to the Baptist church, and at 39 years entered politics. After serving as state senator, Fuller became lieutenant governor in 1886 and governor of Vermont in 1892.

Fuller married Abbie Estey, daughter of the owner of Estey Organ Company, which produced fine organs for many years and distributed them throughout the world. Fuller was vice president of the company and held this position for many years.

Jacob Kempf's brother was born in an apartment over the barn, at the Fuller

Estate, in the 1920s. His parents worked at the estate.

A lady named Katie O'Connor came over from Ireland and was the maid at the Fuller Estate for many years. The children in the neighborhood all loved Katie. When she retired, the Fullers built a house for her, which she lived in until she passed away. In her new home on Oak Grove, she often asked the children in the neighborhood over when she baked pies or cakes. We enjoyed sitting and talking with her and eating her delicious pastries.

When we returned from Europe, where Everett was stationed for four years, in 1963. The house was torn down, and they were building Eden Park by the early 1970s.

We have many happy memories of growing up on Oak Grove Avenue and playing at the Fuller Estate.

—Phyllis Nixon Gorton

The Octagon House

The gray octagon house at the intersection of Greenleaf Street and Western Avenue, where the dental office now stands, was a West Brattleboro landmark. It was at one time the parsonage for the West Brattleboro Baptist Church and became the home of Edgar Henry (known to his friends as E.H.) Davenport.

Edgar Henry Davenport was born to Calvin Newton and Lucy White Davenport on November 22, 1846, in Leyden, Massachusetts. He was one of nine children. As a young man, he moved to Wilmington, Vermont, where he married Emily E. Barnard on November 12, 1873. He farmed, raised sheep, and dealt in wool. They moved to West Brattleboro, where they remained for the rest of their lives. They had five children.
E.H. was well known around Brattleboro as a lawyer and a member of the Windham County Bar, being admitted in 1871. He was a shrewd businessman, buying much valuable property. At one time he owned the buildings on Elliot Street that housed the Lawrence and Wessellhoeft Watercures. He died at home of pneumonia on May 28, 1925, after an illness of five years. At the time of his death, it was reported that he owned the general store, three houses in West Brattleboro, and timberlands in Marlboro and Newfane.

Edgar's wife, Emily, died June 14, 1938, at the age of 87. Eventually, the house was owned by my uncle and aunt, Roger and Emily (LeRay) Chapman. I was just a little tot of three the first time I laid eyes on that magnificent, unique eight-sided building. I thought it was magical, with its cupola on top containing eight little windows to allow light to filter into the circular staircase that snaked up through the center of the house. The cupola had no floor, but I remember asking if there was a way to climb up and look out. Of course, the answer was always no. Still, I persisted in asking over the years, hoping that one day (perhaps out of annoyance) Uncle Roger would say, "Oh, for heaven's sake! If it will keep you quiet, I will get the ladder and take you up for a look!" It didn't happen.

The main part of the house had eight rooms, four over four. Each room had eight walls of varying sizes. I remember one wall being approximately two feet wide. This made it difficult to position furniture, particularly a bed. Usually there was only one wall wide enough to place a bed without blocking off the windows.

Downstairs there was a dining room, living room, den, and a bedroom. Upstairs there were four more bedrooms. The kitchen, bathroom, and pantry were in the ell of the house that had been added on after the original house was built. Also in this addition were two more rooms. One was sort of a storage room, and the other became Roger's radio-TV repair workshop. It had an outside entrance, so it was perfect for business use. There was a small foyer leading from the living room and dining room onto the porch. Surrounding the door were rectangles of various colored stained glass. When the house was sold for demolition, Roger saved them, but they have since disappeared. The family thinks he may have sold them.

The porch stretched halfway around the original house, extending just past the kitchen door on the addition. It is thought that at one time the porch may have gone further around the house. There was a small porch upstairs facing Western Avenue that could be reached from an upstairs bedroom; it had no roof. The railing had been removed, but the platform remained. I seem to remember being told something about snow falling off the main house over the years, causing the railings to weaken and rot.

There were stairs leading from the dining room down to the cellar, where the coal furnace was located. I remember Roger had devised a way, without shoveling, to transfer coal from the coal bin to the furnace as it was needed. There was also a room used as a kind of root cellar, where Emily stored her home-canned goods on

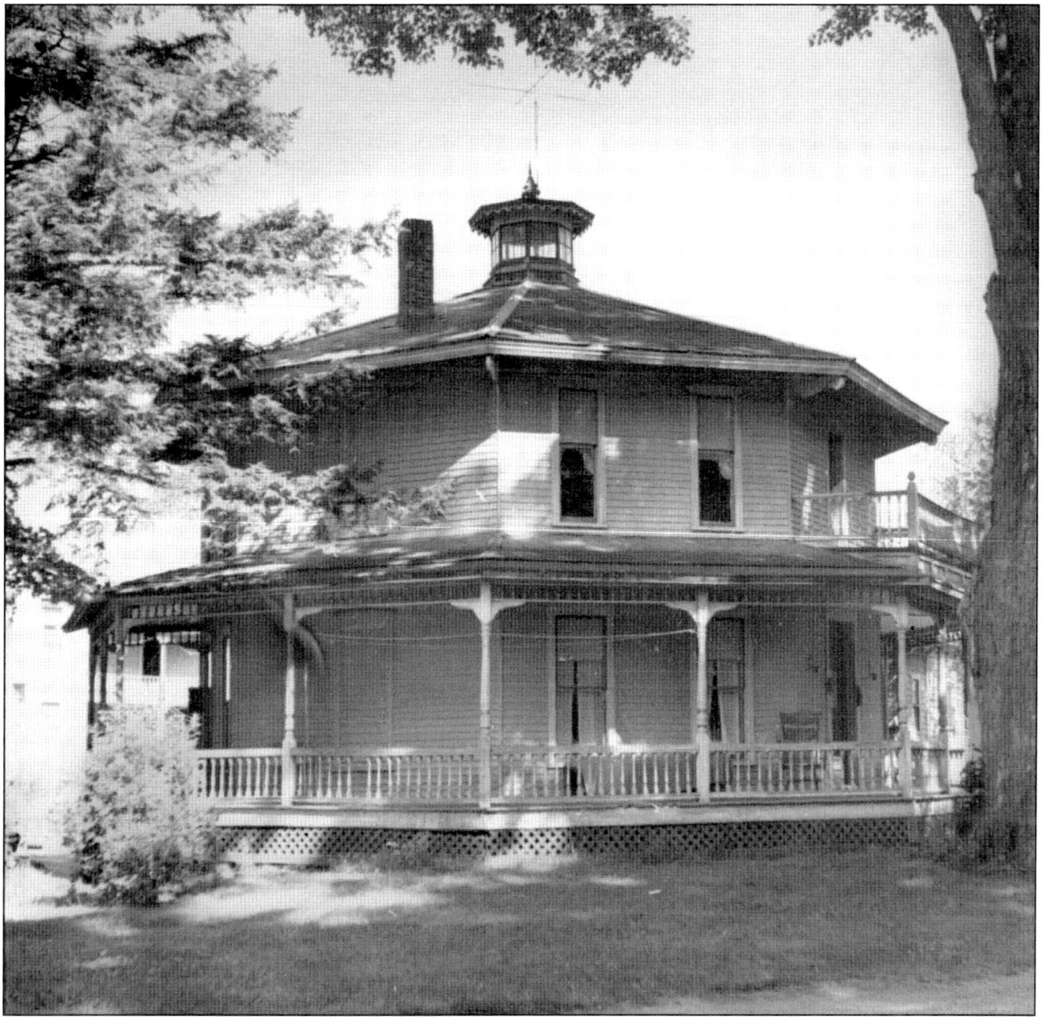

This c. 1900 photograph shows the Octagon House, located on Western Avenue.

shelves. It was very cool there.

Roger was always inventing something. Not having a garage for his car and having winter temperatures dropping far below zero, he got tired of not being able to start the car in the morning. So, by using a timer and other items, he rigged up a system that would start his car at various times during the night and let it run for a short time. Thus it was prewarmed in the morning. Today, you can buy car starters, but back then Roger used Yankee ingenuity. He was probably the most intelligent person I ever knew. I always asked him for help with homework containing difficult science and math problems. He would take time from his busy schedule to sit and gently try to make me understand what I was doing wrong.

There was a large lawn stretching between the octagon house and the house owned by Donald LeRay, Emily Chapman's brother. In the middle of the lawn was a tall pole similar to a telephone pole. It was used by both families for clothesline pulleys, which held clotheslines connected to each family's porch.

Emily had several beautiful perennial flower gardens at the back of the house that contained flowers in shades of pink, purple, yellow, and blue, as well as red and orange.

As a small child, I would follow my aunt as she worked in her flowers, asking her to tell me their different names. I would repeat them after her, delighting in my ability to pronounce dianthus, hollyhock, lobelia, and portulaca and giggle at the thought of such a beautiful flower being known as a bearded iris. On a sunny day, if the light was just right, I would lie in the grass behind the flower garden, close my eyes to a narrow slit, and the morning dew sparkling on the blossoms created a magical rainbow of color like something right out of *The Wizard of Oz.*

We played tag, red light, and croquet on the lush green lawn and had not a care in the world.

The property was eventually sold to the Galanes family. I believe they offered to let someone come and take the house down and move it. But no on came forward. Thus, the beautiful, unique eight-sided structure that had been home to many and that had been a special part of my life was torn down and lost to the ages.

—Dorothy Class

Chapter Three
Playtime

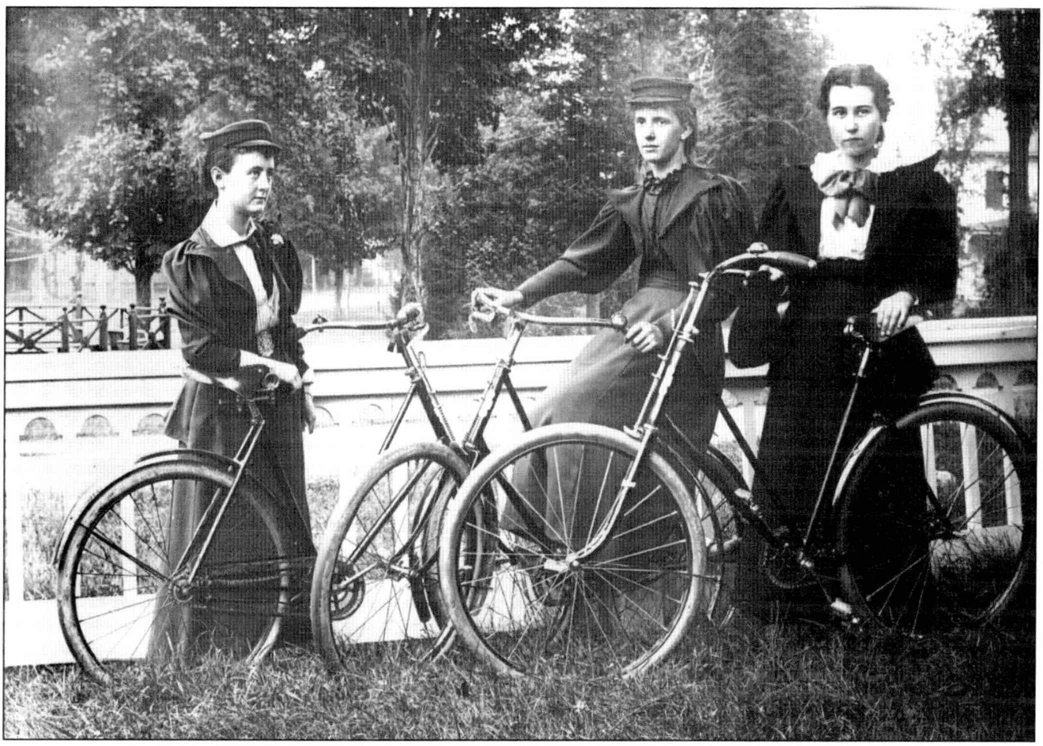

Taking a break in their ride, these young women pause for a rest by the West Brattleboro Common. Their attire apparently does not deter them from participating in cycling, although managing to keep a long skirt from becoming entangled in the bicycle mechanism and avoiding heat exhaustion from the confining costume styles of the day must have been a challenge. The bandstand (back left) provided a raised platform for performing concerts, a favorite entertainment and social activity in the late 19th century and into the 20th century.

The fact that the neighborhood included the only two Swedish churches in town plus a lot of Swedes probably accounted for its name. The Swedish Lutheran Church was at one end of West Street, and the Swedish Congregational Church was located on Strand Avenue. Several adjacent streets were considered part of the area, as the homes were occupied by families of Swedish descent.

I can remember as a grade-schooler coming home in the afternoon and hearing all the ladies of the neighborhood chatting away in Swedish over coffee and cookies on Anna Johnson's front porch. I had a wonderful opportunity to learn the language, since it was spoken by nearly all the families. Alas, like all the kids of my generation, I was just too busy. It was something I regret to this day. My uncle who lived up the street and could play almost any musical instrument you handed him tried in vain to get me to learn to play the piano. Once again, I was just too busy.

Sunday after church was a great socializing time. The churchgoers came from all over town and didn't see each other that often. They would gather in small groups on the street after services and catch up with the latest gossip and news. This lasted for an hour or more. The fact that most of the men worked at the Estey Organ plant or in the printing trade made them a tight-knit group. Everyone looked out for and helped everyone else. You could go away for a week and never lock a door.

I attended Sunday school at the Swedish Lutheran Church, as well as attending every Swedish meatball supper they put on. Those suppers were legendary and had to be run in three sittings to accommodate the crowd. At Christmas our family celebrated twice. We had a traditional one and a Swedish one with all the Swedish foods of the old country. Christmas on two consecutive days wasn't too hard to take when you were a kid.

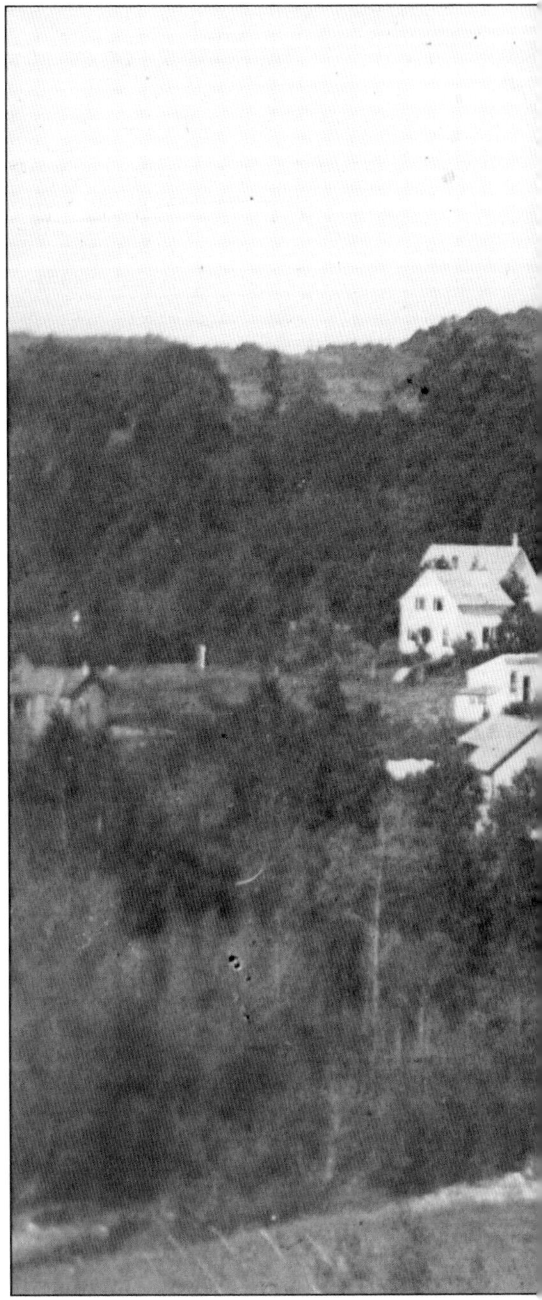

I remember the big maples that lined both sides of the street and provided welcome shade on summer days. The last of those was taken down this past fall. In the evening people spent a lot of time on their

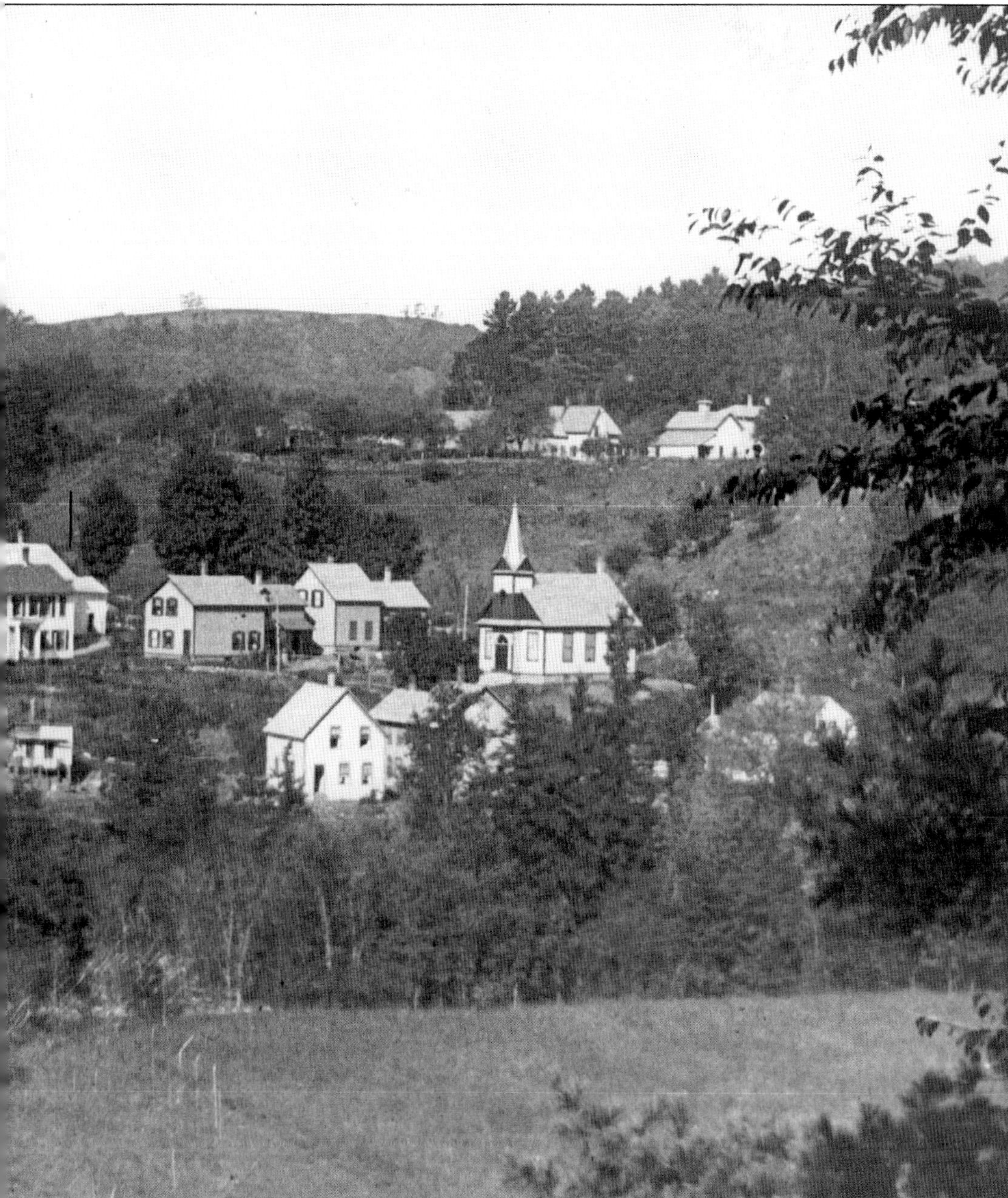

This part of town was known as Swedeville. The Swedish Lutheran Church (right) was built in 1894 and was torn down in 1948.

front porches sitting in porch swings and rocking chairs, which is something you never see now. Going across the street to sit and visit was commonplace.

Where did those days go? The "good old days" you hear older folks talk about really deserved the name in many respects.

—Carl M. Anderson

Island Park

There were outdoor porches and you could sit outside, walk around and watch the activities on the river.

The dancing took place inside the pavilion.

I remember going down to the river to see the damage caused by the flood of 1927(?). The bridge to the island was gone and there appeared to be a lot of damage to the pavilion. It was so sad.

—Mary Brackett

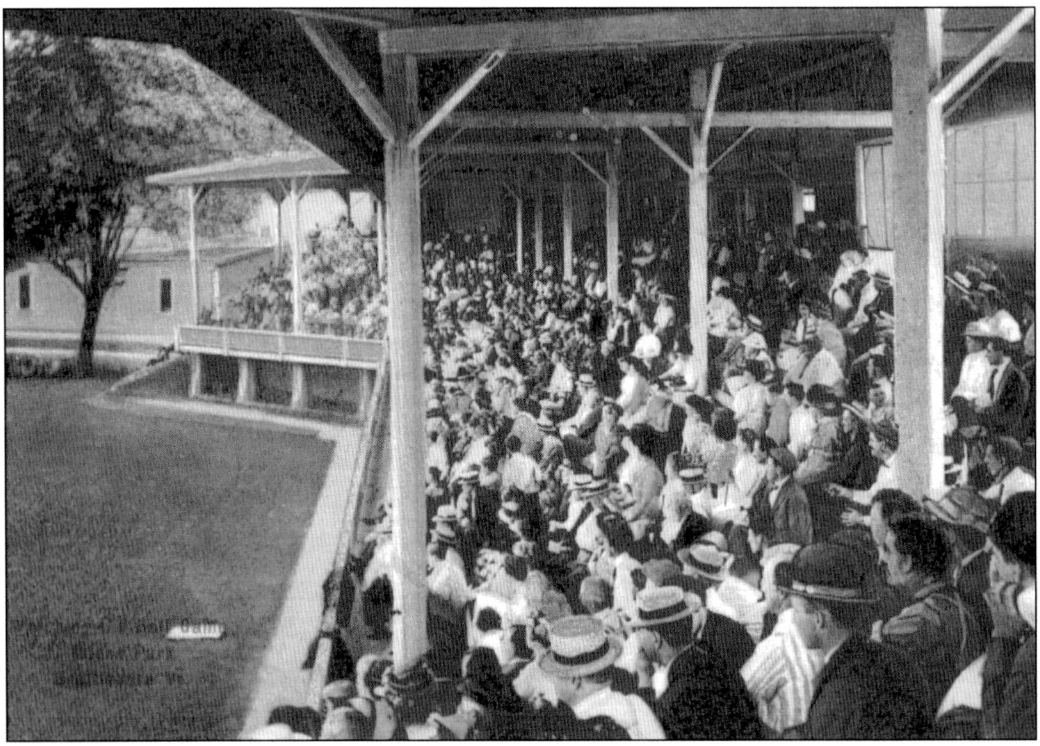

The folks in the bleachers are watching a baseball game at Island Park c. *1910.*

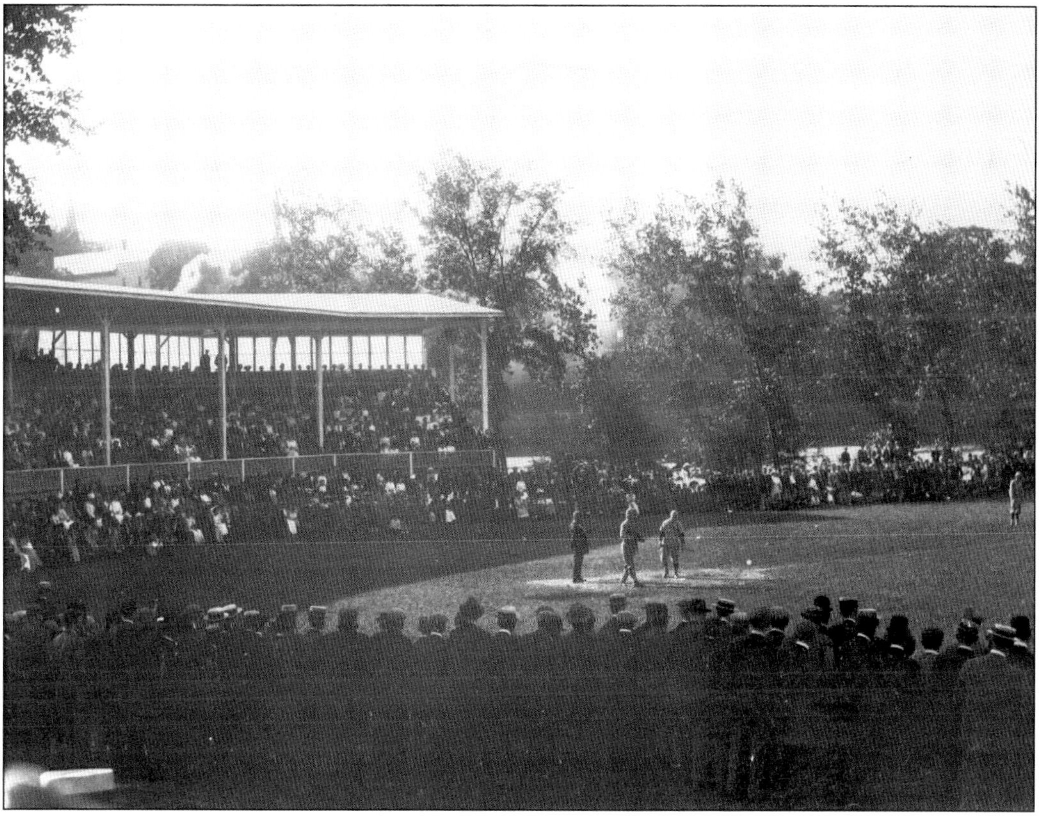

This view shows a baseball game in progress at Island Park c. *1910.*

SUMMER OUTINGS

My dad was a railroad man. He used to awaken me at midnight and let me see them unload the circus train.

They had dances as well as circuses and there were lots of baseball games. I went to lots of baseball games as a little girl. My older sister Ruth (10 years older) used to go to the dances, and my mom took her into the balcony to watch the dancers.

The baseball games were a lot of fun.

—Mary Brackett

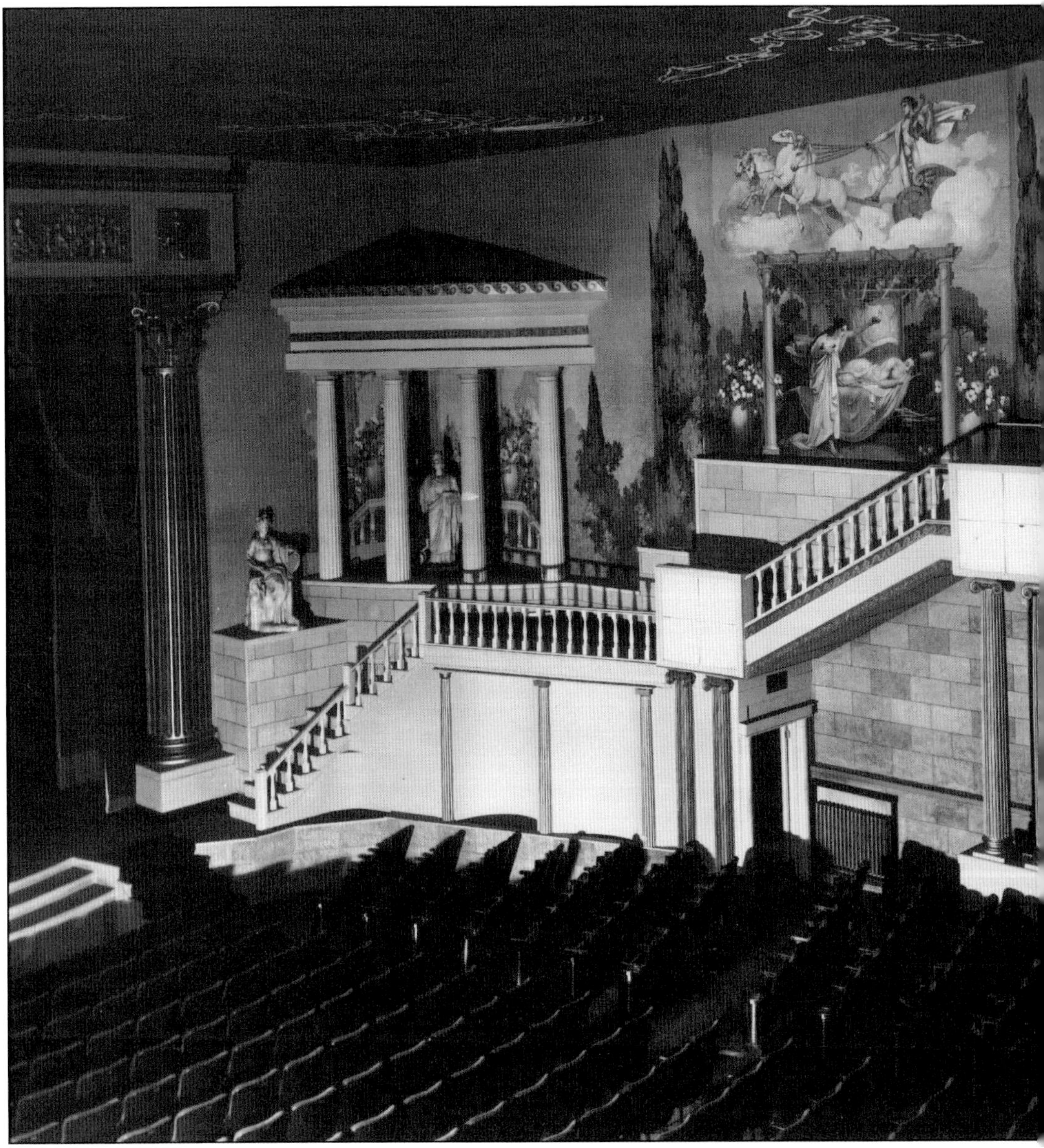

On the wall of the Latchis Theater was a Greek myth pictorial, seen above.

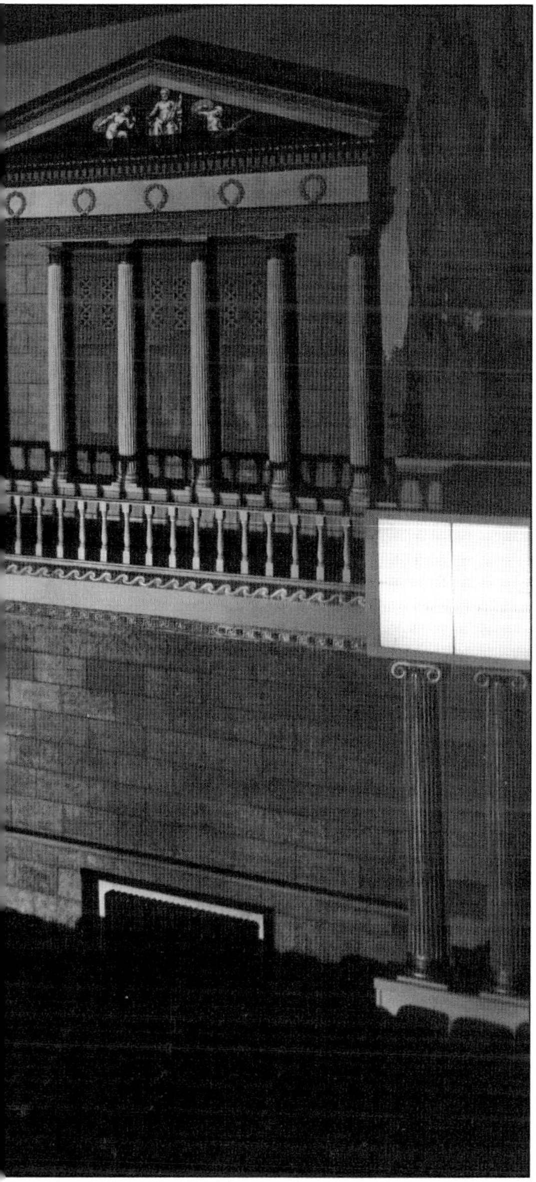

The theater was built in 1938.

Going to the Movies

When I was a kid in the 1950s, the highlight of the week was when Mom dropped us four kids off on Main Street for the Saturday matinee. My oldest sister would be given money for tickets and popcorn for all of us—a dollar or two, I think. And we'd head into the Paramount or the Latchis, the two movie theaters.

Both were scary buildings, with their high, dark ceilings, but my favorite was the Latchis, because of the fountain in the entrance. We'd each put a penny in and make a wish. I always wished for straight, blonde hair, but it never happened.

The movies were usually Disney flicks. *Snow White* I clearly remember seeing, from the balcony, and being quite scared. We didn't realize how safe we were, between the theater manager keeping a close eye on us, and every mom in town knowing our names.

Occasionally, we splurged on sno-caps or gummy bears, which we'd get between the Popeye cartoon and the main feature. I remember buying a can of beans sometimes, when they collected for the poor, and the theater would hand out pencil boxes just before school started. I got a red one with a pen and a pencil, a wooden ruler, an eraser, and a pencil sharpener in it one year. And I still have it.

I'll bet they don't hand out pencil boxes at Disney World!

—*Jane Douglas*

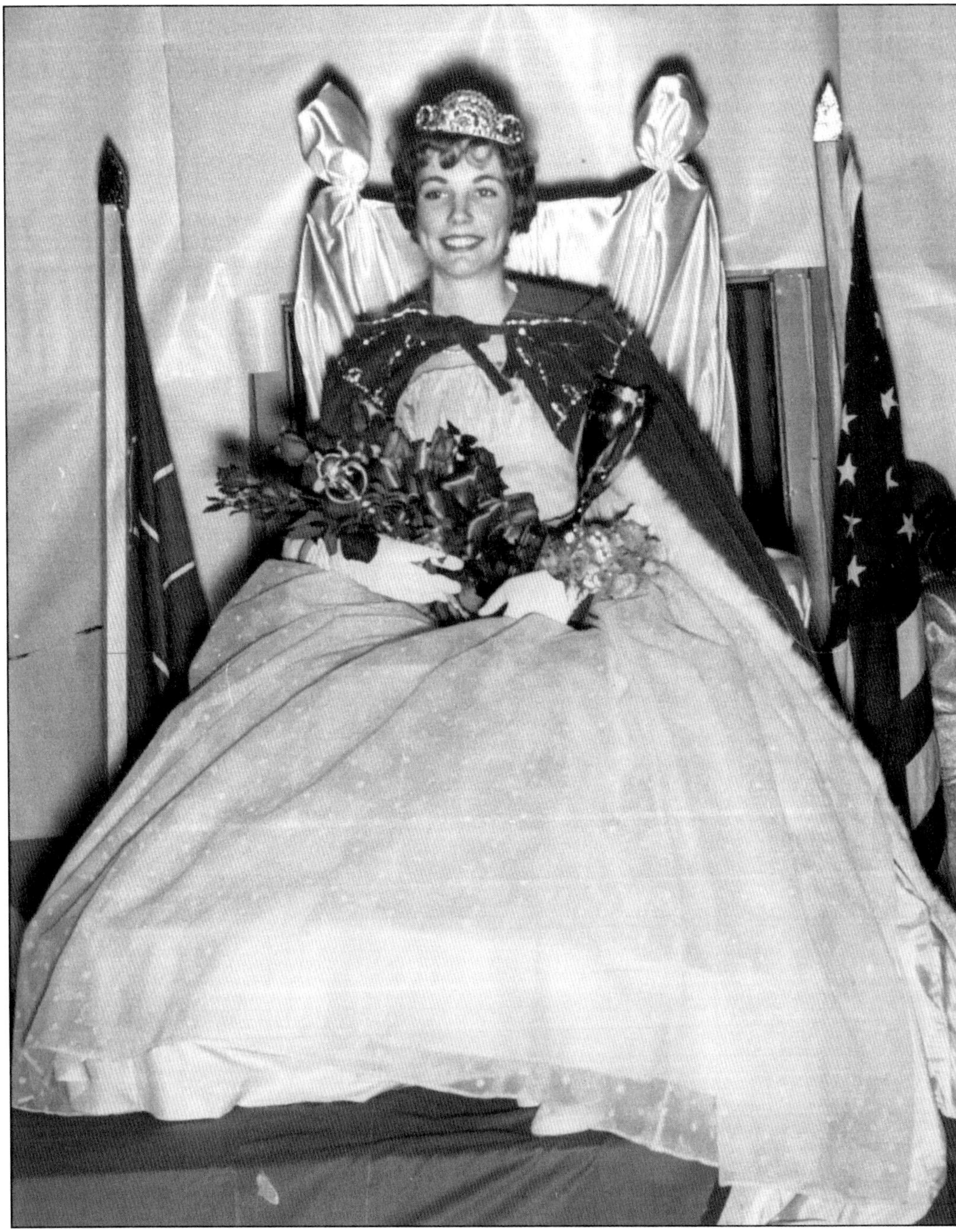

Debbie Estey smiles after being crowned queen of the 1960 Winter Carnival.

The Winter Carnival

When I was a kid in the 1950s and 1960s, the highlight of winter was the Winter Carnival. Back then, we didn't have the money to go to Disney World during February vacation, so we all had to find amusement right here in Brattleboro. So someone had come up with Winter Carnival.

The fun-filled week had a ski jump, where everyone would eat hot dogs and soda, and us kids would take turns running up and down the 436 stairs to the top (I counted them, too!).

There was a talent show, where talent was less of a requirement than courage, and I seem to remember a dance, too. Local kids would play, trying to be as good as Elvis.

But it seems to me, the highlight of the week was the Winter Carnival Parade. The high school band would play, and each of the candidates for Winter Carnival queen would have her own float. These would be quite fancy things put together by their sponsors, covered in napkins stuffed in chicken wire.

After the parade was finished, we'd all troop into the Harmony Lot for a sugar-on-snow feast. The meal included the sourest dill pickle, to offset the sweetness of the maple syrup, and a homemade lard-fried donut so heavy I could hardly chew it. But it was that huge dish of snow I remember most! They'd drizzle hot syrup over it, and we'd wish to get it all wrapped around a plastic fork before it solidified into a hard, sweet lump. We'd twirl it onto the fork like spaghetti, and lap it off like a lollipop.

—Jane Douglas

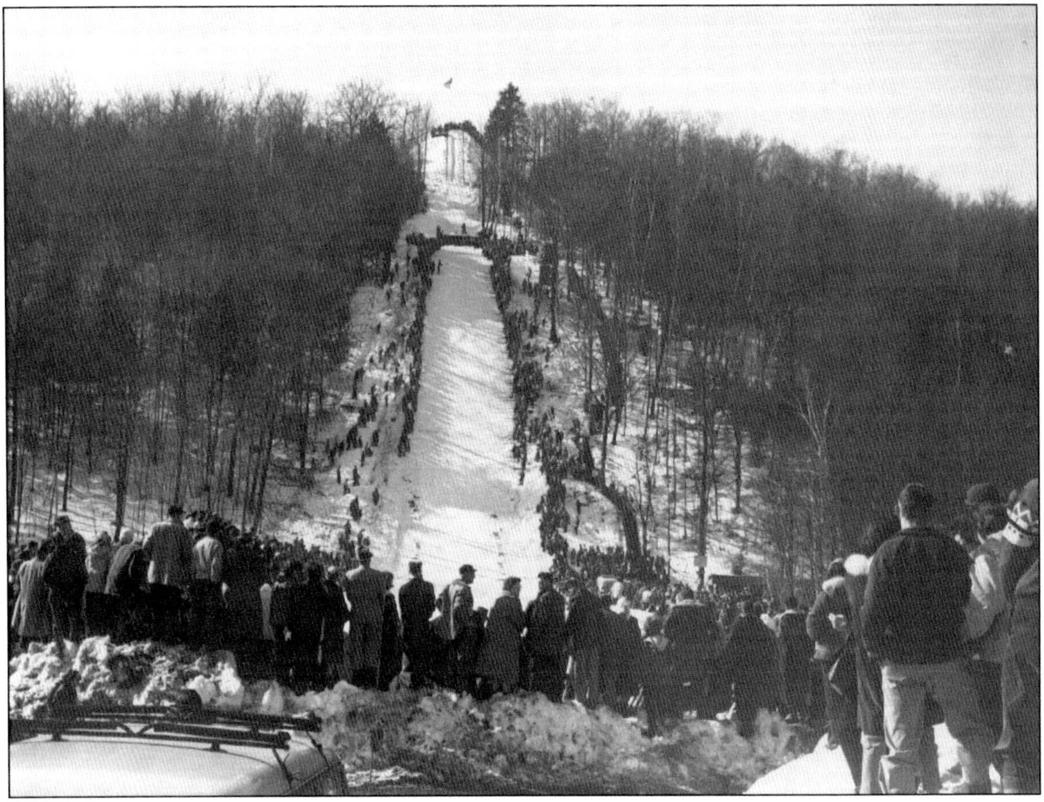

This view shows the annual ski jump event at Harris Hill.

Ski Jumping

As a 10-year-old, I donned my old jacket and overalls and three pairs of socks under my boots. Old folks talked about how cold it got, just standing there in the snow.

Walking over from Western Avenue with a couple of friends was exciting, but we walked everywhere in those days. The traffic down Cedar Street moved slowly. Most folks who drove had already parked on Spruce or one of the side streets. They didn't want to pay 50 cents to park on the Retreat cornfield.

This picture was probably taken in the 1970s, after the top of the takeoff had been extended. Every year the jumpers landed farther down the hill—some dangerously close to the red caution lines drawn in the snow. Eventually, the landing hill was redesigned.

People crowded the edges of the landing hill, jockeying for a good view of the skiers. Markers up the steep sides of the hill had long poles which were lowered as the jumper passed them—the last one marking the place where he eventually landed. The judges at the takeoff watched and calculated distance in meters and feet.

But the most exciting part was when someone fell—skis flying—the skier tumbling over and over. The ski patrol rushed out and checked him; the skier hobbled or limped to the side, to applause, sometimes louder than that for a good jump. Almost always, the previous year's record was broken.

We were enthralled by the jumpers name Torger and Nils, who came from Norway or Lithuania.

Later, crowds wore colorful ski jackets and boots—these folks are wearing everyday coats.

That line of black going up the north side of the hill was a stairway. Jumpers had to climb back up for the second round. I once climbed them and counted 360 steps. There were places to stop along the way. And you had to be careful of the boards that were loose.

Trudging home later, cold, with wet feet, we defended our favorite jumper.

—Marguerite Douglas

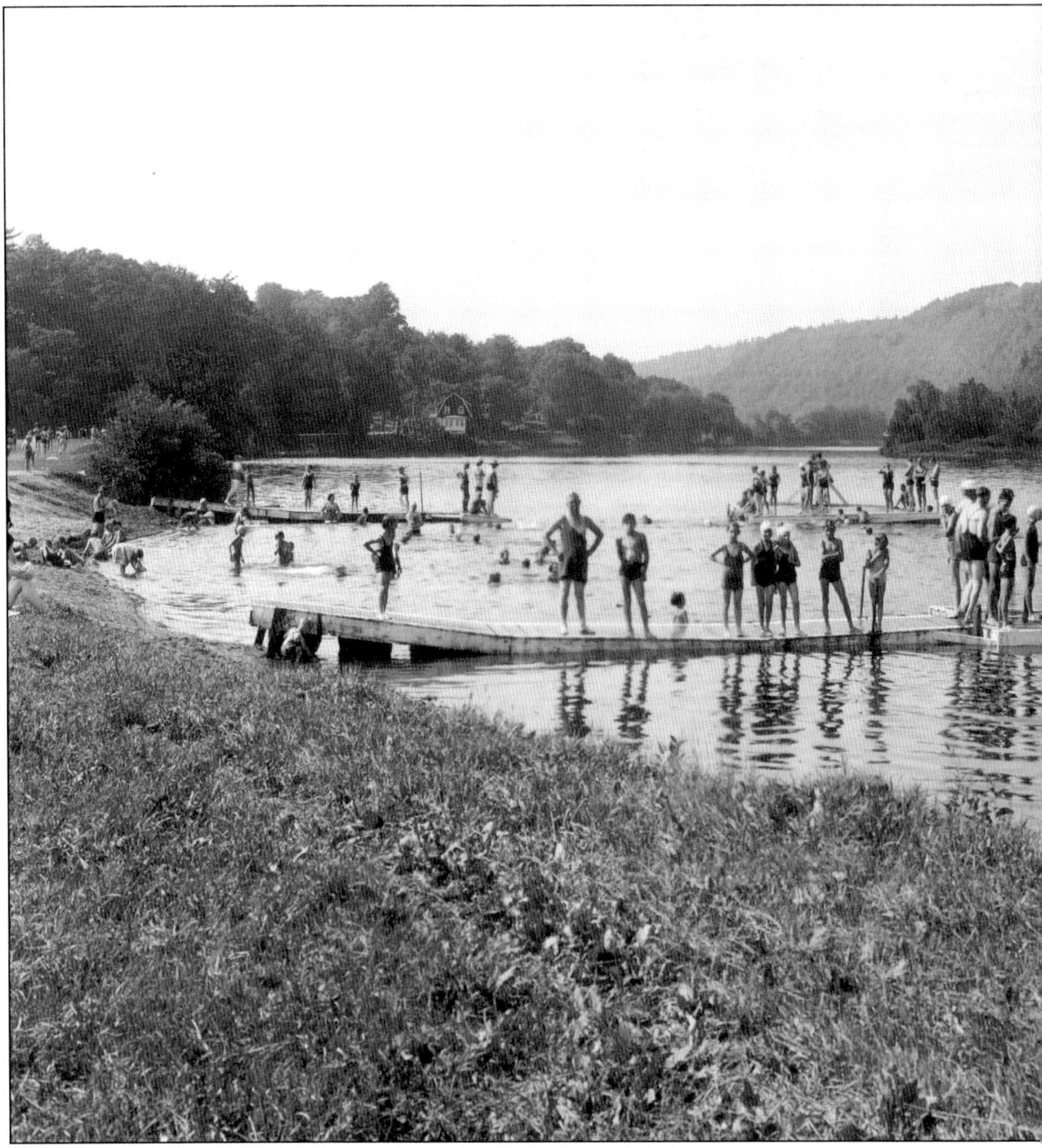

Photographed c. *1940 is the Retreat Meadows public beach, on the West River,*

SWIMMING IN THE WEST RIVER

This is the bathing beach down at the West River. Lester Lovell and his wife were college students, but they were in charge of lifesaving for the area.

Now this area is right out there where the Retreat Meadows is, where the pumping station is now.

They put in two bathhouses, and then they built these piers and they had a bathing raft out there. This was the Town of Brattleboro's public bathing area. They sponsored it and paid all the bills for it.

This was at the time when infantile paralysis was prevalent. And I remember they closed the bathing beach one year. They thought it might have something

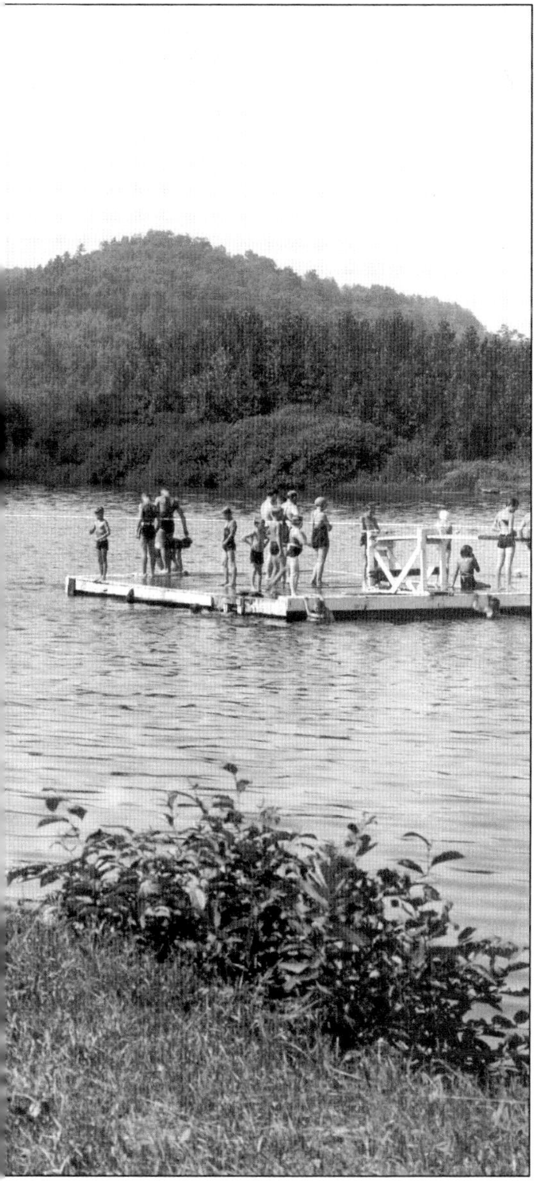

a popular spot for swimming.

to do with bathing.

Lester Lovell and his wife taught swimming lessons for any child in Brattleboro that wanted to go down and take the lessons free. That's how I learned to swim. They did a marvelous job of teaching as well as maintaining the safety of every child there.

—*Wallace Briggs*

Town Beach at the Retreat Meadows

Looking at a photo of the old town beach on the West River brought back many memories. I learned to swim there and got my lifeguard certification there also.

I remember the docks and the float, which seemed a great distance away at the time. On the upstream side of the first dock was an early chlorinating device, which we never messed with, but I am quite sure it dissipated as much chlorine to the whole area as to the beach itself. There were two bathhouses up on level ground and a place where we could check our clothes for safekeeping, getting a small numbered pin in exchange. In front of the bathhouses were the two lifeguard stands where I spent hours broiling in the sun.

Serving as a volunteer lifeguard was great fun. During my break I used to take the path across the field where the wells are now and climb the Retreat Tower to eat lunch. The tower was open full time in those days.

There were a couple of other informal swimming holes upriver, one of which was equipped with a great rope swing, which enabled us to drop about 20 feet into the water. Lots of fun at the time but seems a little crazy to me now.

No one knew what air-conditioning was, so the beach and the swimming holes were our only escape on hot summer days. It was particularly crowded on weekends with whole families coming out to cool off. I know the facilities were overtaxed, but no one seemed to mind at the time. I believe there was a certain tolerance for such things in those days. No fancy pool, very few rules, and the only requirement was to have a good time and enjoy the water.

All in all, the two summers I spent there were most enjoyable, and though it was many years ago, I remember it well.

—*Carl M. Anderson*

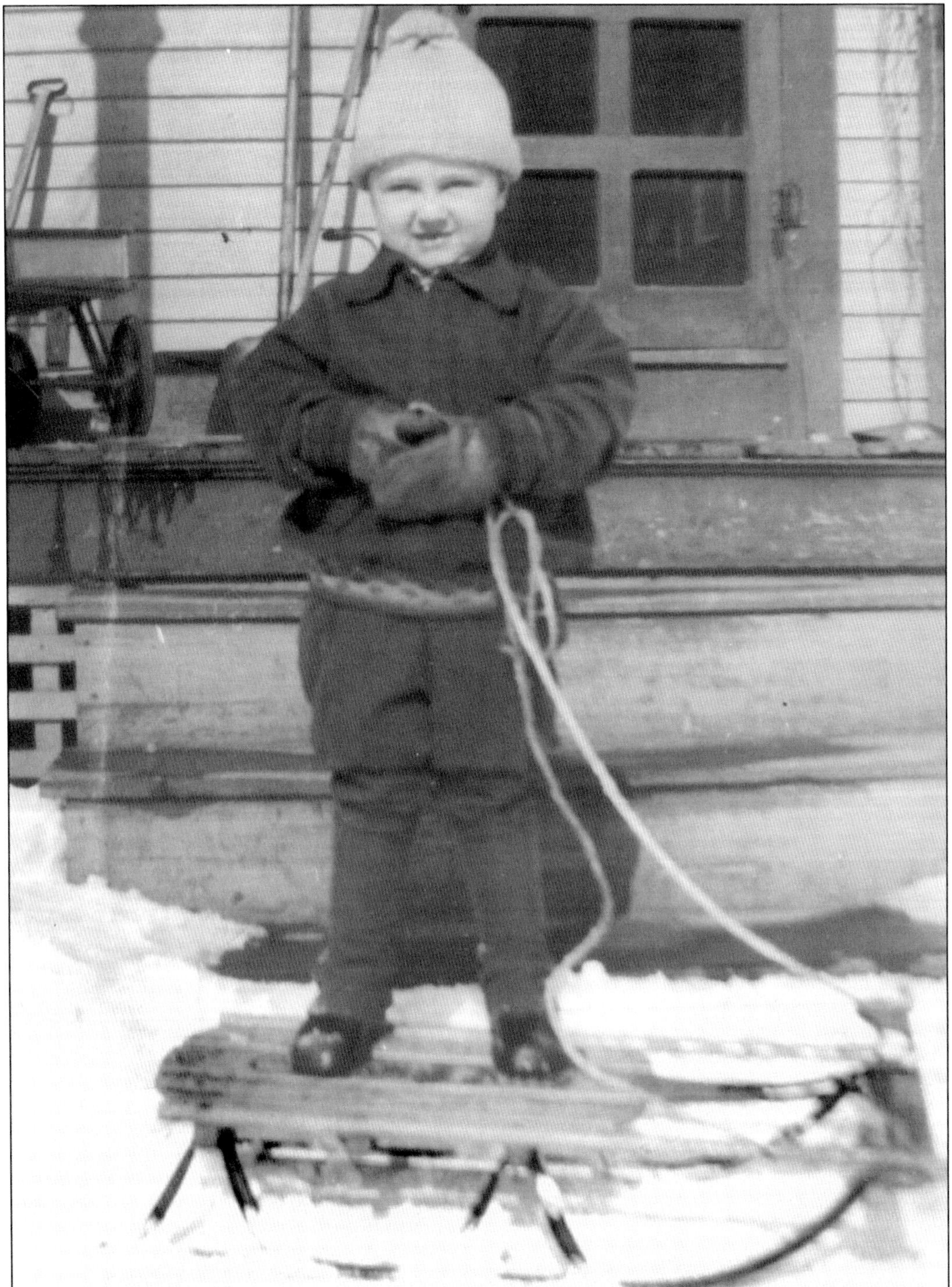

Sledding has endured through the years as a winter activity for all ages. In the winter of 1930, this three-year-old anticipates speeding down the steep hill in his neighborhood. As traffic increased and streets became too dangerous, sliding was relegated to certain areas such as Memorial Park and open hillsides.

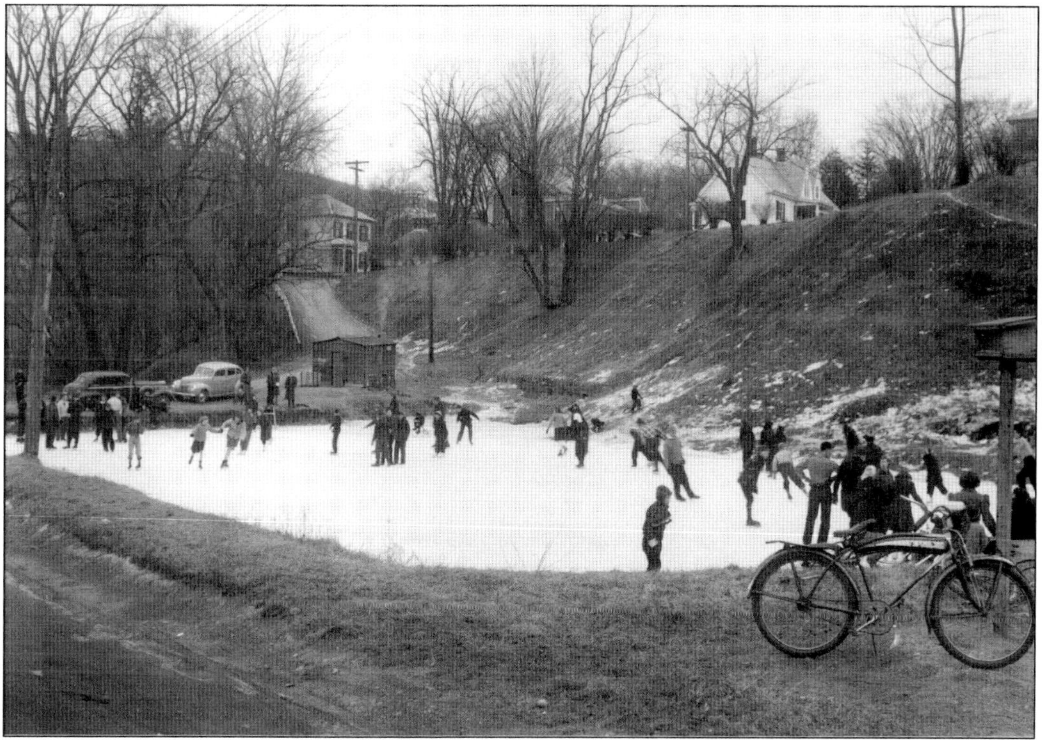

This 1946 photograph shows ice-skaters on Whitney Pond, off Frost Place.

SLEDDING

The winter was a special time for us kids in Brattleboro. I used to go sledding with the King sisters on the hill behind their grandfather Haskell's house on Western Avenue [now, the Max Carr Funeral Home]. We were all bundled up and didn't seem to mind the cold one bit, we were having so much fun. The town would close Green Street so we could take advantage of the hill with our sleds.

Those were good times, and they are good memories.

—Harriet Ives

SKATING ON CRYSTAL ICE

One of my earliest memories of being allowed, as a child, to go off somewhere unaccompanied by an adult was to go ice-skating. Most of the kids in the neighborhood would walk over to Crystal Ice & Fuel Company on Frost Place and spend an entire Saturday afternoon there. Sometimes when we got there, we would go sledding down Brook Street, which was blocked off to traffic in the winter, but mostly we would skate. I can still remember twirling on the ice until I was dizzy and playing tag in my old pair of hand-me-down skates. Then, when we were so cold that we thought our toes would fall off, we would race to the warming hut. But, either the shed wasn't heated or we were too impatient to stay inside long enough to thaw out, because in addition to remembering all of our great fun, I can still recall the cold!

—Annette LeBlanc Cappy

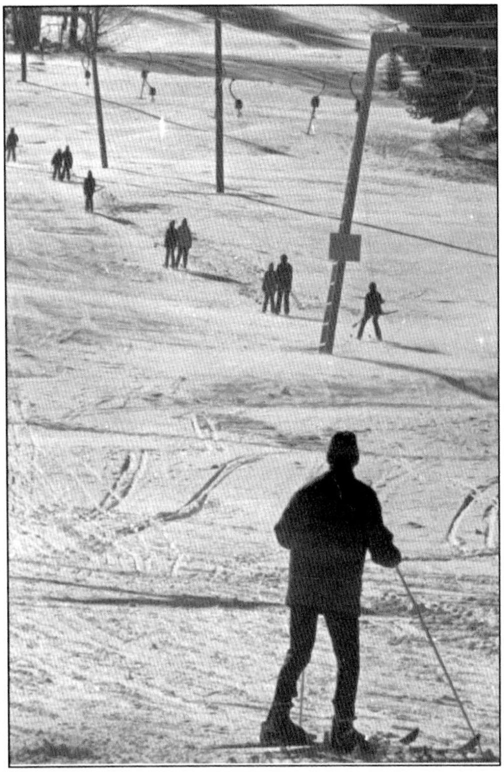

The ski tow at Memorial Park is pictured in January 1977.

THE DOPPELMAYR T-BAR LIFT

The Hogback Ski Area in Marlboro purchased two Doppelmayr ski lifts and the town of Brattleboro purchased one. The shipping of the three ski lifts was paid for by the Hogback Ski Area. The lift at the Memorial Park was installed, and the funds to pay for it were raised by the Brattleboro Recreation and Parks Board in a private fund drive.

The Memorial Park Ski Area has an interesting history. It started about 1935 on private land owned by the Clark family off Guilford Street. The area was called the Guilford Street Ski Tow, with a 1,100-foot rope line for skiers.

The rope tow had its limitations. It took a degree of skill just to get on it and ride to the top. The skier would grab the bottom rope and let it slide through his two hands while gradually increasing the grip enough to hold onto the rope. If you tightened too quickly, it would jerk you off your feet. Many times on a wet day the rope would get thoroughly wet and it would leave a mark on your ski sweater as it slid by in front of you. When the lift halted and you were on the hill, the rope would be heavy in your hands, so you might drop it and have to start over when the rope began to move again. It was a lot of squeezing.

The new Doppelmayr T-bar was a great improvement. It was located on a new site to the right of the old site and provided more land to ski upon and made a longer and higher ride to the top of the ski area. A new ski hut at the top of the hill was provided by the Hogback Ski Area [the building was moved intact from Hogback to the Park, where it was affectionately called "the Castle" by the ski patrol].

To use the T-bar, a skier would get in position on the lift line and wait for the T to come from behind and the bar would ride up against the back of the thighs. The spring tension on the T-bar would make a gradual start, not a jerk as the rope tow would do. At the top the skier would pull forward on the T of the bar and would give them impetus to ski off the bar to the left. It was a relaxed ride once on the T-bar.

At one time there was an amplifier which would provide music for skiing. With the white snow, the great view, and the lovely music on a moonlit night, it seemed almost heavenly.

Due to several seasons of poor or little snowfall, the opening of the skating rink which attracted so many young skaters, and the alternative skiing at Maple Valley, the T-bar lift ceased operation in 1994.

—Frank Dearborn

CHAPTER FOUR

DINING IN OR OUT

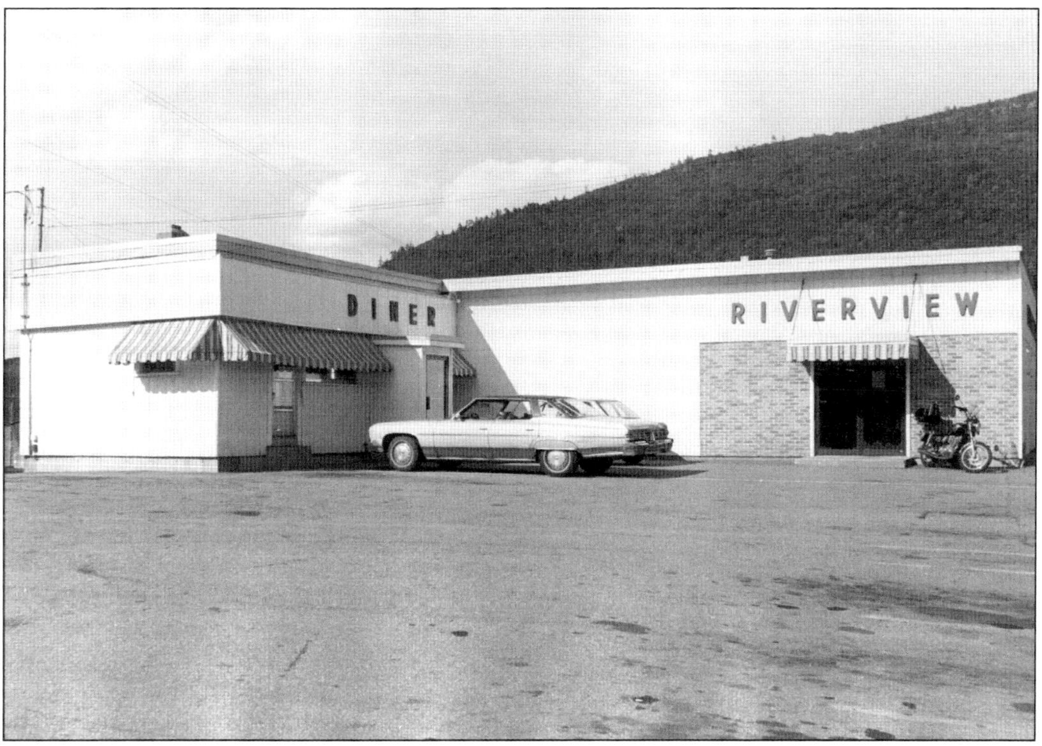

Dining in or dining out aptly describes the options at the Riverview Diner after it was moved from Bridge Street hill and relocated across the railroad tracks on the edge of the Connecticut River. An additional dining room was attached to the original diner, and an outdoor deck area was constructed to provide seating for viewing the river. Weather permitting, patrons have their choice of eating "in or out."

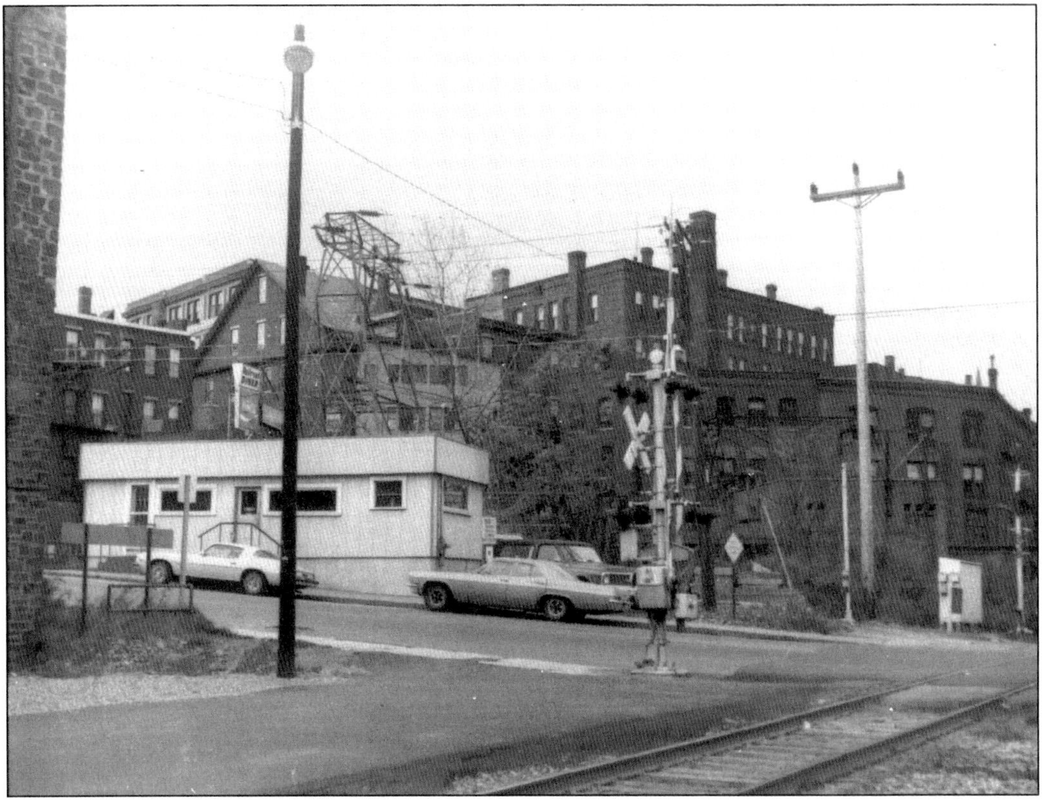

This c. *1970 photograph shows Railroad Diner, located on Bridge Street.*

RAILROAD DINER

Railroad Diner, currently part of the Riverview Restaurant. My dad owned it. It was originally in Putney, and he moved it to the area near the railroad station in the mid-1940s.

In order to support the structure, steel beams were put up, as it was virtually hanging right over the Whetstone Brook as it went into the Connecticut River.

My dad leased it to Ernie Bishop, who ran it for many years. In 1952, I took over management of the diner. The Hinsdale Racetrack paid us $300 a year to have a sign on the roof showing directions to the racetrack. I also got a free pass to the racetrack.

Ray Lanois moved it to its present location [now part of Riverview Café] in the late 1950s.

—Matt Speno

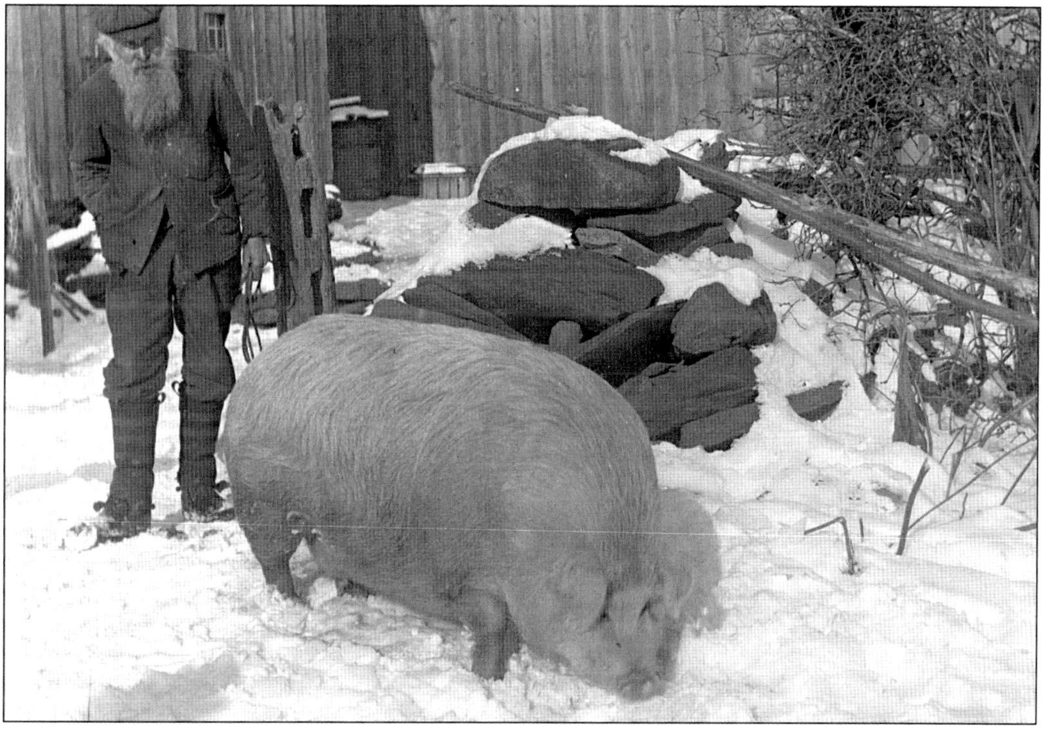

Wes Rockwell shows off his prized 500-pound sow c. *1919.*

Dinnertime

Back in the late 1960s, my husband, Leonard, and a friend thought it would be a great idea to raise a couple of pigs for winter eating. Howard had the barn and the space for a pen. We pooled our money, and Howard purchased two small piglets, got the necessary feed, and constructed the pen. Over the summer I watched them grow, turning their once neat grassy area in the pen to a smelly, muddy hog wallow.

It was now November and turning cold, getting close to the time when the two pigs would have to be slaughtered. Howard decided they had gained enough weight, having raised hogs before. So one Saturday morning it was future dinnertime.

Foolishly, I decided to watch. The former pigs were turned into their yard, one at a time. Howard got his revolver out. BANG went a shot. Right in the head. It killed the pig almost instantly but not before squealing so horrendously it made my stomach turn. The pig dropped. Leonard and Howard carried it a few feet to a rope thrown over a rafter. The end of the rope was looped around the pig's neck, and he was hauled up until the carcass was off the ground. Howard took a knife and slit its throat. The blood gushed out of the slash in torrents. This is an important part of butchering, to have all the blood drain out completely so there is no residue in the meat.

Then Howard took his knife and slit the animal lengthwise so it could be gutted—another important step in the butchering. All the guts slithered out, some of which had to be manually pulled out. The pig came down off the rafter, and the rope was taken off. Then the guys carried the carcass to a huge boiler of water that had been heated to the boiling point. Howard had rigged up some sort of block and tackle to load the pig into the hot water, and in it dropped. The pig sat in the water for a short time and the scraping of the bristles began until the hide was clean. The carcass was hauled out of the vat and carried onto the back of Howard's pickup to be driven to Bushnell's to be cut up, wrapped, and stored in Bushnell's freezer locker.

It certainly made for very good eating on a cold winter night, the aroma of a loin roasting in the oven permeating the entire house. But it was extremely difficult for me not to remember how this roast pork originally came about.

—Mary Lou Buchanan

Living in the 'Hood

In retrospect, growing up directly on Main Street in Brattleboro provided a very secure childhood.

During the 1950s, Main Street was a totally different downtown from today. One could leave my house (next to the existing library) and walk to three chain grocery stores—the A&P, the Grand Union, and the First National. Errands were run downtown on a regular basis because there was no need to shop elsewhere. Major chain stores were all downtown, and it was the center of activity.

My favorite time was Sunday supper. If I had been well behaved for the week (which was a loosely defined term in my case), I was allowed to cross Main Street by myself and go to the Royal Diner to order a hamburger and french fries. This was a supreme treat, as the taste of those hamburgers is something I still remember. It was even better when I brought the take-out order home to eat because I was allowed to set up a TV tray and watch television in the living room. Of course, all the other meals for the week were family meals at either the kitchen or dining room table.

Later, as the 1960s started, things changed drastically. The thruway opened and, despite the worries, brought more traffic to town, and business started moving from downtown. My parents were finally forced to actually buy a car in 1961.

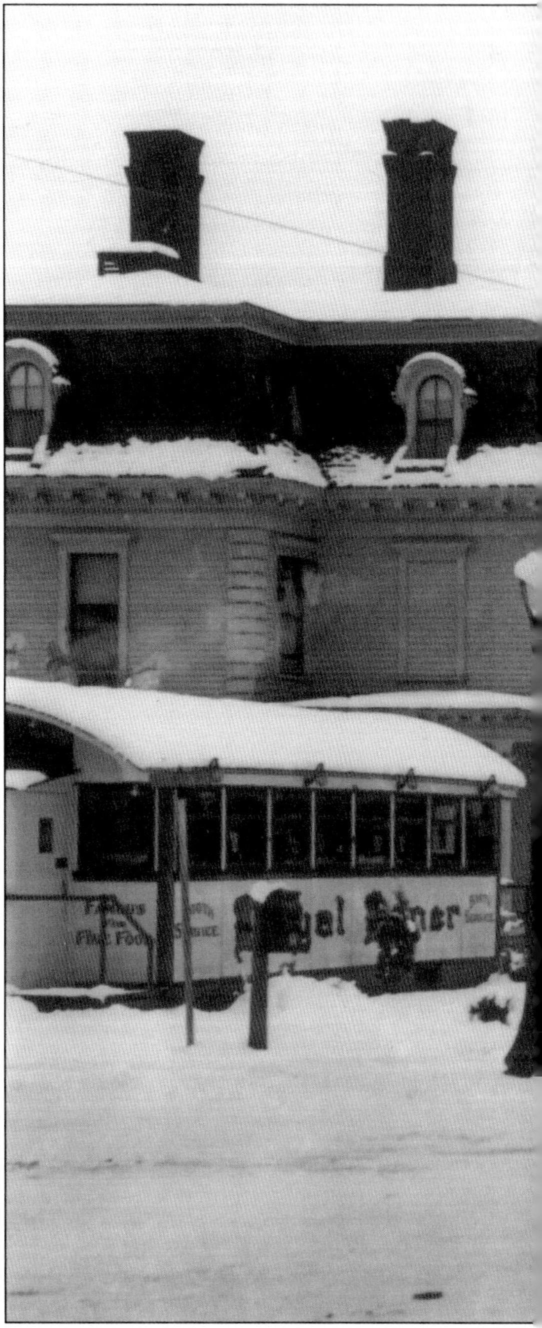

The quiet Sunday evenings of years ago have vanished, but we still retain our sense of that community. Times and technology have changed, but perhaps we should still remember and cherish the past.

—Jerry Remillard

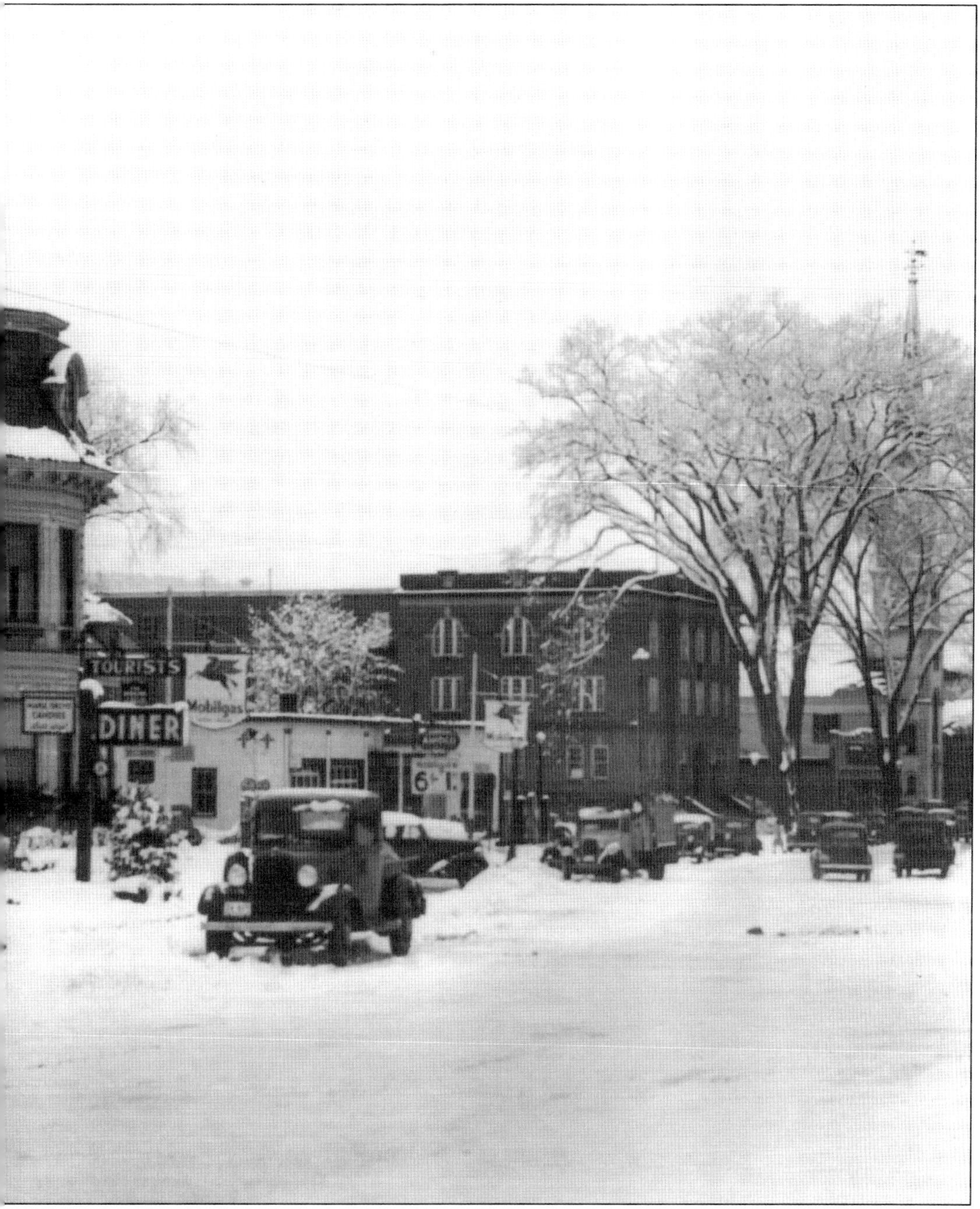

This snowy street scene shows the Royal Diner, a candy shop, a gas station, and automobiles that appear to be parked at random.

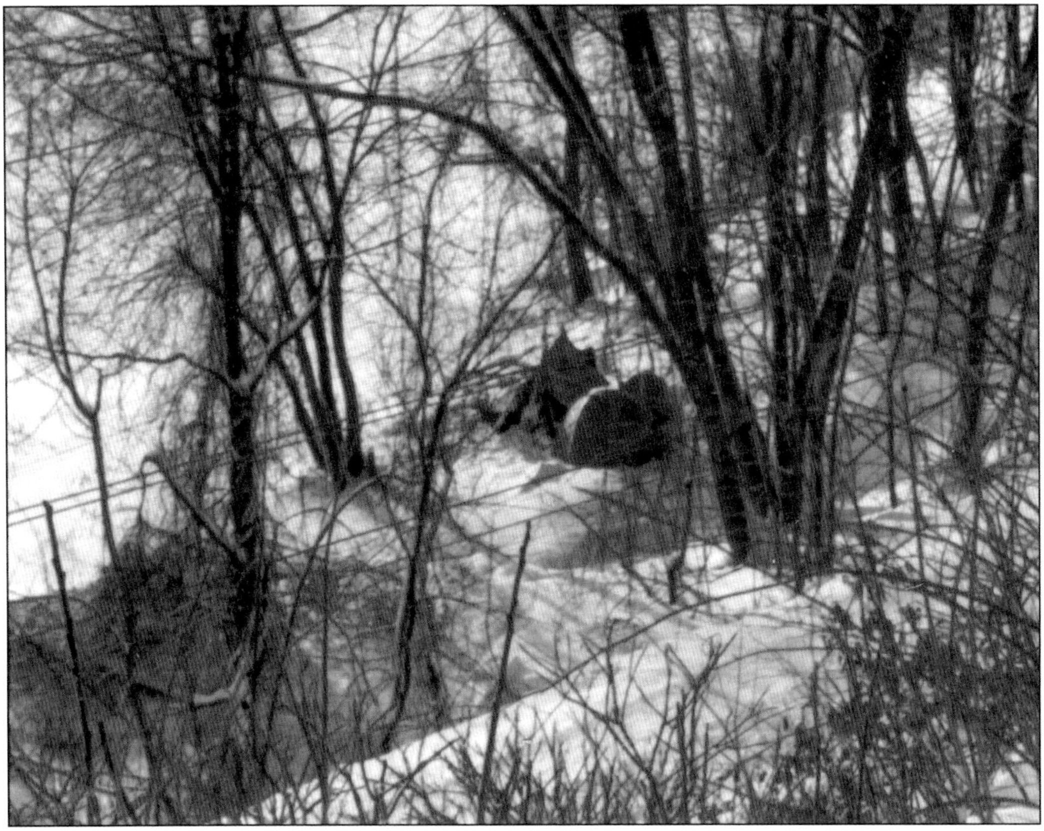

Two tents are pitched along the riverside.

No. 999 Walnut Street

I realized we had new neighbors when I smelled smoke in the backyard. In investigating, I saw white tendrils coming from the edge of the river. New folks had moved in and set up camp on the land that is located across the railroad tracks. It was February, and the fire was attempting to provide a semblance of warmth. From an article in the newspaper, I learned that one of the gentlemen, Earl, had left his job a few months previously because of disabling pain and refused to seek any means of welfare support, as he considered it demeaning. The other fellow, Larry, had just gotten out of jail and joined Earl, since he was homeless, penniless, and friendless. The location of the camp tended to reel in folks who were down on their luck.

The previous spring a pair of white geese had arrived mysteriously and had spent the season on the water. The pair had built a nest on the opposite shore, and Linda, the female, had laid eggs. But high water would come every so often and flood the nest. The pitiful girl would sit and sit with no results. Finally she gave up and Larry, the male, and Linda spent the rest of the summer cruising the river.

Now it was cold, and the river, for the most part, was frozen. The geese were having a difficult time finding food and continually getting enmeshed in ice. Earl and Larry noticed their predicament. Since Larry was the smaller of the two, he was elected to creep out on the ice to free the birds. Successfully, the birds were released from their icy prison. Leftovers from local food kitchens kept both Larry and Earl and

Linda and Larry fed for most of the winter. The two men were resourceful and had built themselves a quite adequate shelter from cardboard, scraps of wood, and tarps; they had a grill on which to cook food and pallets on which to sleep.

It was almost April, and the ice was just about gone from the river. With open water the geese didn't have the need to stay around the camp. A new spring and perhaps a new nest was coming around the corner. Paddling up and down the river that bordered the river camp, the geese were able to forage for their own food. Later that summer the geese drifted to the site of the marina farther down the river. Rumor had it that the owner of the marina tried to lure the geese into a shelter for the winter but was unsuccessful. The geese disappeared and were never sighted again.

I felt a sense of loss on losing the geese, as I had kept a periodic check on them the past two summers. The fact that two homeless individuals cared enough about the birds to take care and feed them also touched me. I knew there was still some sense of caring and charity left in the world even if it was just feeding geese with leftover bread.

Unfortunately, Earl's health problems intensified, and he died in April of complications of diabetes. Larry continued to live at the camp until the railroad company decided he was trespassing and evicted him from the premises. But I will always remember the two guys and the geese that inhabited 999 Walnut Street, even if it was only for a short time.

—Mary Lou Buchanan

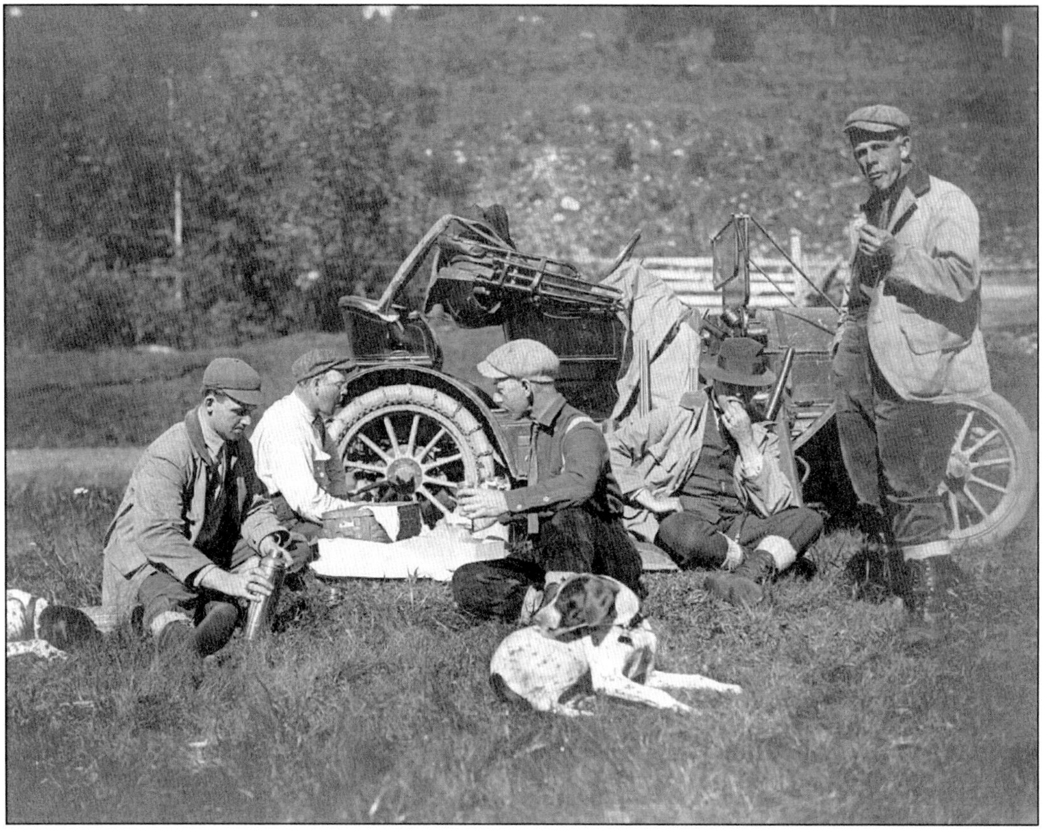

This group takes a break after a morning's hunt. Those pictured are, from left to right, Lawrence Barber, "Doc" Aldrich, Ernie Perry, Sam the dog, unidentified, and Charlie Harris.

Family Picnics

As a child, I would often visit my Grandfather Bancroft, on Western Avenue across from the water tower. The tower is now gone. Grandfather worked for 60 years at the Estey Organ Company, and he would let us visit him there. I remember it as a big and busy place, with all kinds of smells. Later, I learned from some of the Estey records stored at the Brattleboro Historical Society that he worked in building No. 3, where they made the keys for the instruments.

He was a kindly gentleman, and he and my mother and aunts would plan picnics for us at Stickney Brook. We would buy the groceries at Chase's store on Western Avenue [now Avenue Grocery] that was not far from their house.

With Grandfather's help, we would build a fire in the rocks by the brook to cook the picnic dinner. While the food was cooking under my mother's and aunts' watchful eyes, Grandfather supervised our wading in the brook. When the food was ready, we were called and we would all enjoy the meal. Somehow the food always tasted better at those picnics.

—Harriet Ives

CHAPTER FIVE
WORK

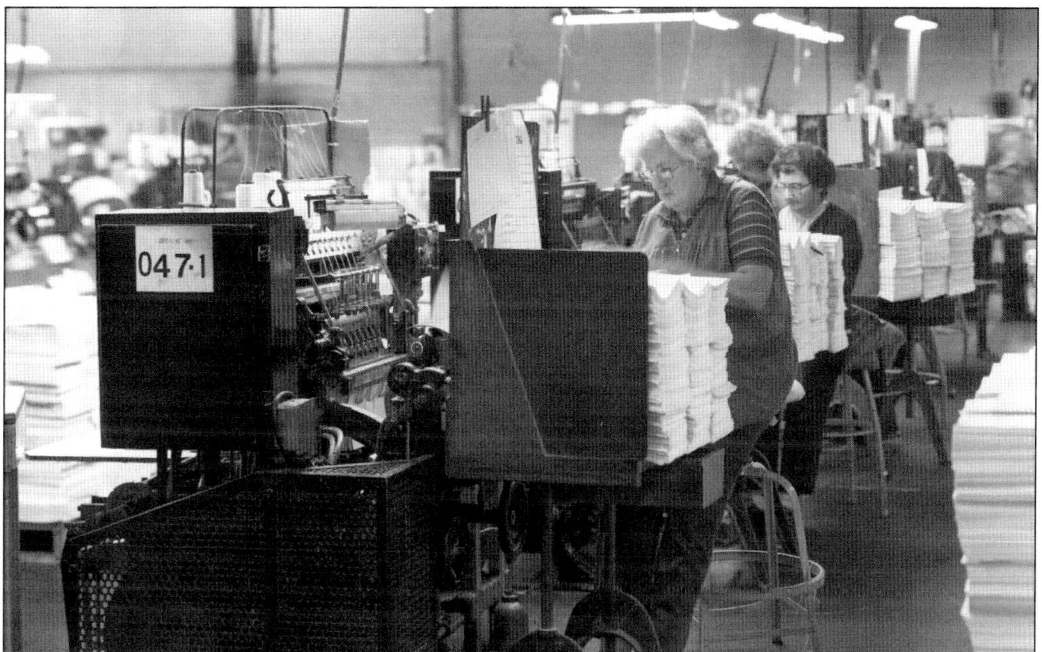

The Book Press was one of Brattleboro's larger employers within the memories of many residents. As the operation changed ownership through the years, a variety of books, including best-sellers, were produced at the local plant on Putney Road. From the early days of the community with publishers Holbrook and Fessenden, printing and publishing have provided vital sources of income for workers and recognition in the literary world for the one and only Brattleboro. Firms such as E.L. Hildreth Company and Stephen Greene Press emerged over time as important publishing and printing houses but have passed into the history books. The printing and publishing business exists in town to this day, although on a smaller scale than the major enterprises of yesteryear.

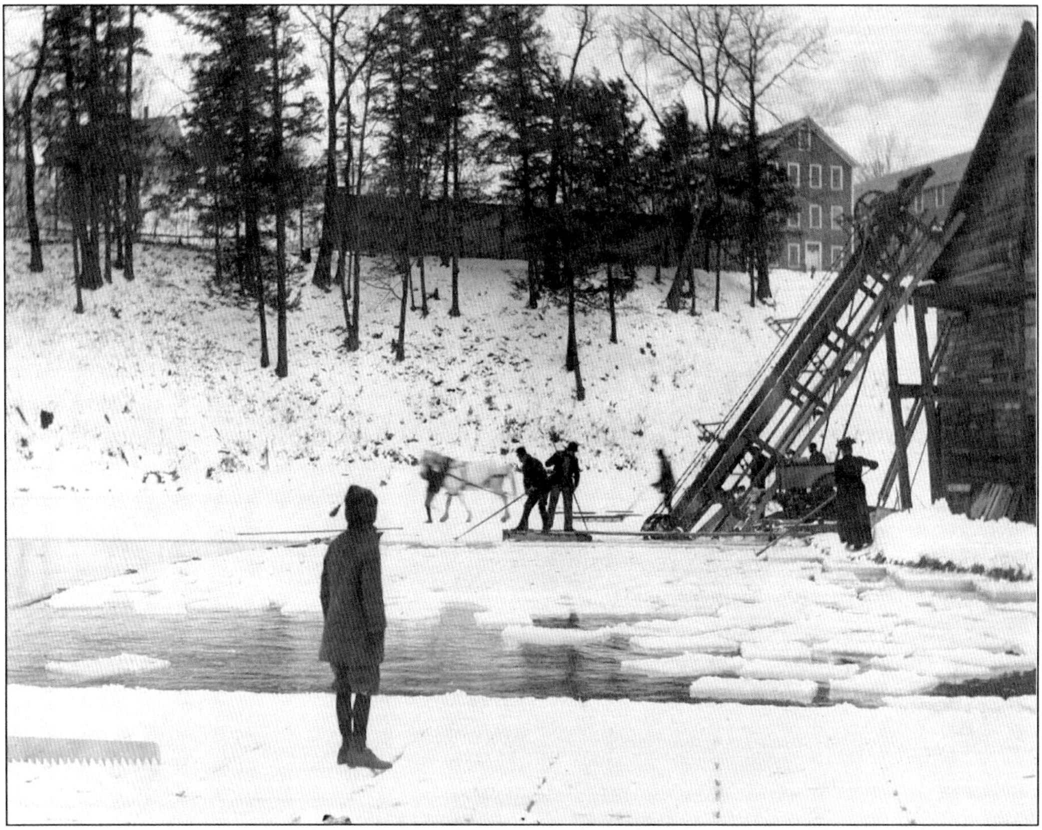

Ice blocks are loaded on the conveyer belt for storage in the icehouse.

The Crystal Springs Ice Company

Olly Whitney owned the Crystal Springs Ice Company on Frost Place. The ponds of the ice company were formed by springs and controlled by sluiceways. In the early 1940s, my father and I came down to see the place from Meburyville, Vermont. We stood on the porch of Mr. Whitney's house. Mr. Whitney was a devoted raccoon hunter. I remember looking at stretched-out coon hides. I didn't like looking at dead animals. I was about four years old. My father bought the ice business about 1944, and we moved into the house that is still there on Frost Place. A large icehouse was out in back of the house. The original icehouse had been torn down. This was about the time that they stopped cutting the ice out of ponds and the actual process of manufacturing ice was done inside the icehouse.

My brothers and sisters didn't care much about the ice business. I was the one who was interested. My father had a delivery truck. He delivered ice to all of Windham County and the towns of Chesterfield and Hinsdale in New Hampshire. I used to ride on the back of the ice truck. Icemen used to wear a large sponge under the back of the rubber apron to prevent water from the melting ice soaking their trousers. My job was to wring out the sponge after each delivery. I used to hand out pieces of ice to children who ran after the ice truck.

I still remember the telephone number of the Crystal Springs Ice Company. It was 438W.

The ice manufacturing business was a true art. I still remember the process in detail. In the large icehouse building, there was a large metal tank about 30 feet by 40 feet set in the ground. That was called a "field." This was filled with brine. The top of the pool was covered with wooden grid work. Each grid would accommodate two 300-pound galvanized steel tanks. These tanks at the end of the process would provide 300-pound cakes of ice each. These tanks were filled with water. A hoist was used to drop them into the brine. An air hose was attached to a bubbler, so that each tank would have water and air bubbling through it. The ice block would form from the outside in. Then there was a coring process that would cause the ice to be crystal clear and easier to cut. Inside the building there was a very large cooler. I knew it well because a couple of times I got accidentally locked in there. The wall of the cooler had pipes with ammonia running through them that were embedded in eight-inch cork.

There was an engine room with large motors and flywheels. As kids, we were never allowed in the engine room because if our clothing got caught in the flywheels, we would be gone!

There were a lot of accidents in the icehouse. More than once or twice workers got their hands caught and injured in the equipment.

The plant ran 24 hours a day, seven days a week. There was a dip tank to loosen up the ice cakes. Occasionally, after a few nips of drink, someone fell into the tank and would have to be rescued.

People used to come to the door of my house to buy ice. I don't remember how much we used to charge for a block of ice, but I do remember that my father used to pay me a penny a bag for bagging up ice cubes.

I remember skating on the pond. The Brattleboro Recreation Department took over the pond and would scrape it off after each storm. They even put lights at one end of it. The pond was used for skating into the late 1950s. My brother now owns the Crystal Ice & Fuel in the same location.

—Linda Hellus

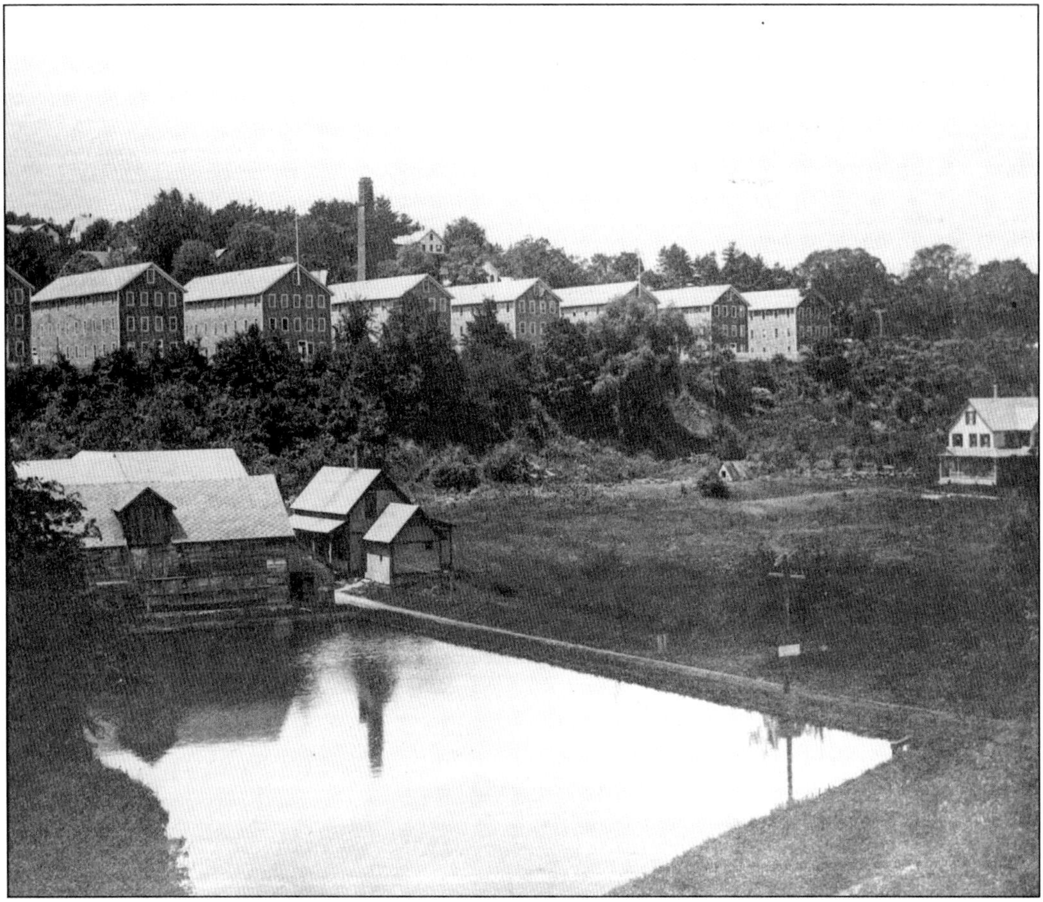

Estey Organ buildings overlook the ice pond, on Frost Place, c. *1930. In winter, ice was cut from the pond for summer use.*

The Crystal Ice Pond

This is the Crystal Ice pond. Years back, the ice was cut in sections and sold to homes for use in their iceboxes. Customers were furnished a large square card with numbers which would specify how many pounds were needed. This you placed in the window for the iceman to see. (Ed had a dog named Zep when he lived on Green Street. Zep did not like the iceman for some reason. One day when the dog was home alone, he took the ice card out of the window and chewed it up.)

We had an icebox in our first apartment, as electric refrigerators were not available for a while after World War II.

This pond was also great for skating and enjoyed by many of us as we grew up, as well as our children. A warming hut or section made putting on and taking off your skates much more comfortable.

The background of the picture shows the Estey Organ Company buildings. My father worked there as a cabinetmaker of the reed organs for about 43 years. I can recall going in there as a young person and being quite impressed with all of the equipment and the work that was being done.

—Dot and Ed Milkey

The Crystal Icehouse and the Estey Buildings

I remember the Crystal Icehouse and the pond created by springs that came down from the hills. I remember my father was a cabinetmaker in one of the slate-sided buildings. He came from Sweden in 1909 and worked for 43 years for the Esteys. I remember going in and seeing the work that was going on. We lived in Esteyville. We had great fun skating on the pond, as did our children.

—Dot Milkey

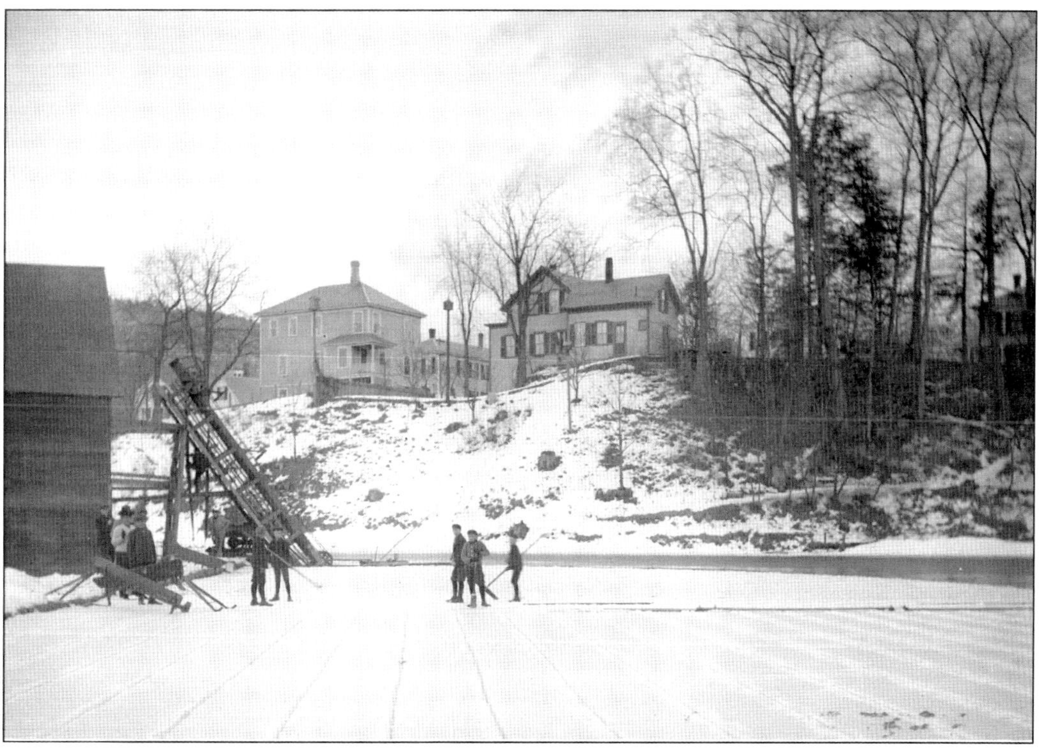

The ice on Crystal Ice Pond, off Frost Place, is scored for harvest.

Life on Elliot Street

I was a child then. It must have been the 1930s. This firehouse was on Elliot Street, which used to be Brattleboro's busiest street, with Speno's Fruit Market, an A & P, and Hammerlund's Fish Market. The harnesses used to hang right over the horses in the back of the fire station. When there was a fire, the harnesses were released right onto the horses.

Dr. Grace Burnett had her office a couple of buildings down, and as a child, I recall getting my smallpox immunization from her.

—*Russell Briggs*

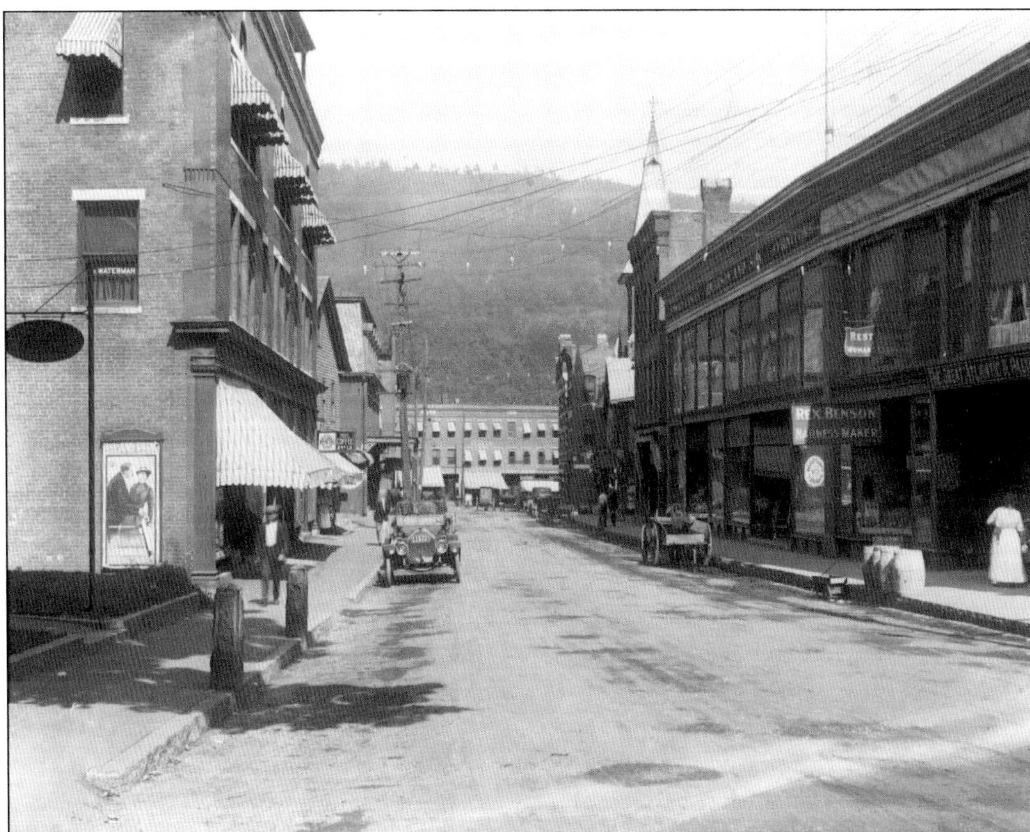

This view was taken looking east on Elliot Street c. *1916.*

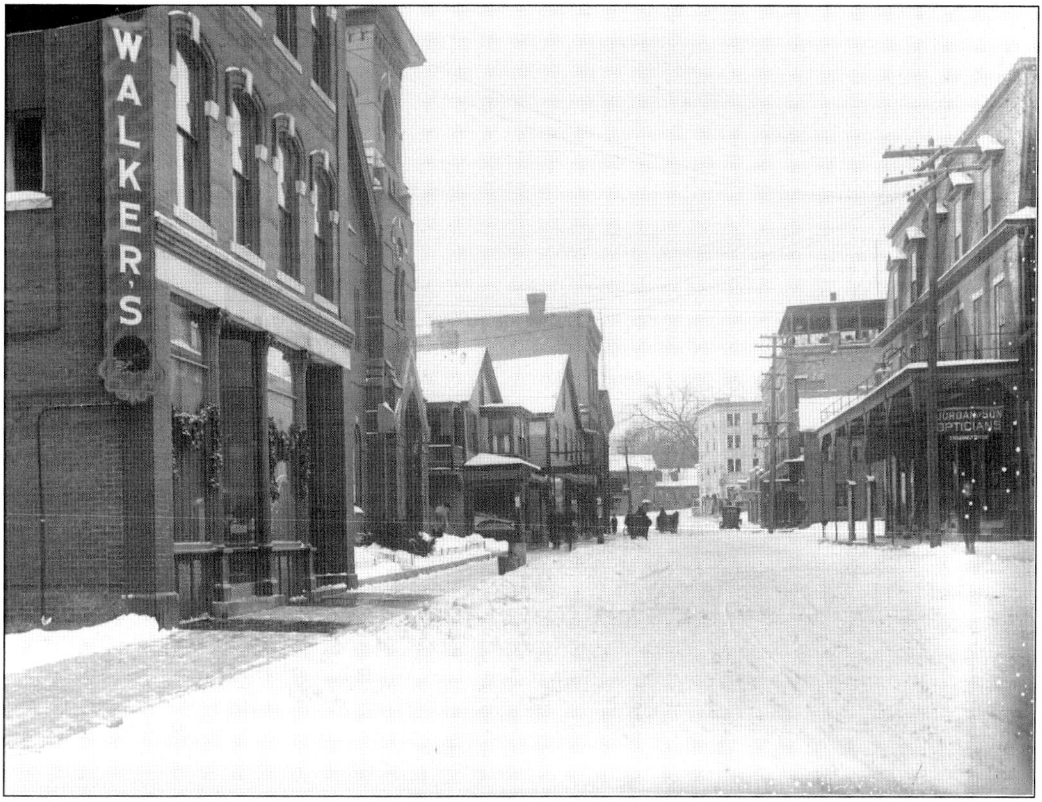

This view was taken looking west on Elliot Street c. *1910. Snowplows were not in use, and transportation was still by sleigh.*

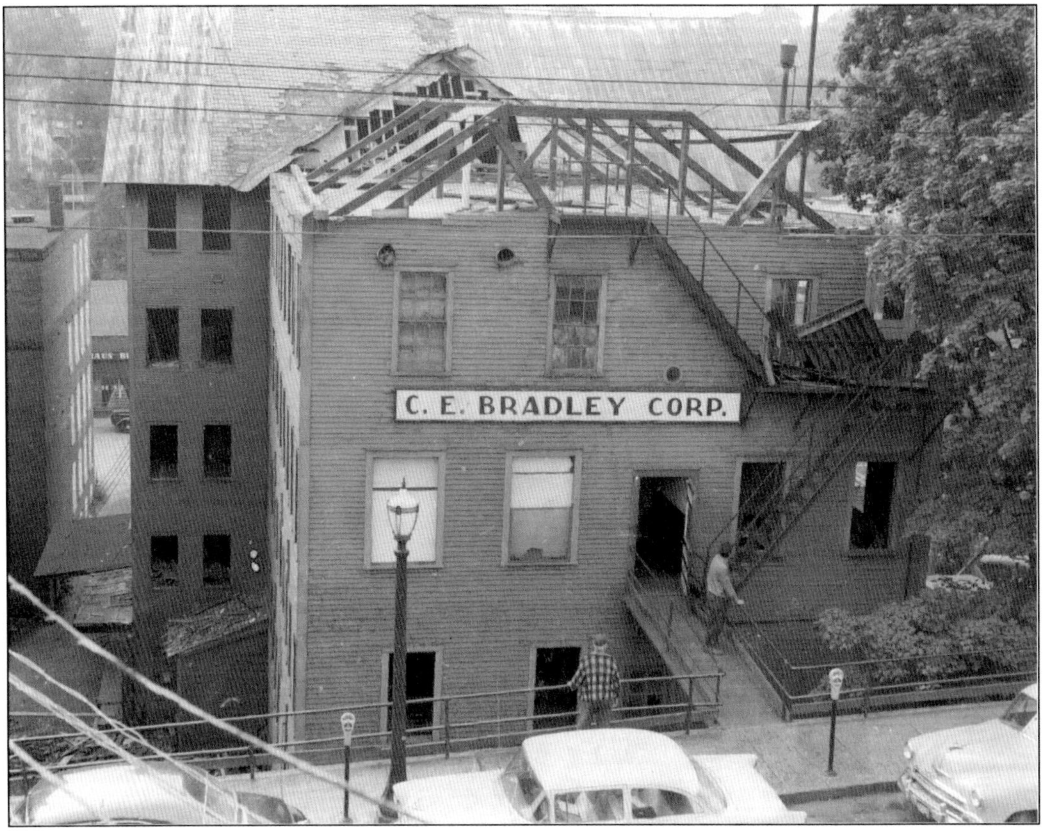

The C.E. Bradley Corporation is being demolished c. *1955. The site is now the Bradley parking lot.*

WORKING AT BRADLEY'S

This is where the new parking garage is going to be.

They dipped penholders, paintbrushes, pencils, and things like that in the lacquer. My brother Warren worked in the lacquer department on Williams Street. Mr. Roland Bonner was the head chemist.

The men worked by piecemeal. I think women also worked there. They blew the whistle in the morning, at noon, when to return from lunch, and in the afternoon at quitting time.

This building came up from Flat Street.

One time there was a fire at the plant. It was caused by the colors being ground. The colors would come in chunks, and they would grind them in a machine. The red was the hardest to grind. The machine got overheated and caught fire. The firemen parked a few feet away at the corner of Elm and Frost Streets at the C. H. Eddy plant.

My brother got his education working at Bradley's.

—*Russell Briggs*

Where Dad Worked

My father became manager at Emerson's in 1901 and stayed there for 53 years. They kept their carpets displayed on the second floor in a unique way so you could see the whole carpet. As I remember it, the store was laid out over the years as follows: the top floor—one above Elliot Street—contained rugs, carpets, linoleum, Congoleum, and parlor sets. Elliot Street level was mainly crockery and related items. One floor down was stoves, cedar chests, gliders, and a small toy department. One flight down from this contained dining room sets, bedroom sets, bedsprings, and mattresses. Another flight down was used as storage (for example, mattresses), repair space, and room for outgoing and incoming furniture—this was on the Flat Street level. The basement was also used for storage—for example, crockery, and Glenwood stove parts (the most complete anywhere around)—and a large boiler room to heat the whole block. All floors were served by an elevator.

—Ed Milkey

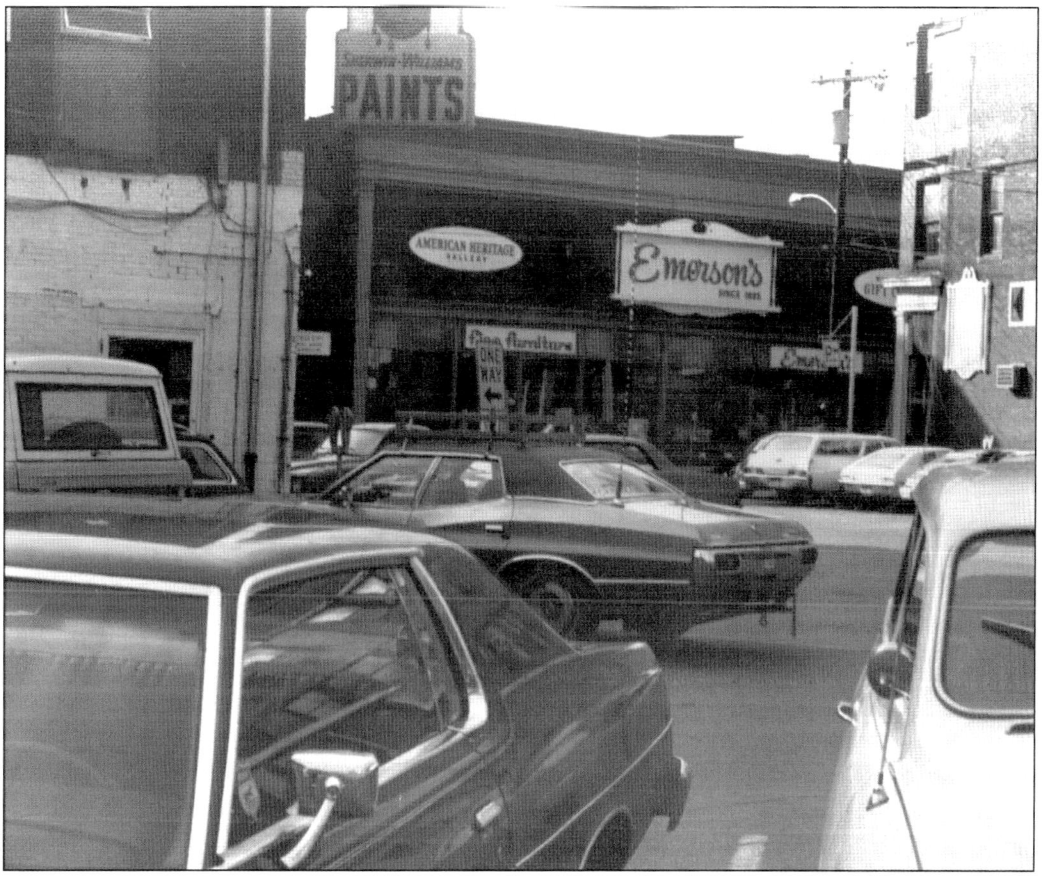

This view of the Harmony parking lot was taken looking toward Elliot Street c. *the early 1970s. The lot is still in use. In 1951, Frank W. Milkey celebrated 50 years of employment with Emerson's Furniture.*

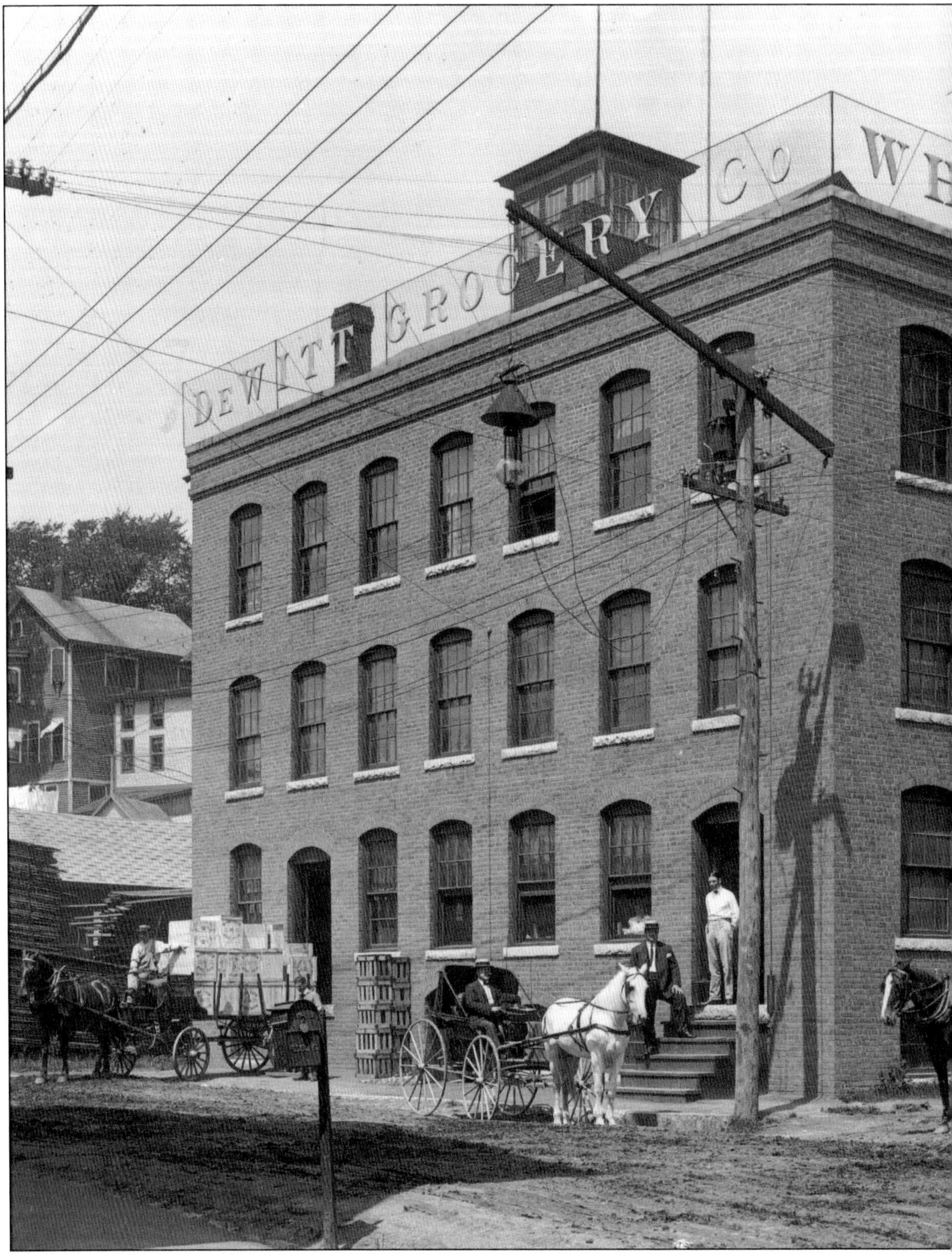

This shows DeWitt Grocery Company Wholesale Grocers in 1906. A fire in 1922 caused considerable damage, as the automatic function of the sprinkler system failed.

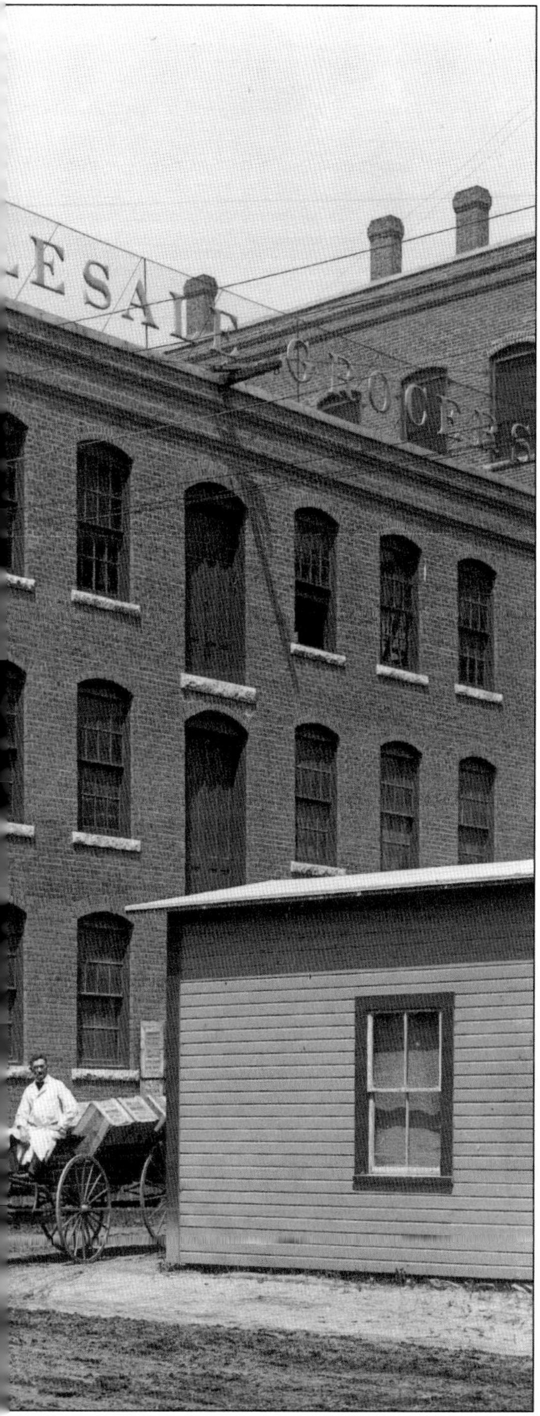

Bookkeeping

During the summer of 1944, I looked for a job at a bank because I had some experience working in one when I lived in California. My job search at the banks in Brattleboro was unsuccessful, so I answered an ad for a job as bookkeeper at the DeWitt Grocery on Flat Street. I worked with Dot Chickering, and the two of us had to use the bookkeeping machine. Dot and I were a whiz at that noisy device. I guess teenagers must get the same kind of kick using their computers today.

Another memory of my job at DeWitt's was Moxie soda. Coming from California, I had not heard of the drink and was amazed how popular it was. DeWitt's sold many cases each week. I knew all this because I worked in the bookkeeping department.

—Harriet Ives

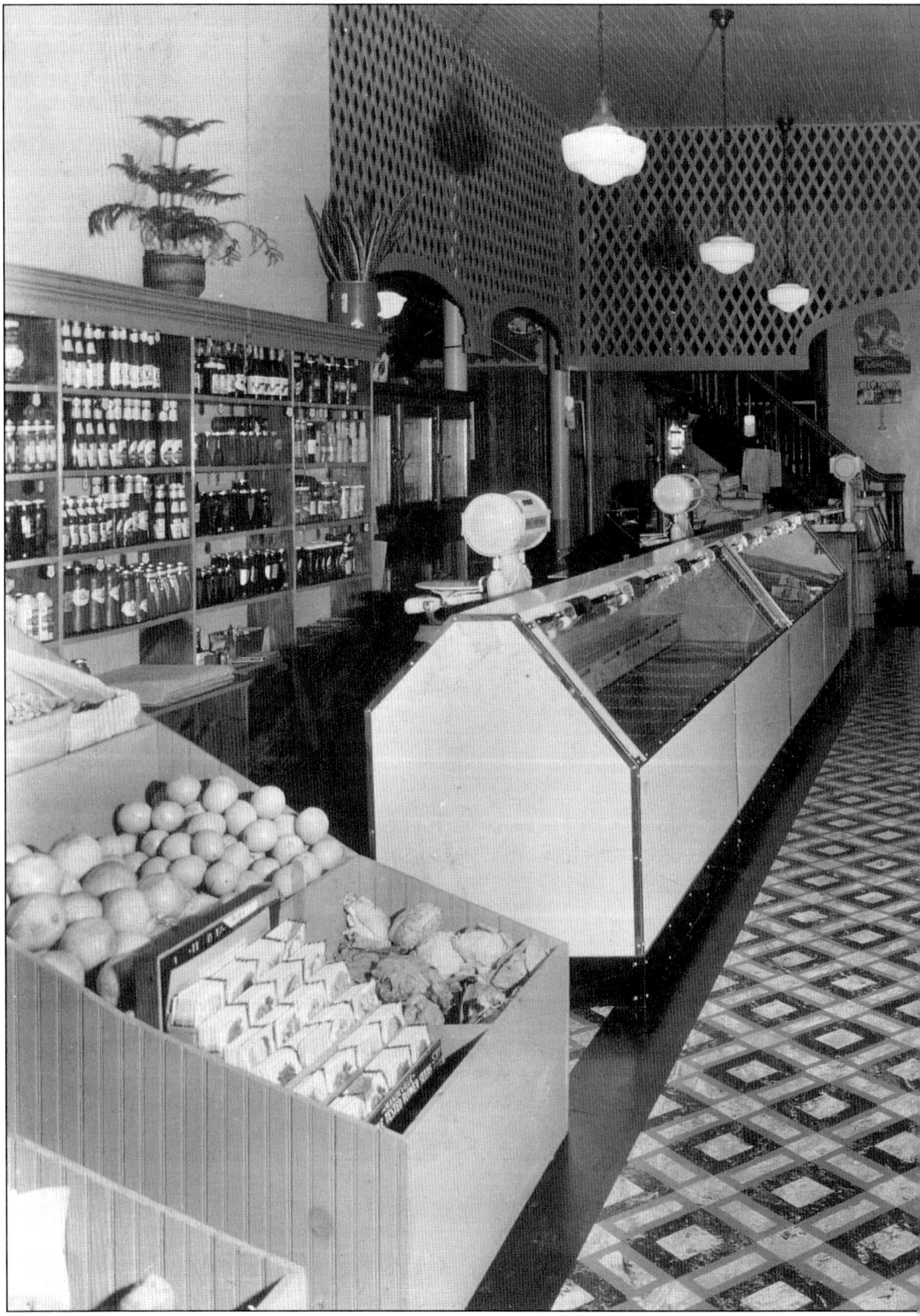

This May 1933 photograph shows the Brattleboro Public Market, on Main Street, which

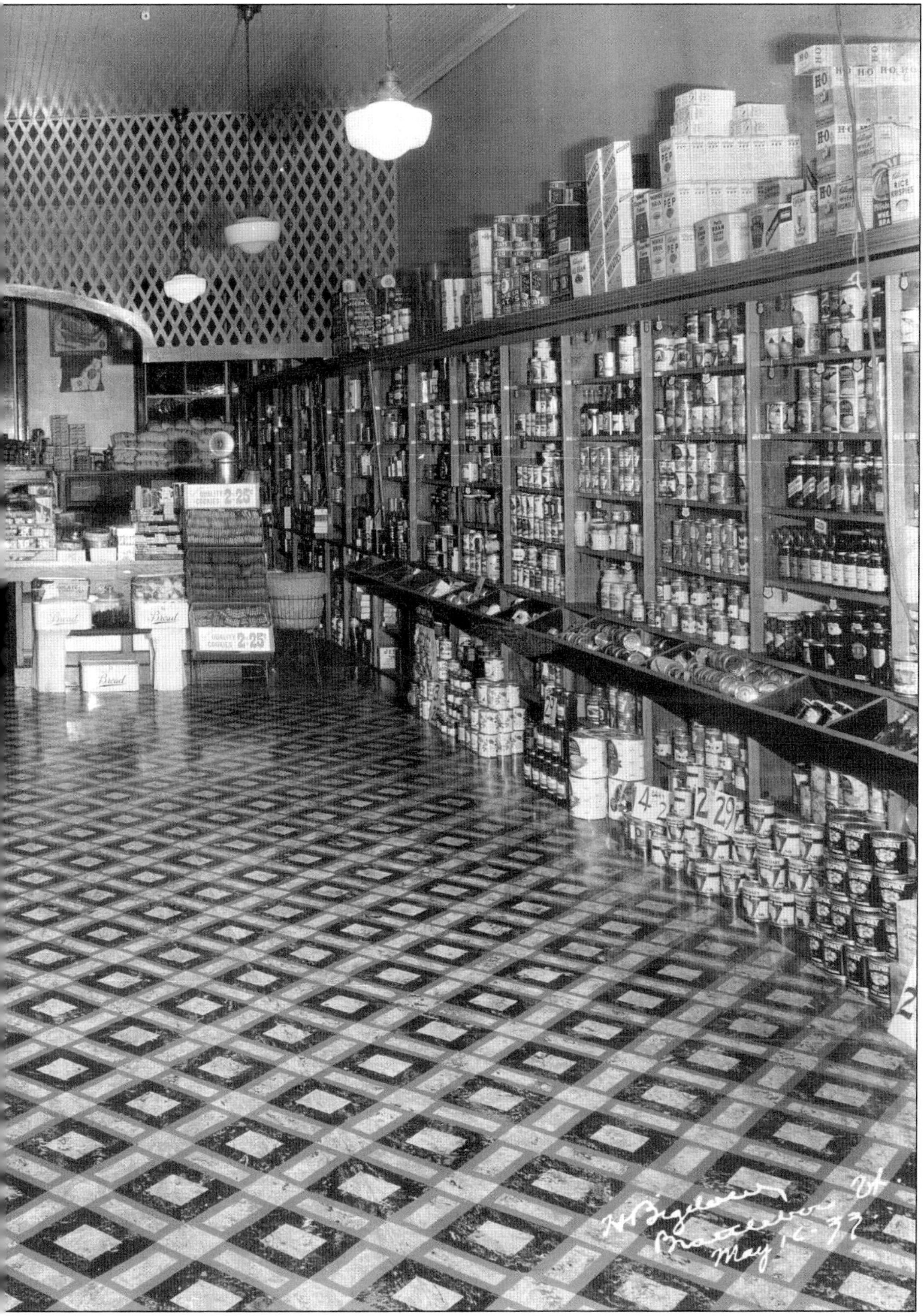

was owned by Michael Broutsas.

Dad's Store

My father, Michael Broustas, came to this country as an immigrant about age 11 and went to Lowell, Massachusetts, where many Greeks lived, and worked there in the textile mills. He lied about his age in order to get in and watch the spindles. He was intelligent and industrious. Where there was someone else who was lazy, he would watch someone else's spindles as well as his own.

Later, he started the Greenfield Public Market. He worked very hard and it was very successful. As the landlord saw his success, he kept raising the rent. So, my father decided to move north and he stopped at the first town in Vermont. This was at the beginning of the Depression. My father bought a farm in West Brattleboro. I believe it was the Federal Land Bank that allowed him to get low-interest rates.

At the same time, he bought 57 Main Street, the Ullery Block. He determined it would never happen again that people would raise the rent on him. Of course, he called it "the Brattleboro Public Market." I think the reason it survived despite hard times was the tremendous personal attention he gave to his customers. He really loved people.

We had regular customers who read religiously the Friday *Reformer* ads which he placed. Mrs. Phelps, who worked there, took orders over the phone on Friday evening for free delivery on Saturday morning. When I was 16 and started delivering orders myself, a regular customer called. She forgot her little square of Fleischmann's yeast. A little square cost 3 cents. My father said, "Get in the truck and deliver it." People's houses were open back then. Somebody would say, "Put the butter and milk in the icebox. Leave the other things on the kitchen table." Some customers wanted raw milk at a time when it was already pasteurized, and so we made raw milk on the farm. We're talking about personal service here. Anna Johnson lived in Swedeville. Well, she baked fabulous things every Saturday morning and she always gave me pastries.

Another reason the store prospered in difficult times was our farm in West Brattleboro. We raised turkeys, chickens, apples, peaches, cherries, and all sorts of vegetables. Before I could drive the truck, I'd be weeding. I'd get a call in the farmhouse. "We need 25 bunches of carrots, 30 bunches of radishes." The deliveryman would then drive up to the farm to pick up the produce.

Our regular customers would ask, "Is this from the farm?" even though our sweet corn was not better than others'. Even our egg cartons said "Arcadia Farm." My father came from the town of Arcadia, in the province of Arcadia, in the Peloponnesus Mountains.

The market was kown for its quality meat. Swift and Squires were the biggest suppliers. A lot of staples came from Dewitt Grocers, where Sanel Auto Parts is on Flat Street. Salesmen from other suppliers also came by the store and took orders for canned goods, beverages, bakery goods, and other items. These salesmen would come by with their books and wait till my father was free. Some were patient; some were not. They delivered by truck.

There was a walk-in cooler, a great big wooden thing. Salt pork was in a barrel and cut to order, a pound or a half-pound. Oysters were also sold in bulk and scooped out of a small barrel into those white containers now used for take-out Chinese food. There was a sign on the counter saying "Oysters R in Season" because they were only safe to eat in the months that have "R" in them. As a child, one's standards for wit were not very high and I thought that was so terribly clever.

One time I was working in the store and my father pulled my sleeve and he said, "That's Dick Gale coming into the store. He's a Democrat." Richard Gale was one of the finest and most respected gentlemen in town, but at the moment his distinction was that he was a Democrat in an overwhelmingly Republican community, and my father wanted me to see one.

The farmers came in on Saturday to shop for staples. Everything else they raised. One time the telephone rang in the back there and it was for one of these farmers. We had a French phone, the kind with the receiver we have today. My father brought him to the desk, and he didn't know what to do with it. He seemed confused and humiliated. It almost broke my heart.

He sold the store to Neil and Russell Briggs, whom he liked very much. Being an immigrant, he wanted his children to go to college, get an education, and we did. My father was active in civic affairs in Brat. He became chairman of the board of selectmen and town representative to the state legislature. He was the first immigrant to be voted into the state legislature.

When we would have family gatherings on the farm, my father would always tap on a glass to get people's attention and say, "The United States is the best country in the world, Vermont is the best state in the U.S., and Brattleboro is the best town in Vermont."

—Constantine M. Broutsas

THE BRATTLEBORO PUBLIC MARKET

The Brattleboro Public Market was purchased by the Briggs brothers [Russell and Neil] in 1952. Rather than being just another grocery store, we wanted to be a little different, so we bought the highest quality we could find plus many items that other stores did not carry, such as caviar; snails; wild rice; pate de foie gras; marzipan; imported jams and jellies; English, Belgian, Swiss, and German cookies; an extensive line of teas; olives; and imported chocolate bars.

At Christmas we had large assortments of gifts, cheese sets, jelly sets, S.S. Pierce gift boxes, imported chocolates, fancy mints, fruit cakes, chocolate oranges, and marzipan assortments. Vermont cheese and maple syrup were shipped all over the country.

We also were sort of a test store for new items. A good example of this is the story of the man who had a small restaurant in his home in Winchester, New Hampshire. On request from his customers, he packaged some of his items for stores. The first ones were O.K. Fairbanks in Keene, New Hampshire, and the Public Market. It was sold under the Black Horse label. His business was so good he opened a shop in Keene. He sold his business to Pepperidge Farm Company. So when you buy raspberry turnovers, patty shells, etc. , from the frozen food case, they got their start in Winchester.

We had large insulated bags "courtesy of the Grand Union" to use when we delivered to Marlboro College, Marlboro Music School, and our deliveries to Dummerston.

When Woolworth Company opened on upper Main Street, they wanted us to supply their lunch counter. They wanted to tell us how to make their hamburg. We believed that there should be only one grade of hamburg—the best. We didn't have their business.

We had an exclusive on English cookies and candy for the coronation of Queen Elizabeth II. This was the most popular item I had ever sold in my 50 years in business.

We sold the store and block in the1970s. Now I have wonderful memories of all the nice people that I met and did business with for many years.

Just a note: No advertising signs for tobacco, etc. , were allowed on windows or inside of the store.

—Russell Briggs

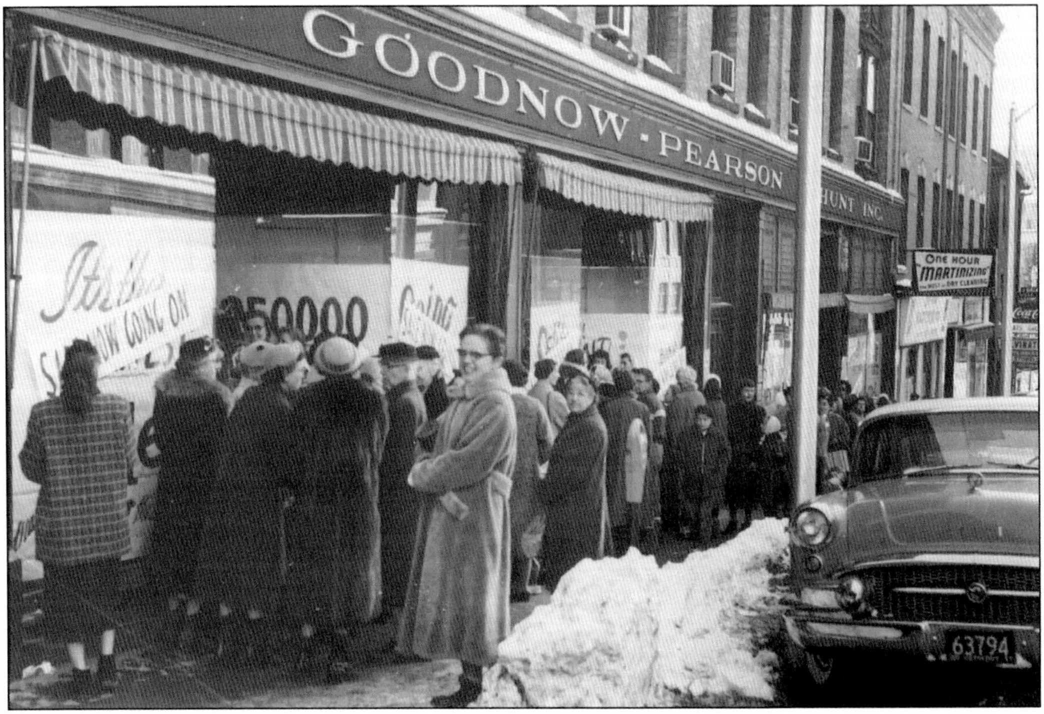

This 1957 view shows the closing sale for Goodnow, Pearson and Hunt, at 63–71 Main Street.

WORKING AT GOODNOW, PEARSON AND HUNT

This was a department store on Main Street. I worked there in 1944 every day after high school when I was 16 years old. There were several interior levels to the store because of the incline as you move up Main Street. I worked in the upper, first level in ladies' lingerie and hats. Then, you would walk down two steps to another department, where there were dressy dresses and women's coats. Walking down three more steps took you to the men's department, and in between the dresses and the men's was clothing for children. They had everything there.

One of the favorite things I loved was seeing the displays that Mr. Thayer, the window dresser, created. Sometimes I was able to go into the room where he had all his materials for displays. I really loved seeing what he could do with all of that.

—Regina Witalis

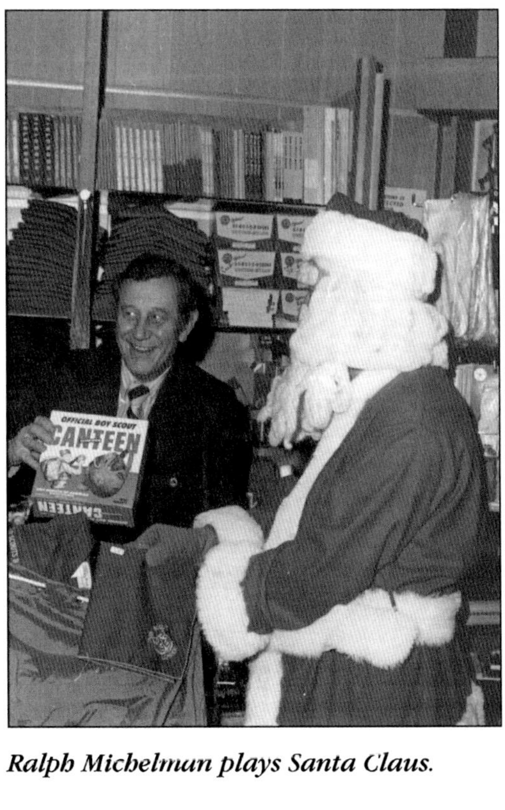

Ralph Michelman plays Santa Claus.

How Dad Made His Living

Dad was a familiar face in the life of Brattleboro's Main Street. He could be found at his men's clothing store from 1939 until it closed in 1976. He was born in Greenfield, Massachusetts, in 1913, and moved to Brattleboro and opened his store with Mr. Willard Beebe. In 1940, he married my mother, Lucille Rosenzweig, and just a few years later was serving in the Pacific in World War II. After returning, the partnership with Mr. Beebe ended, and the store became known as Michelman's Inc. , which proudly sold quality men's and boys' clothing "for style-minded men," so the advertising proclaimed. I was born around this time, and our family settled into the routine of post–World War II Brattleboro.

The store moved to larger quarters in June of 1962, taking over most of the Union Block where Fishman's had been. His neighbors in the block were the Dutch Bake Shop and DeAngelis Shoe Repair. Some of the employees of Dad's store through the years included Bill Mellen, Nelson Blouin, Corinne Langmaid, Ruby Lucier, Brenda Doyle, George Brown, and John Brosnahan.

Dad became active in civic affairs. He was a selectperson, a member of the school board, and active in the chamber of commerce and fraternal organizations. When I look at Main Street now and see the clock, I think of how involved Dad became in saving it.

—*Richard Michelman*

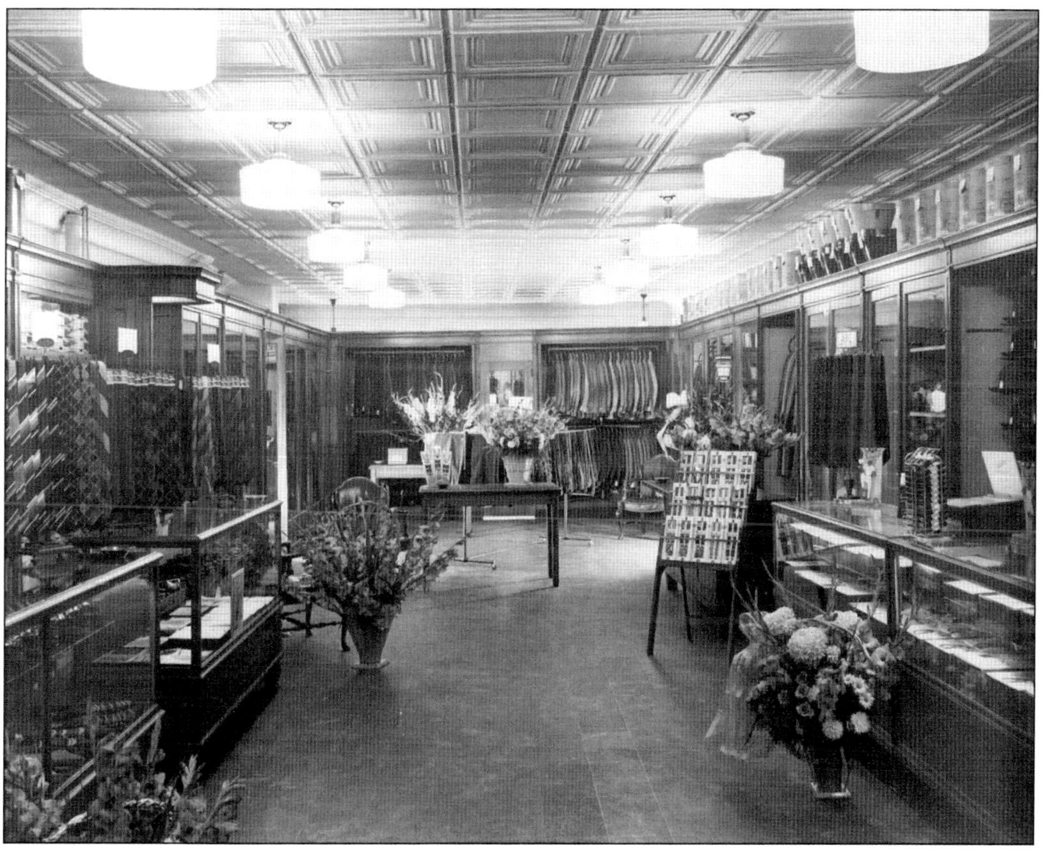

Michelman's Retail Men's Clothing opens for business in 1949.

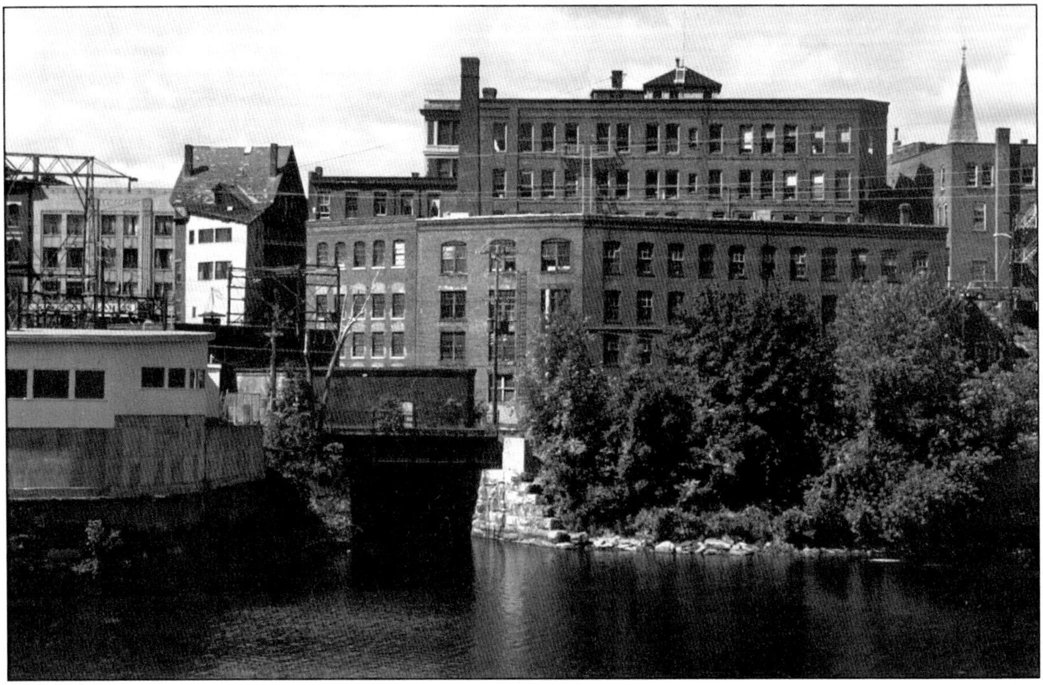

This view looks west across the Connecticut River at Brattleboro. The Riverview Restaurant is on the left, the former site of the gasholder tank.

DESTINATION BRATTLEBORO

It was a sunny, cool March day in 1975 when I first saw Brattleboro. Desirous to leave big city living, my brother and I and our wives were looking to settle in a small town. My brother had seen an ad for E.N.T. in a journal and had visited here first. Now it was the time for our wives and me to weigh in.

We exited the interstate at Exit 1 and drove north up Canal Street. When we reached Main Street, David headed across the bridge to Hinsdale, New Hampshire. After a short ride, we turned around and, as we came back over the bridge, my brother pointed ahead and said, "There's the Brattleboro skyline." We all laughed at that. After all, our hometown of Chicago was reputed to have the finest skyline in the world.

But, as time went by and as I got to view the skyline again and again, it did not take long for me to fall in love with it. Each building is unique, yet they all seem to fit together. Furthermore, the river side of the buildings are such that unless you know each building, it is difficult to match the fronts of the buildings with the sides that face the river.

As our community starts to develop the riverfront, the wonderful resource of our downtown buildings and their river-facing sides will become increasingly appreciated by the local citizenry and visitors alike, and we will all be the better for it.

—Robert Fagelson, M.D.

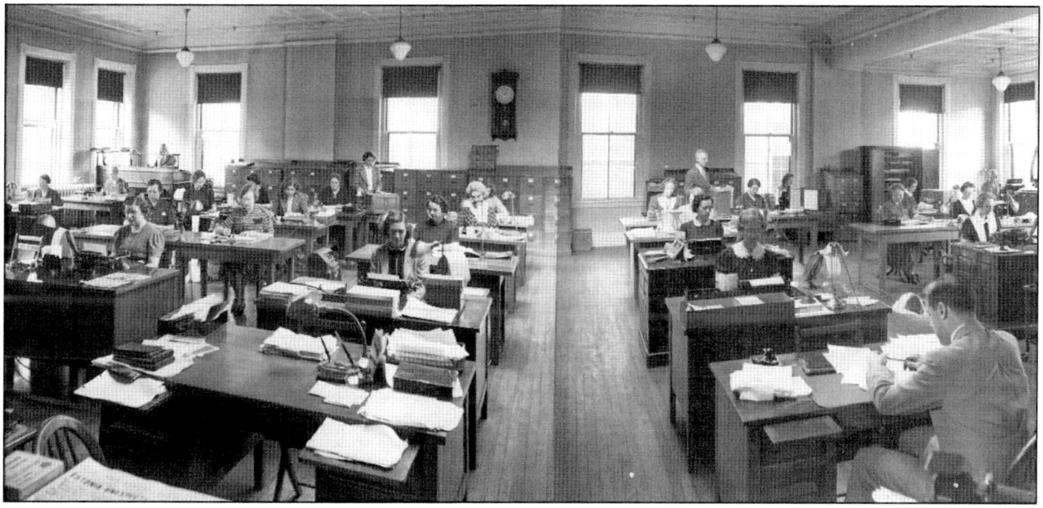

Dunham Brothers office workers are shown at work, at 139 Main Street, c. *the 1940s.*

ROMANCE AT DUNHAM BROTHERS

Graduating from high school was a big day in my life; out into the real world, finally. So, I filled out applications and was so excited to get an interview at Dunham Brothers. Up the two flights of stairs at 139 Main Street, the main office was filled with desks, chairs, and rows of filing cabinets. George Denyou was office manager, along with Harold Dunham, a descendant of the original Dunhams.

So, I joined the gang of girls who typed and filed and calculated. All this supported the warehouse in the lower floors of the same building. Orders for shoes and boots came into the office and were sent on to the warehouse, where workers assembled cases of footwear and shipped them out by truck.

The alley between our building and the bank next door was just wide enough for a truck to back in. Of course it meant stopping traffic on Main Street while the truck maneuvered. More than a few times, the truck would scrape the buildings on either side. It was a real test of the driver's skill.

One day I noticed a warehouse man up in the office on some errand. Later, he offered me a ride to work. Things progressed, interrupted by his stint in the Army Air Corps, and we were married as soon as he was released from service.

I left Dunham's then to raise four children; but when they were all in school, I went back to the office job. The extra money helped put the kids through college. Stay-at-home mothers were the norm in the 1940s, so I baked bread and beans and tended a garden. Money was always scarce, but we made a lot of our own entertainment. It was a good life.

—Marguerite Douglas

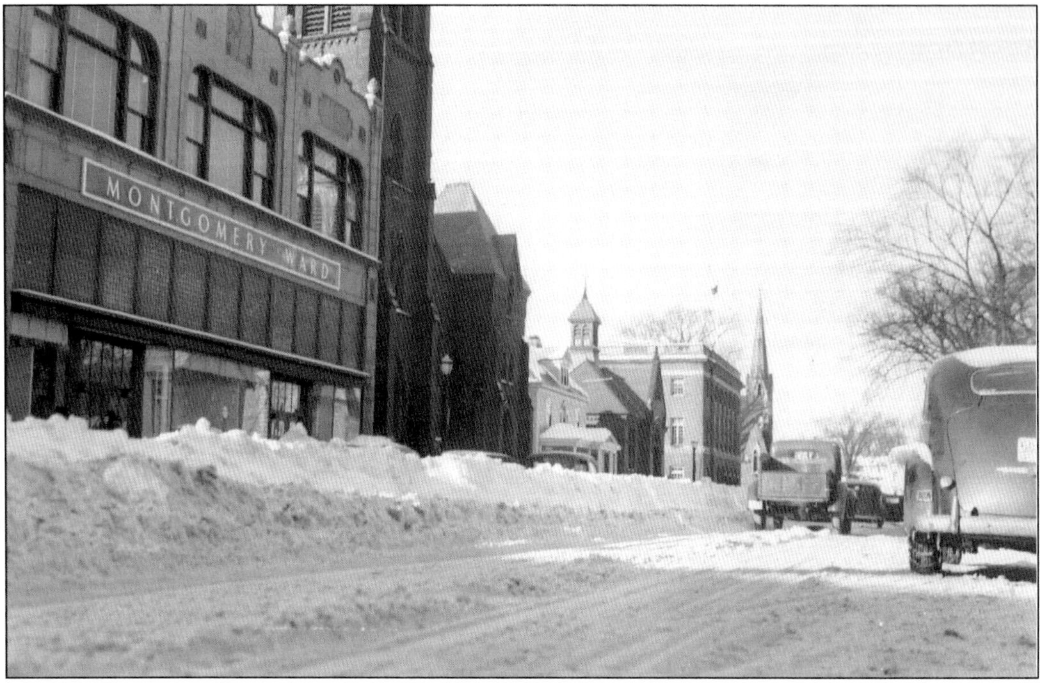

This December 1946 view shows the Montgomery Ward building, on Main Street. The building is the present home of Brown and Robert's Hardware.

"MONKEY" WARD

I worked probably afternoons and Saturdays, when I was in high school, at Montgomery Ward. After that, I might have worked just part-time. That was during the Depression. I can't remember when I started to work steady.

I got a watch in 1971 for 25 years at Montgomery Ward. I worked the main floor, although I had to help out in various departments. We all did that.

The fellows played jokes on me. They picked on me. They thought it was fun. I parked my car in the back one day, but it wouldn't back up. I tried again. It wouldn't back up. People were laughing in the doorway and at the freight elevator. The fellows had jacked my car up on blocks. They thought it was funny.

I worked at American Optical during the war. I inspected lenses, colored lenses, used for pilots. I quit because the work was steady and it was indoors. I enjoyed store work, though, meeting people and like that.

I liked to ride horses on the Old Guilford Road. The Old Guilford Road went to Algiers before they put the park in.

My house is on Moreland Avenue. I've lived there nearly all my life. I'm still living there.

—Allethaire Smith

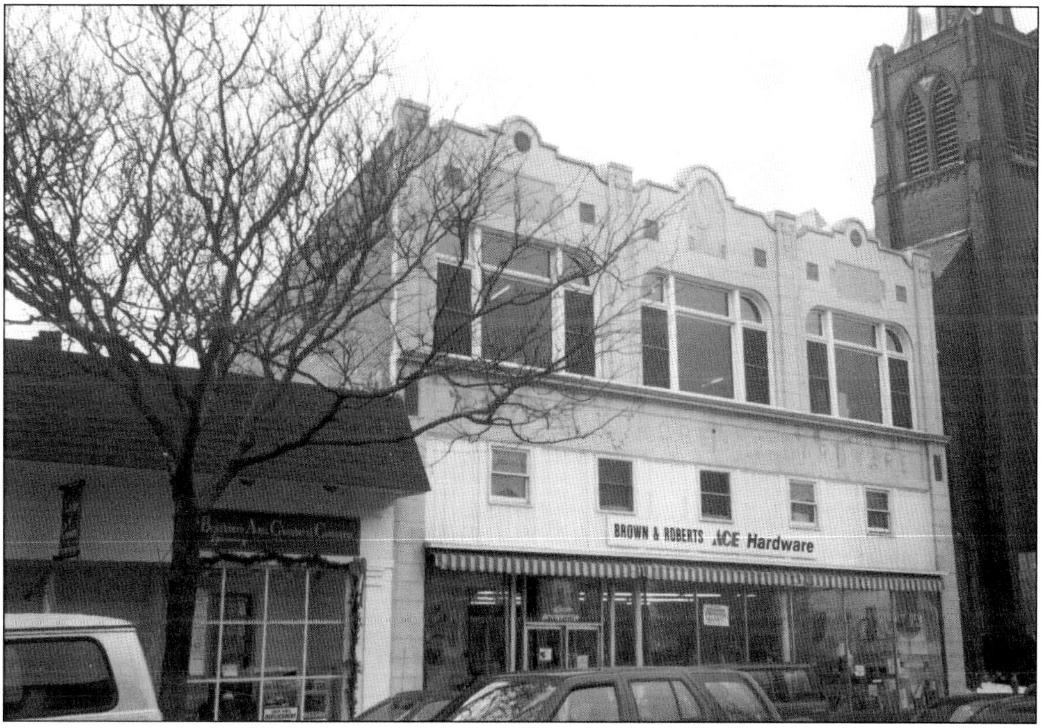

This is a current view of Brown and Robert's Hardware, on Main Street. The building was originally built in 1929 for Montgomery Ward.

WORKING AT THE HARDWARE STORE

My son, Christopher, got his first "real" job at Brown and Roberts Hardware Store after school. This was in the mid-1980s. He had delivered the *Town Crier* before that, but he wanted to do something more "grown-up." He had to take a test to be hired, which he worried about, but apparently he did all right. He floundered around a bit at first, because he really didn't know much about hardware or how to build or repair things—and there were a number of adventures with the freight elevator which they may or may not have known about—but they were very patient with him, and gradually gave him various responsibilities, which made him feel valued.

The neat thing about the job was that the Putnams were such caring people. They took a personal interest in their employees and treated them like family. For Christmas each year, they gave everyone a ham. Christopher eventually went on to other pursuits, but they always remember him and ask about him to this day. The great thing is, Christopher is only one of a long line of young people who have cut their teeth at Brown and Roberts, and been nurtured in the same way.

—Veronica Johnson

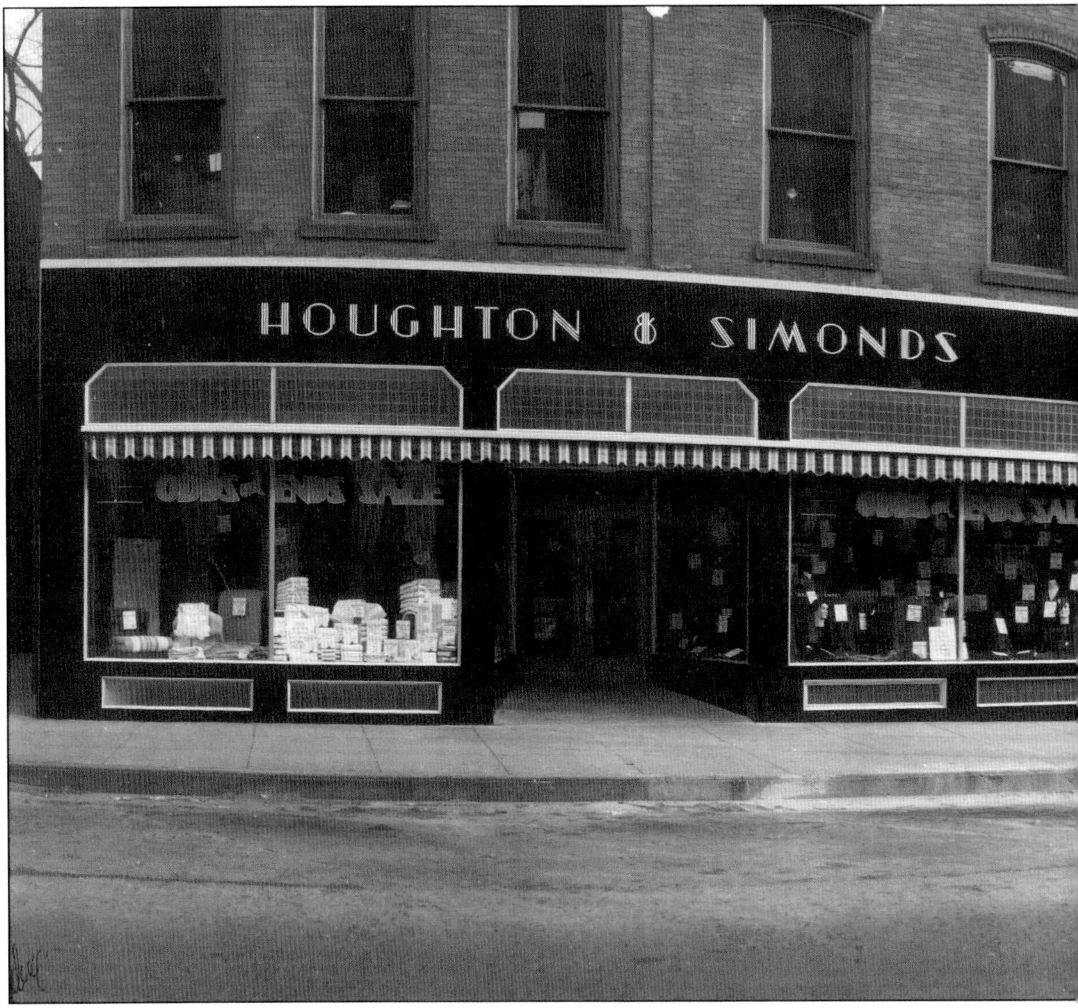

This is a c. *1930 view of the Dunham Brothers Company building, located at*

My First Job

Following graduation from the old Brattleboro High School, I obtained a position as a salesclerk at Houghton & Simonds dry goods store in the summer of 1947. At that time, beginning clerks were paid less than $20 for a six-day workweek. Of course, the store granted a discount on all purchases by employees, but paying on an account often depleted one's wages considerably. I worked in the notions and fabrics departments for the most part; however, any clerk could be called on to help on other counters on the main floor, such as hosiery and handbags, cosmetics, and handcrafts.

Close scrutiny of the photo indicates that the store is in the midst of its semi-annual Odds & Ends sale. These sales were anticipated events for local shoppers, as there were similar stores on Main Street that scheduled major sales within a few days or weeks of each other. Opening day of the sale would find the entryway filled with eager shoppers ready to dash for a sought-after bargain that they had checked out the previous day.

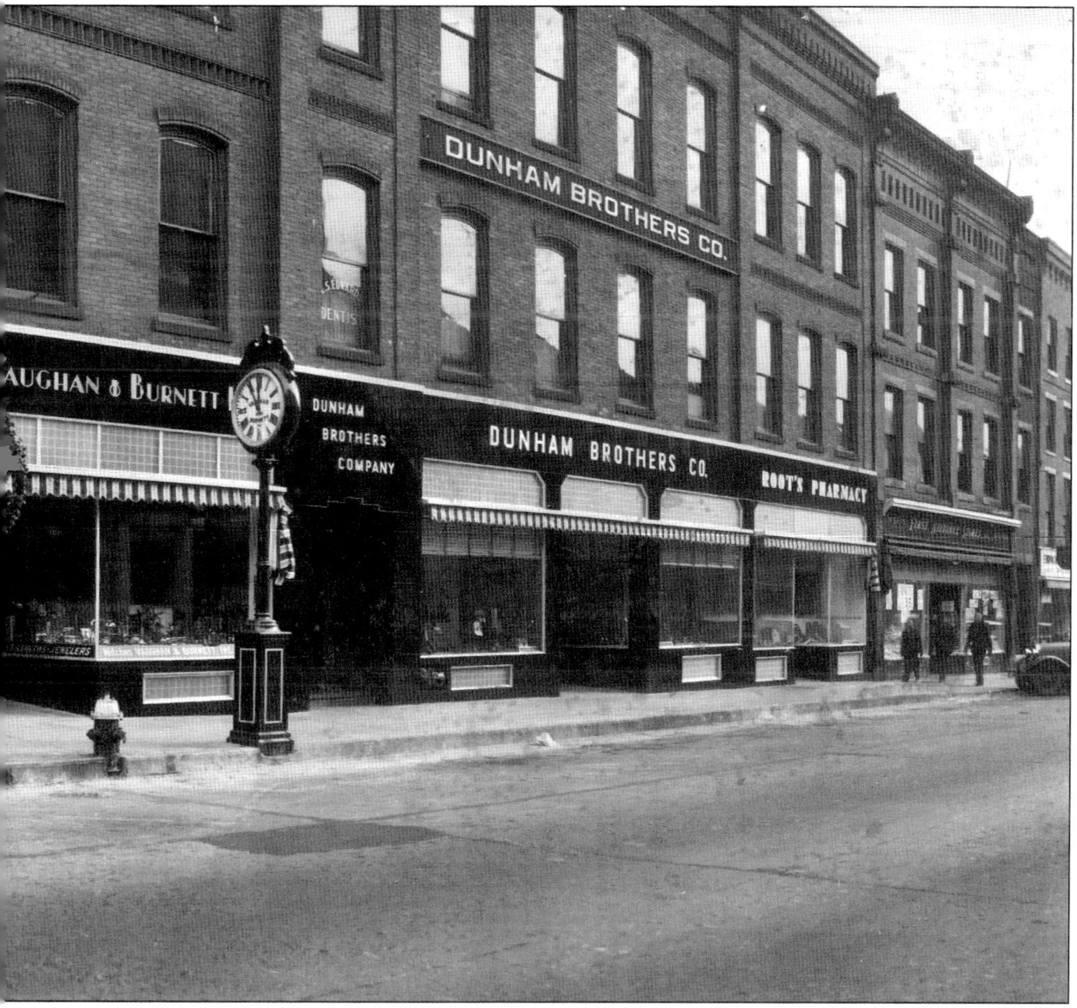

139 Main Street.

Once the winter sale was over and stock was depleted, it was time for inventory. Even though the thread on each spool was not measured, as was the story told to new employees, it was necessary to count every spool, every button, every package of needles, snaps, several types of tapes, and numerous other items.

Houghton & Simonds occupied three floors of the building. Quality ready-made women's clothing was on the second floor, the previously listed items were on the main floor, and domestic goods and home decorating fabrics were found on the basement level.

Vaughan & Burnett's jewelry store was located next to Houghton & Simonds for many years. I recall the gleaming silver and beautiful china, pewter, and glassware that lined the walls and filled the display cases. Watch sales and repairs were an important part of the business when it was owned by Messrs. Brown and Foster.

Dunham Brothers retail store was an excellent place to purchase shoes and boots. Many residents were employed by Dunham in either the retail establishment or the shoe and boot wholesale distribution business.

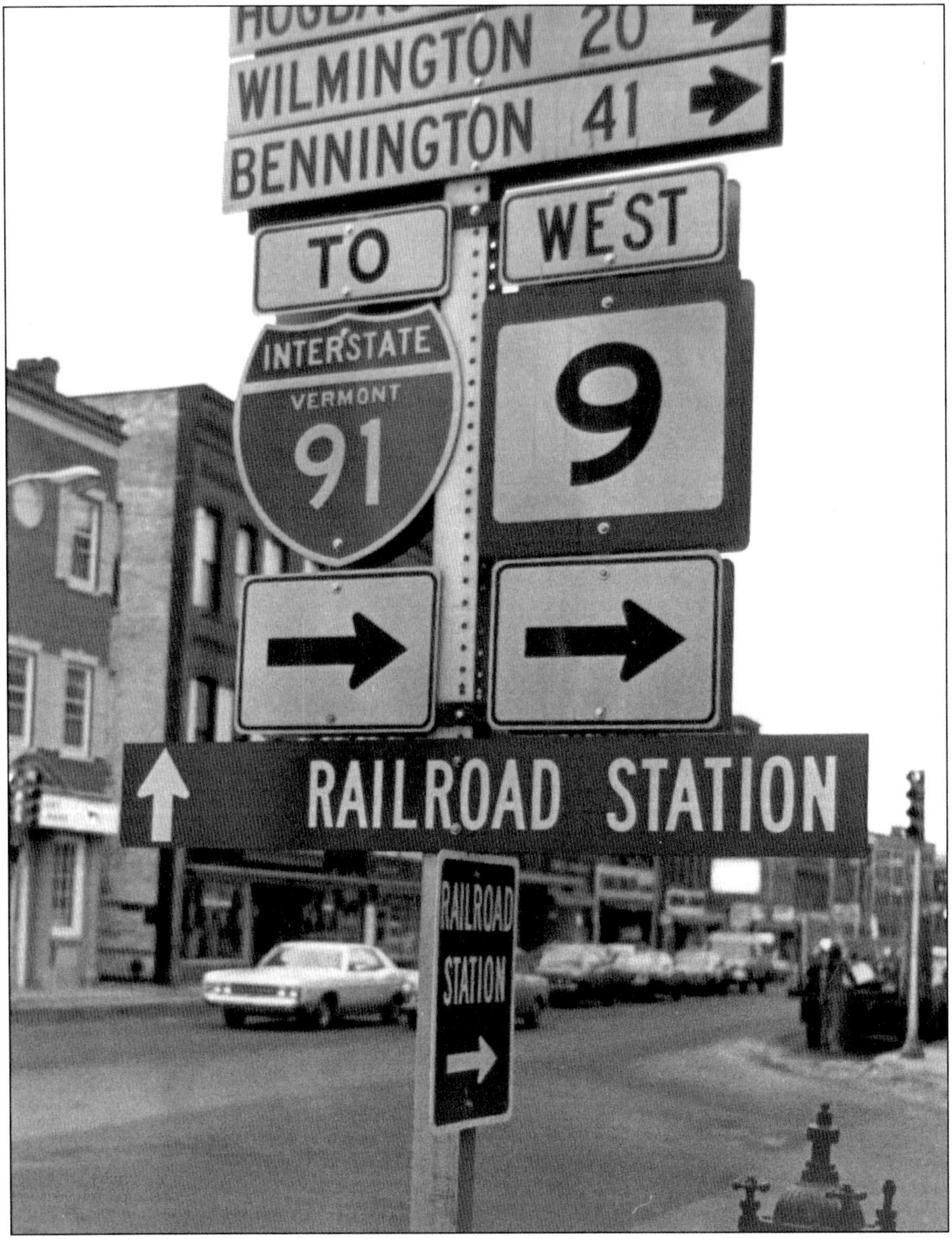

These signs were located at the intersection of High and Main Streets, downtown, c. *1970.*

I remember Root's Pharmacy, with its enticing soda fountain just inside the door and several metal tables and chairs in the center aisle waiting to accommodate customers while they enjoyed a break or waited for a prescription.

All the storefronts have changed since this late 1930s photo. On occasion, even the clock has been missing when it fell victim to being exposed to the weather, but at the present time it is the one enduring feature in this Main Street view.

—*Hazel J. Anderson*

THE WARTIME TICKET AGENT

In September 1943, I walked into the Brattleboro Railroad Station to take the position of second "trick" ticket clerk. The hours were from 3:00 p.m. until 11:00 p.m., seven days a week. Ordinarily, whoever did this job also handled the baggage, but since I was a young woman, this was done by the janitor. I did the paperwork; he did the lifting. Also because I was a woman, I had to sign an agreement that should a man become available, the railroad could hire him and fire me! (I *do* like equal rights!) Because of the war, no able-bodied male wanted to take over. They were either in military service, in exempt positions, or working in war plants—maybe in Springfield, Vermont.

The law mandated that those working an eight-hour shift had to be allowed 20 minutes for lunch. Since I lived close to the station, the station agent, William Moore, allowed me to go home after the 6:00 p.m. train departed. Before I went, there was a waybill to be delivered to the telegrapher downstairs. One evening I received a phone call at my home. Where was the bill? So, I went flying down South Main hill to the station and brought it downstairs. Just once did that happen.

Life in the ticket office was interesting. More so since the country was at war. There was gas and tire rationing, which severely restricted the use of automobiles. Almost everyone traveled by train. This, of course, included military service personnel and their relatives, sweethearts, and spouses. I always suspected some training areas were situated so travel to them would be difficult—people went anyway. One area was the Finger Lakes section of New York State.

Unlike big-city ticket offices, we sold passage to local and long-distance destinations. A lot of variety looking up routes and tariffs. At first, it was a little bewildering, but with time, experience, and the help of the day ticket agent, Mr. Huff, and the people in the taxi stand across the hall, it became fun and interesting.

We kept an eye out for passenger trains to see if they were flying small flags on the engines. Green meant that there was a second section to a scheduled train. White meant that it was a special. This could be a troop train, a prisoner-of-war train, or a secret one for important political figures. I would look down on the troop trains and wonder how many soldiers would return.

On the local scene, every Saturday a bus came down via Route 30 from the valley towns. This was the night the stores stayed open until 9:00 p.m. The passengers would wait in the station for the return trip. One young man played a harmonica. Another time a man brought a cage with an owl in it.

The 10:20 p.m. train connected to northern New York State. Some of these passengers thought it hilarious if, when they named New York as a destination, I would take out a ticket to New York City. Not quite my idea of humor!

The 6:00 p.m. train was local and stopped at Putney. When I was new at work, a woman came in to check her dog. I went out to the baggage room, yelling for the janitor. He came up, and we squared the ticketing of the dog. Later, he came back and told me the conductor had his laugh for the day—I never sold the *lady* a ticket. One Sunday evening, a man, J.N. Cook, manager of the local plant of the Sterling Drug Company, dashed in to catch the southbound 9:00 p.m. train. He watched the train pull out, then came with a grin on his face and asked for its next stop. Then he dashed out to his car. Meanwhile, another man came to the ticket window and blasted me for not making the train wait for Mr. Cook. Ah! If only I had had that much power!

People were concerned with the war, naturally. A man, while waiting for a train one evening, was conversing about the army, etc. The young taxi driver from across the hall came over. With a straight face, he proceeded to explain that he was 4-F. I don't know why he did this. Actually, he was in the Battle of the Bulge, had been a German prisoner of war, and had come home weighing about 80 pounds. To me, human nature is still a puzzlement.

One man purchased a ticket to the nearest station to Valley Forge Hospital. So someone told me. Also, they did plastic surgery. This man had a patchwork face. Something one never forgets.

An international flavor was provided periodically by a British Merchant Marine sailor. Usually, he would check in to say hi or to stop and visit. He tried to convince me that the British system of the lord of the manor looking after his tenants who lived in cottages under his care was a better way of life than our American system. I never knew if he was serious or just joshing me. He had an uncle who lived up the West River valley. Sometimes they would meet in the station. Other times, I would tell the uncle he had been in. So, the uncle would say, "I know where to find him," and head for the All States Café.

I went to the Montrealer at 2:10 a.m. to see my brother, Milton, off. He went to Bellows Falls and thence to Fort Devens, Ayer, Massachusetts, to enlist in the air force. My sister, Irene, was in the navy. So the war and service personnel traveling through the railroad station held a personal interest for me.

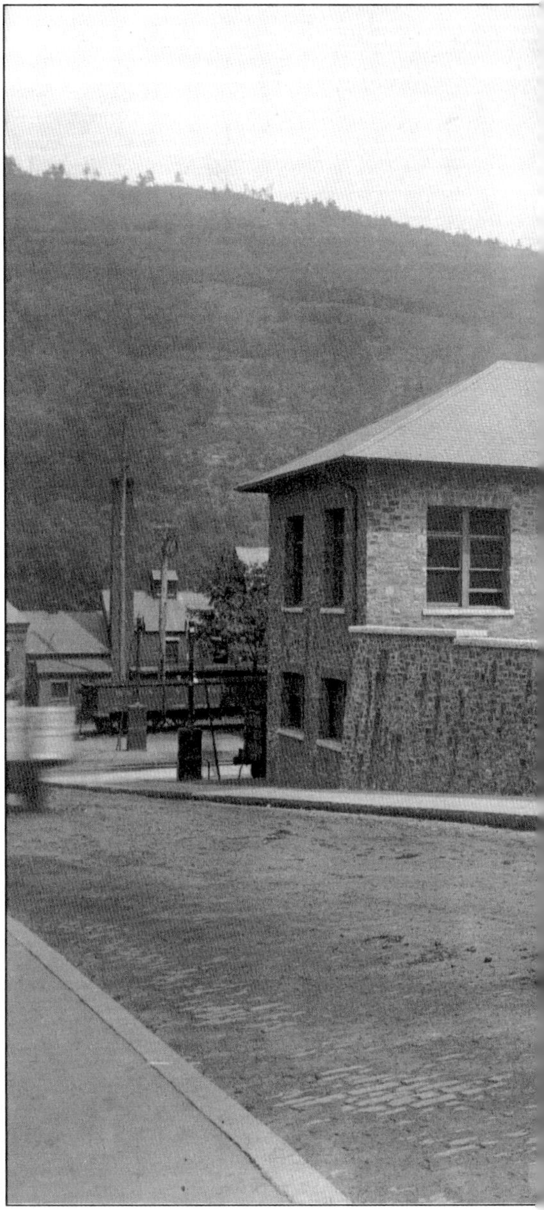

Passenger business persisted after the end

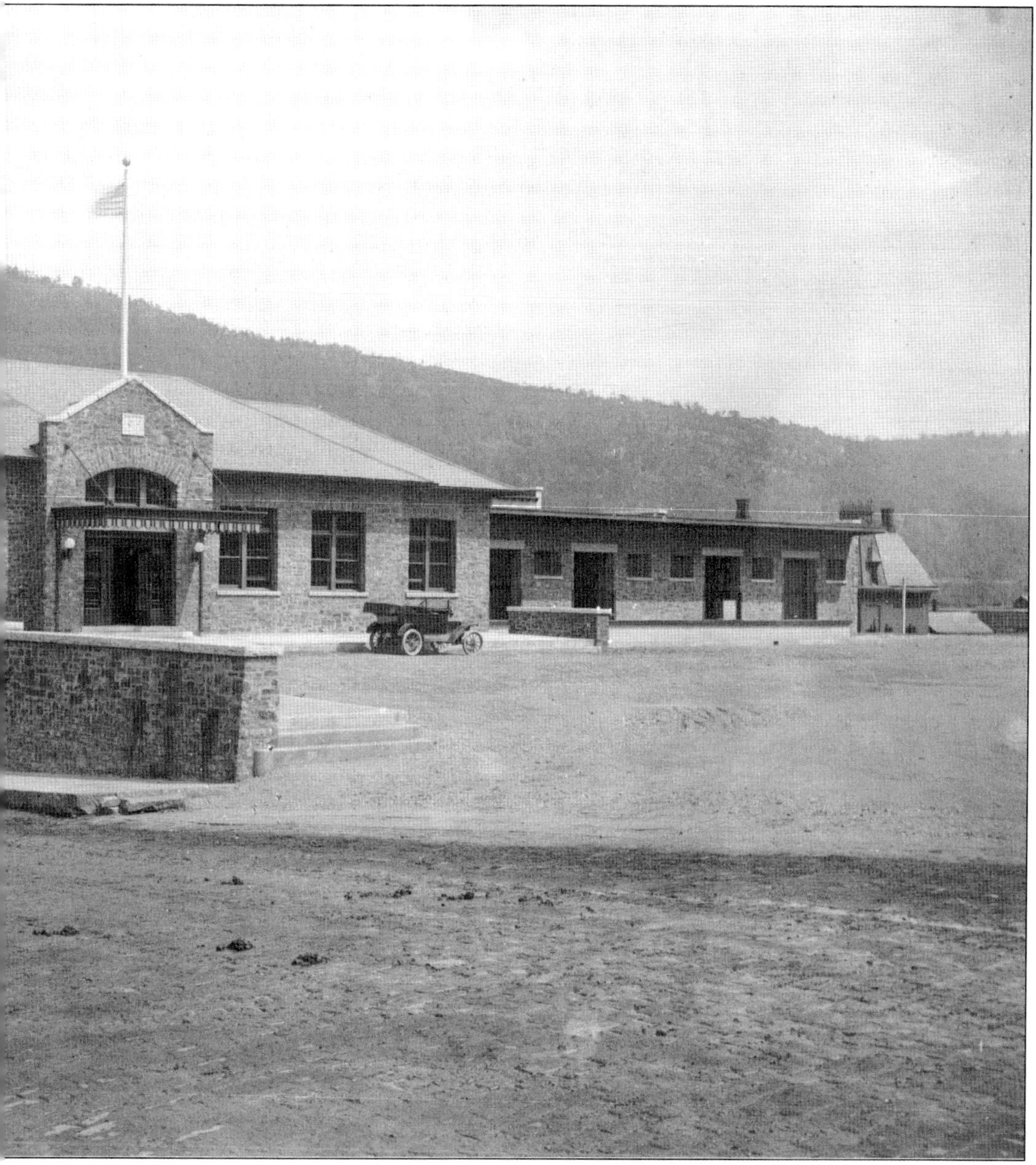

This view shows Union Station soon after its completion in 1915.

of the war until supplies of rationed goods were available. I left the ticket office in May 1946 to be married.

One memory I took with me was the sight of the fireman on the engine at 10:20 p.m. shoveling coal into the glowing firebox of a large 700-class engine. There *is* something romantic about a steam engine.

—*Marion Deaett*

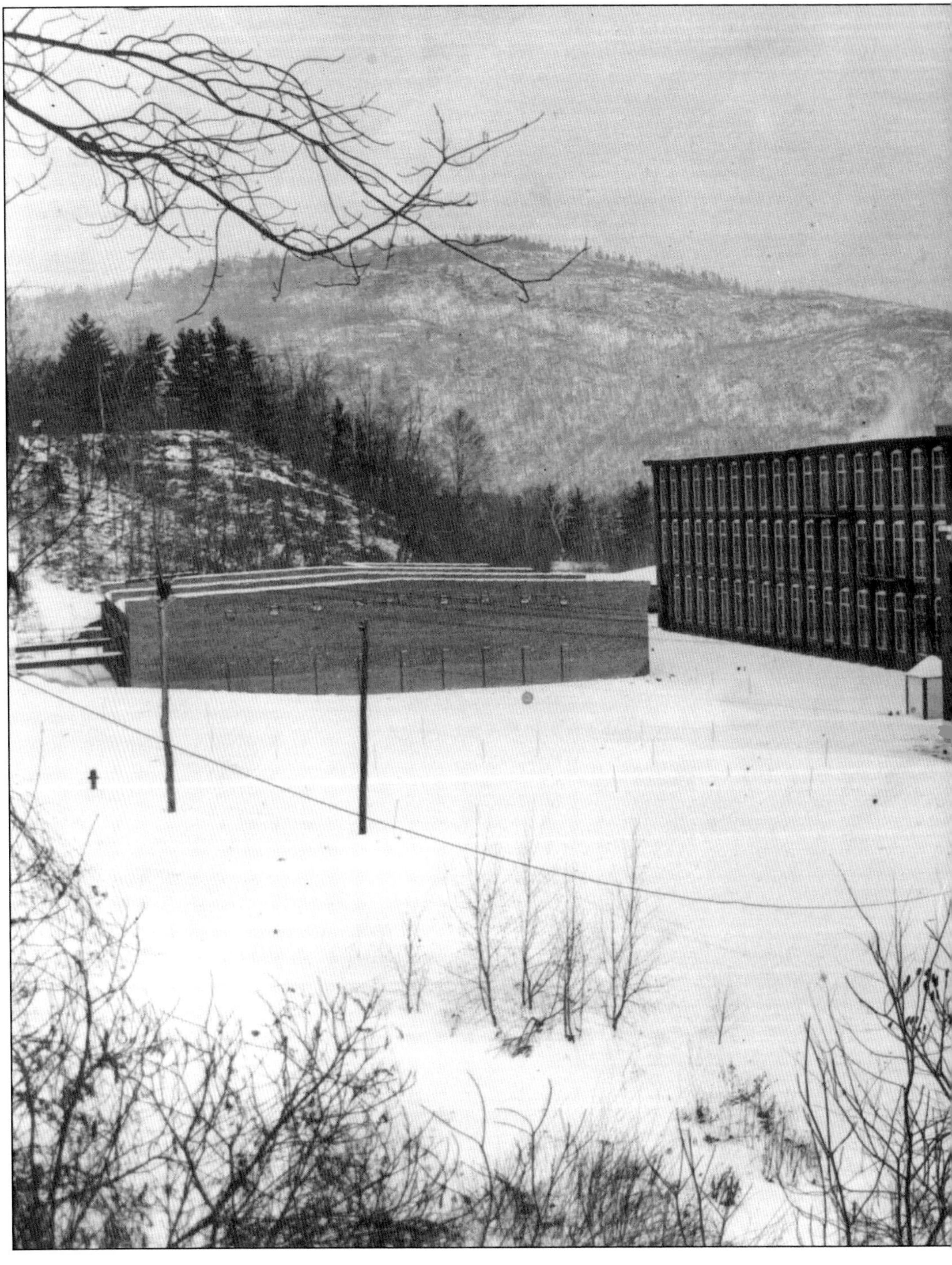

Fort Dummer Mill-Berkshire Fine Spinning was located on Vernon Road.

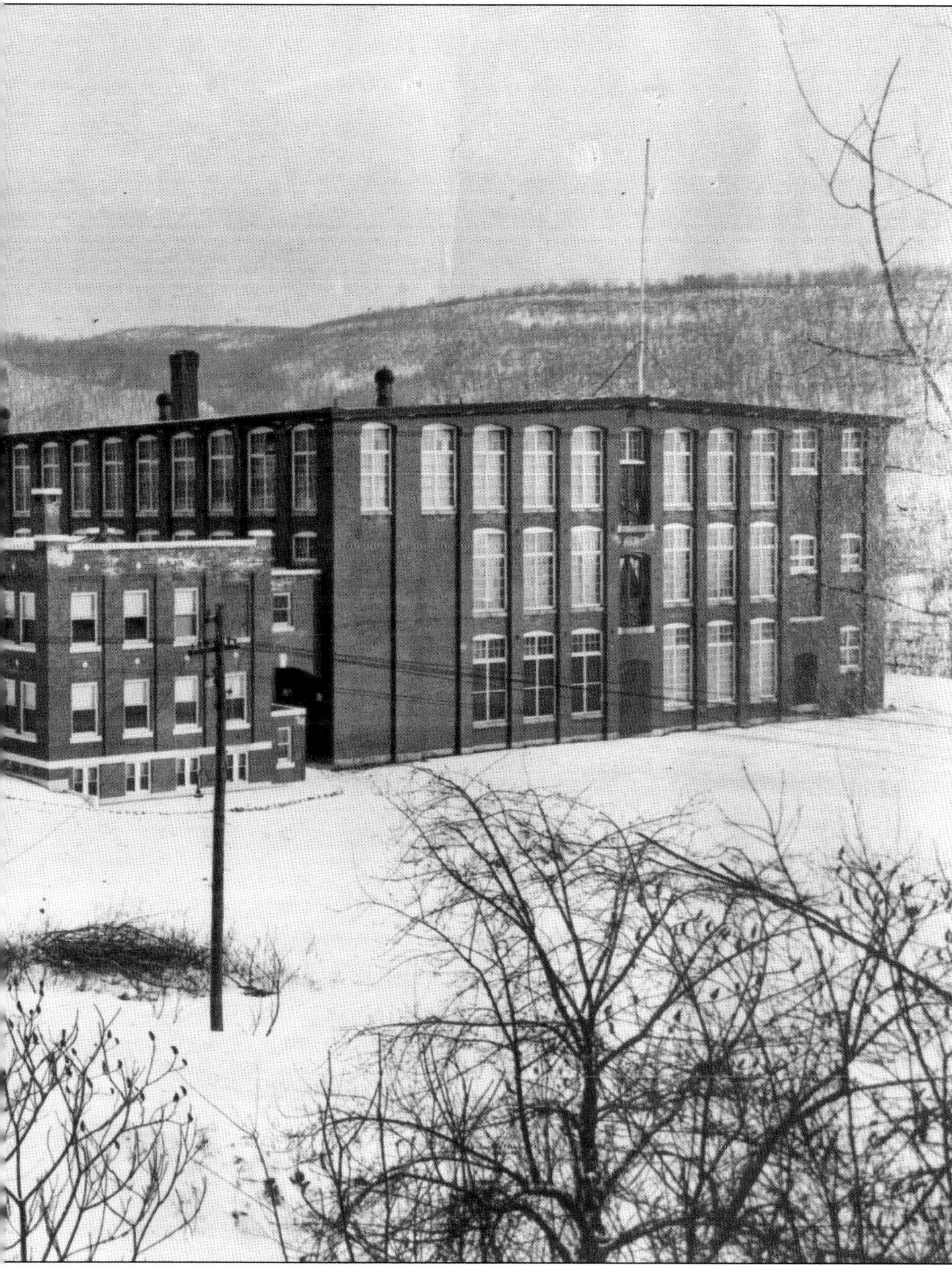

Fort Dummer Mill and Berkshire Fine Spinning

Looking at a photo of the Fort Dummer Mill brings back many memories. This mill was an important part of my early years. It was the reason my family came to this area and was a source of income for several family members.

My grandparents Frank and Catherine Juscen moved to Brattleboro in 1918. My father, who was 14 years of age at the time, began work at the mill alongside his parents. At this time there were no laws governing a minimum age for minors to begin work. My father's three younger sisters cared for each other and entered into school. Such was the life of mill families.

Upon opening in 1912, sufficient workers were available to handle production at the mill. But as time progressed and the demand grew, more workers were needed. People were hired to venture into other states to secure needed workers. It was this method that had brought my father and his family to town.

As their family enlarged, my grandmother felt needed at home. Their home was one of the many tenements provided for the workers by the mill owners. Rent for these apartments was deducted weekly from the workers' salaries. The house included six rooms with a large attic, which was sometimes used by a new worker until their own living quarters were secured.

My mother's family was also drawn to town by mill employment. The Reome family had been recruited from a farm in upper New York State. My mother, along with her sister and brother, also hired on at the mill. Their father came just for the winters initially, although he eventually came to live in Brattleboro full-time also.

My parents met at the mill and eventually were married. Both my parents worked at the mill, my mother returning there after I was born. The first few years of my life were spent living with my grandparents. My grandmother "Baba" Juscen cared for me. She worked very hard cooking, cleaning, and doing laundry. Yet, she still found time to enjoy me. My earliest memories include remembrances of her long cotton dresses and coverall apron. Aside from her traditional household duties, she tended the wood stove in the kitchen. The oven door opened to the side, and she would sit with me on her lap and warm her feet as she sang Polish songs. I walked first for my grandmother, and my mother was sorry she had missed my first steps. My Baba was so proud, my mother later told me.

When I was two years old, my sister, Dorothy, was born. My grandmother also cared for her for a short time until my parents secured their own place. We moved into a new tenement building on the corner of South Main and Cross Streets. Ours was the last one on the end. This change brought new friends and neighbors. An older Irish couple lived next door. The wife cared for us. While we lived there, my brother was born. I still recall our Irish neighbors celebrating with us. He played a small accordion, and his wife did the Irish jig. Within a short time, we moved to Valley Street, just one street from my beloved grandparents. Now, I could see them each day, for having lived in their home for four years, they were a part of my family.

Many times while visiting them, they would argue in Polish. They would speak English to me, however. One day, after hearing them conversing in Polish, I picked up a new word. Feeling proud, I was anxious to share this with my father. Upon repeating the new word, my father replied, "Nancy, don't ever say that word again." I learned I had repeated a profanity.

While living on Valley Street, I entered the first grade at Oak Grove School. My uncle, Stanley Juscen, walked me there on the first day. After that I walked with the other children in my class up the short hill to the nearby school.

I remember the day we received our first

report card. We were all comparing marks on our way home. Grades of A to C were marked in blue pen, while D to F were penned in red. A friend, Norman, compared his card with mine. He told me mine was not as good as his. He was proud of receiving so many red letters. Upon arriving home, I was relieved to have my mother explain how well I had done.

Berkshire (Fort Dummer Mill's owners) had a baseball team. My father played center field. The players were all mill workers. Games were very well attended. As they were near my home, I remember going to each game and cheering for my dad. He was a good player in the field, as well as at the plate. Out-of-town games became family outings.

The summer after I completed first grade, we moved into our own house at 39 Home Street. The move was not too far, just up the hill from our tenement and one street from Oak Grove School. It was convenient for us to come home from school to eat lunch. Both of my parents continued working at the mill. Our family owned a car, and both of my parents could drive, but they continued to walk to work.

By fourth grade, we had become quite independent and had our own chores. My job was to cook the morning oatmeal, while my sister, Dot, made the beds. The dog had to be let out and brought back in before we began our short walk to school.

My teacher, Mrs. Mack, was strict, but very understanding of her student's home life. She would look out the window, and if I was on the playground, she would not mark me late. Our dog, Skippy, sometimes gave me a problem. He like to wander the neighborhood and did not always return promptly. One day, in frustration, I decided Skippy could spend the day on the porch until lunchtime. I hurried to school and was visiting with my classmates when I heard a click, click, click. As I looked up, my dog was coming through the door. Fearing I would be in trouble, I looked the other way, ignoring the uninvited visitor. Of course, Skippy walked right over and sat down beside me. Mrs. Mack asked, "Is that your dog, Nancy?"

I looked down, pretending to be surprised and answered that it was. Her reply, "Well, take him home." Naturally, I obeyed my teacher's command.

My five years at Oak Grove School were happy ones. Many of my friends had parents who also worked at the mill, although there were some children whose mothers were at home, as well as some fathers with other occupations.

After graduating from high school, I spent that summer working at the mill myself in the weave room. I had a small office with an adding machine. It was my job to take the "picks." Each weaving loom had a clock for each worker. Since there were three shifts of workers, there were three different counts each day for each loom. Workers were paid according to the amount of cloth they wove. It was important to accurately credit each worker their production. It was a fun summer. One of the most enjoyable memories I have was of walking to the mill each morning with my dad, who was now a foreman. I enjoyed our time together, even though he was not always communicative in the morning. Upon entering college that September, little was mentioned of the mill when I came home to visit.

However, my dad continued to work there until the mill closed its doors. It was a sad time for many workers, and it was difficult for the community to absorb the newly unemployed. Some of the younger workers were fortunate in seeking other employment, while for others it was difficult. My father traveled to work in North Adams, Massachusetts, setting up machinery for the cotton mill there. Not wanting to relocate, nor continue the long drive, he decided to find other employment. Being in his fifties, it was not easy to find a new job. When I was hired as a teacher later that year, I became aware of an opening for a custodian at Oak Grove School. The custodian there was ill. When the custodian returned to work, my father moved to the Academy School, and eventually to Green Street School as head custodian. A conscientious worker, he enjoyed the children and was able to stay on until he retired.

Yet, it was Berkshire Fine Spinning that had first brought him to this community and created an extended family that lived and played together just up the hill from Fort Dummer Mill.

—Nancy Juscen Goldsmith

CHAPTER SIX
FROM HERE TO THERE

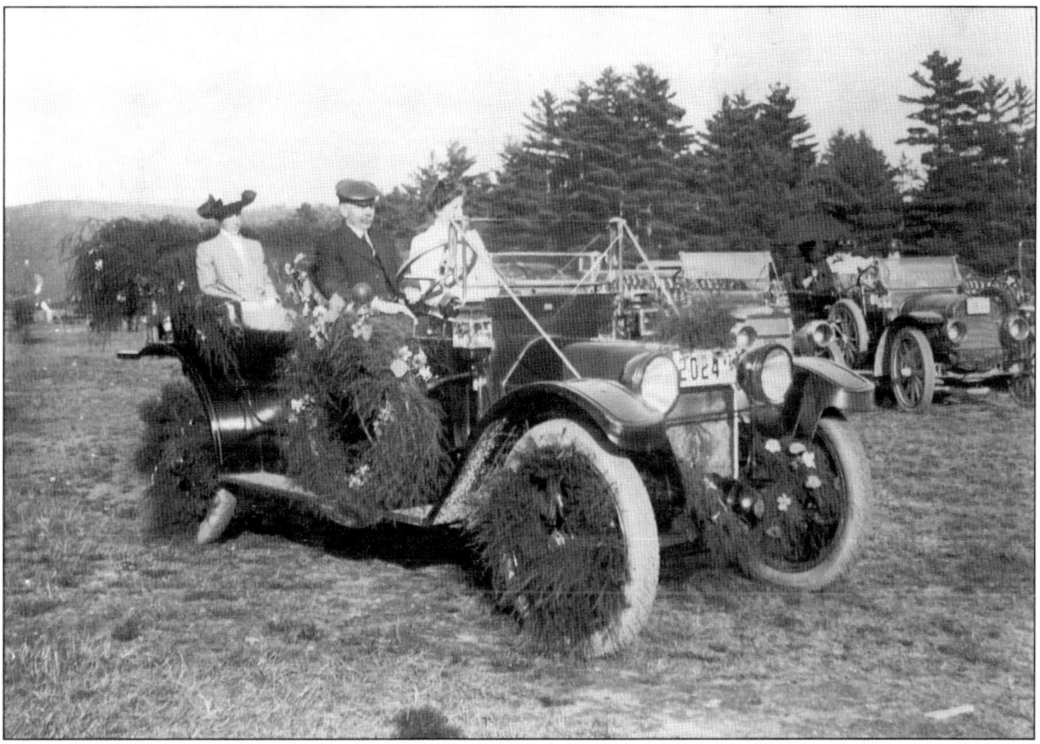

Participating in the Valley Fair was a highlight of the fall season for many years. Pictured in their wreathed Rambler are William and Lillie Vinton, with Mrs. Frank Nichols in the back. Elaborately decorated vehicles of all sorts and sizes made up an impressive parade that wound its way from the north end of town to the site of the fair at the south end, now the location of Brattleboro Union High School. There were activities for all ages at the popular agricultural fair, as well as many special events. Some residents can recall the last years of the fair, which ceased operations in the early 1930s.

Locomotives

I was born in Connecticut in 1933 and moved to Brattleboro in 1969. Most machinery interested me at an early age, but nothing moved me more than railroad steam engines. I lived 100 yards from a main line railroad and one mile from a small steam rail line that delivered crushed rock to barges.

I would beg my mother to take me to see the small steam engine because there was a yard where they often paused to take on water and fuel, which was soft coal (bituminous). She also knew one of the engineers. The engines were like large, black living beings. Just sitting on the siding, they radiated intense heat and smells of soft coal, hot grease, sweet steam, dripping hot water, and an internal groaning and pulsing of its boiler. I can't think of any machine that I've witnessed in my lifetime that had the presence of a steam engine just sitting there. Of course when it moved, the drama increased. There was usually a blast of steam from the cylinders, clanking of connecting rods, and exit of smoke and steam from the smokestack. They really did "thunder" down the tracks. Nowadays, when people describe a tornado, they often say it sounded like a freight train.

The engineers usually wore blue denims, a striped hat, and a red bandanna around the neck. Soft coal is very sooty, and during the hot weather, their faces were often covered with soft coal dust streaked with sweat. How I wish I could return to that time and take some photographs.

—Robert F. George

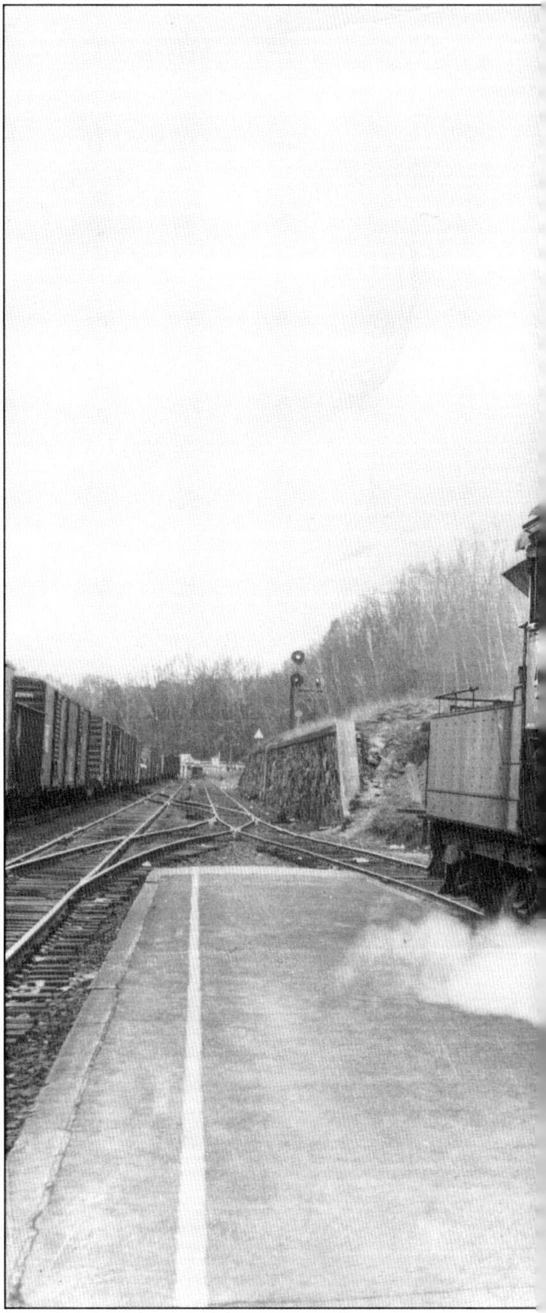

Union Station

I remember the railroad station. When I was seven or eight, my mom took me there to go to Connecticut. I loved walking up the marble steps. I remember the walkway over the tracks. You could stand right over the tracks, and the smoke would come up all around you. I was there two or three times. It's now the museum building.

—Elisha Prouty

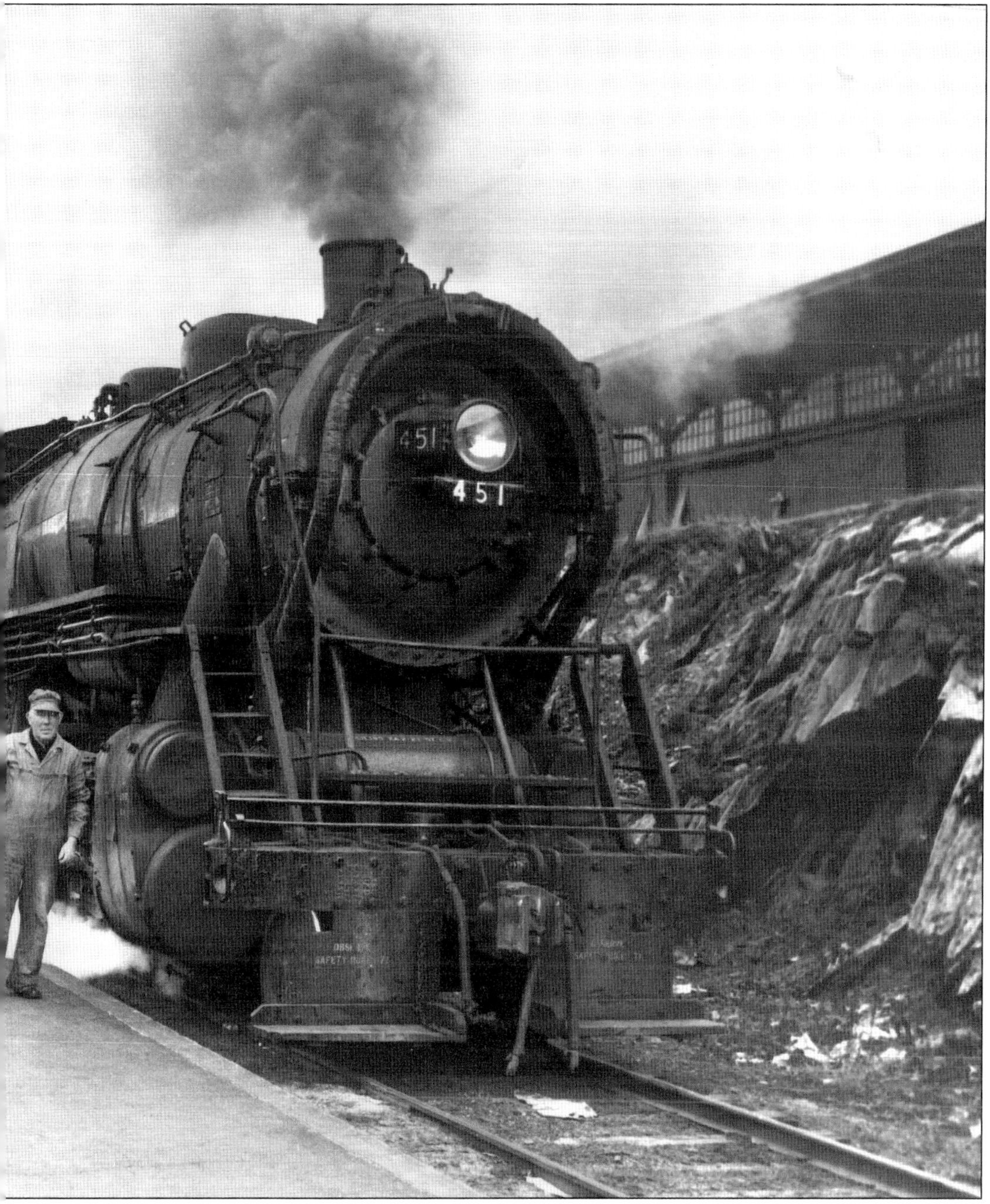

Pat Flynn is the engineer who ran the last steam-powered locomotive to operate in Brattleboro. The photograph dates from 1956.

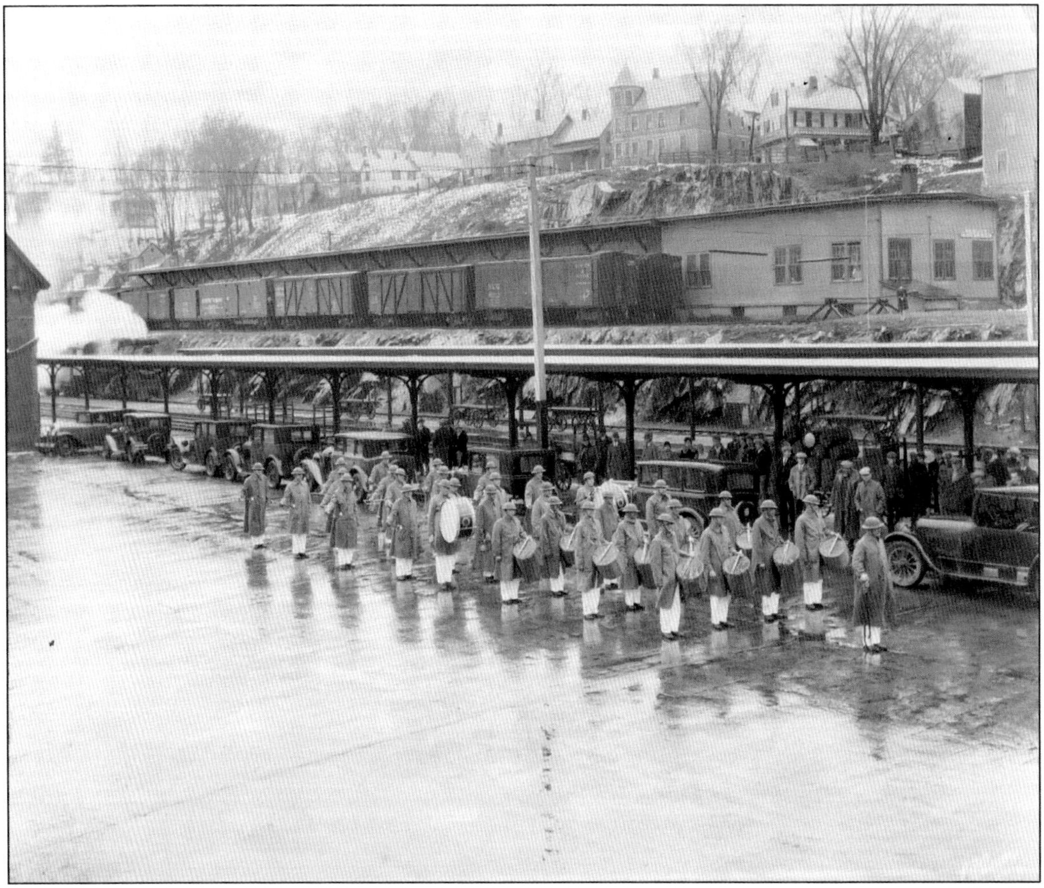

This photograph was taken during the time of World War I. It was common for such drum-and-bugle bands to meet trains arriving in town. Brattleboro's second railroad station is on the left.

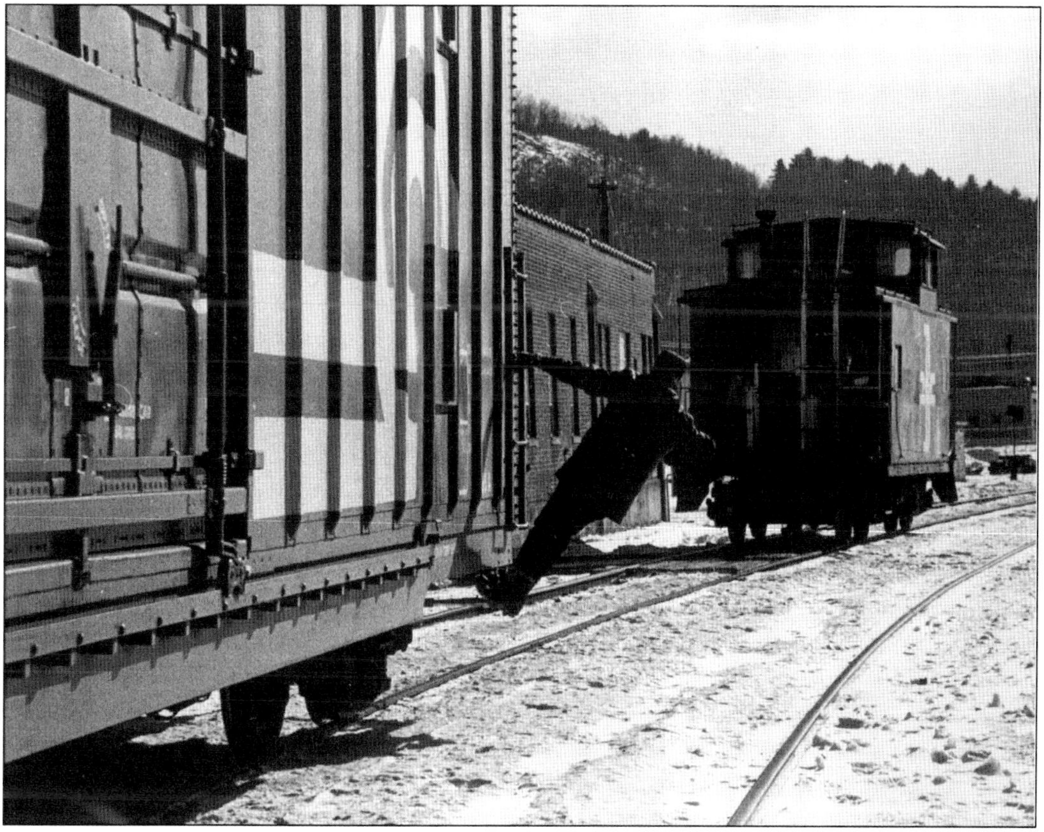

A freight train backs into a Brattleboro siding to connect with a caboose.

Hopping the Freights

It was the summer of 1979. A bunch of school buddies, including me, were in the habit of cooling off those oppressive afternoons by swimming in the West River. It had been a particularly hot day, and we had been swimming and horsing around for a couple of hours. We were also developing a tremendous thirst. None of us was old enough to drive, so of course no one had a car. We used our bikes everywhere we wanted to go.

A freight train was coming across the West River railroad bridge. At this point it always had to slow down because the switch needed to be thrown to direct the train onto the other track. Someone had the bright idea to ride the train to downtown, where we could pick up some sodas and maybe something to eat.

We knew we would have just enough time to be on the tracks when it came almost to a halt. We waited until a flatbed crept by and jumped on. It was great. Just knowing we were breaking the law added to the thrill. The train came to the crossroad by the railroad station and we all jumped off. We got our sodas and had to walk home, as our bikes had been left at the river. My mother got wind of this adventure and chewed me out thoroughly. I got the lecture on danger; it was illegal.

Nevertheless, by the end of the summer, we had probably ridden the rails at least six more times. Always the same destination, but always with the thrill of doing something we were not supposed to do.

—*Tim Buchanan*

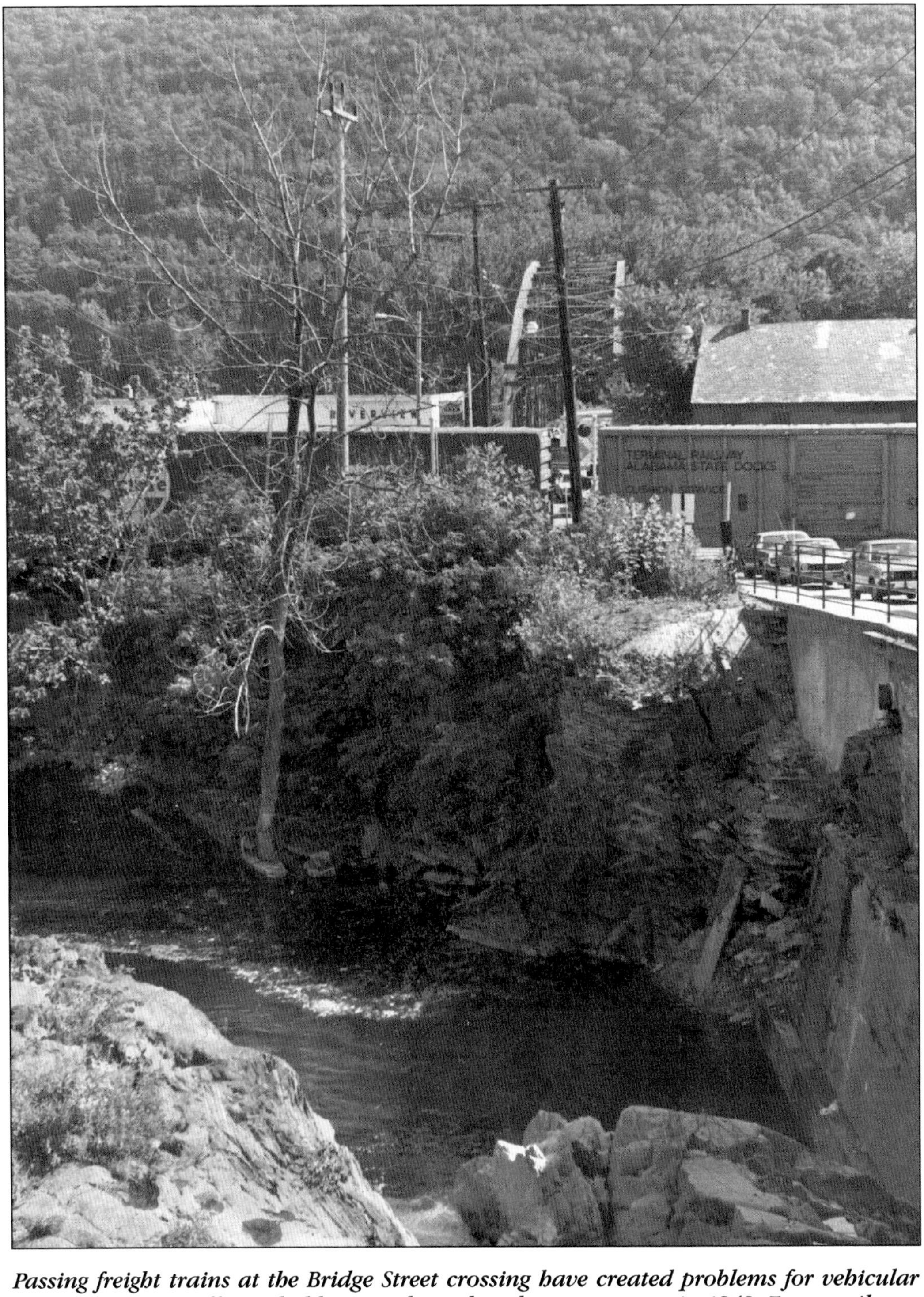

Passing freight trains at the Bridge Street crossing have created problems for vehicular and pedestrian traffic probably since the railroad came to town in 1849. Fewer rail cars making up a train in the early days may have caused a slight delay, but the modern train with its seemingly endless numbers of freight cars tries the patience of the unfortunate individual caught on the "wrong" side of the gates and flashing lights.

Waiting for the Train

The Bridge Street at-grade railroad crossing tried my patience frequently when I returned to town from my teaching job in Hinsdale, New Hampshire. Although it was difficult to predict when a freight train would slowly wend its way through town, it seemed that invariably late afternoon was prime time. When the gates were down with the train approaching and two diesel engines came into view, a long wait was a sure thing.

Sitting in the car watching the train rumble by, I could study the various types of freight cars from the Midwest, Canada, and other faraway places. The cars included the familiar boxcars, refrigerated units, tankers, flatbeds, and bulk cargo carriers. Counting the cars provided some mental exercise, if I felt so inclined. Usually, something distracted me and I lost count. The traditional caboose was still in use at the time, so when it finally passed by, the track cleared, the gates moved slowly upward, and the rhythmic sound of wheels on rails subsided.

I could then proceed up the hill to the famous, or infamous, intersection at the south end of Main Street, that to this day remains the nemesis of motorists and pedestrians.

—Hazel J. Anderson

Moving to Brattleboro

In May of 1993, my girlfriend and I were living in New York City and I worked at the New York Public Library. We decided to visit Vermont, where I had spent some time during the 1960s and 1970s. After some bike riding, we sat on the porch of the Grafton Inn, where we were staying, and I started to read the *Brattleboro Reformer.* I always look at help-wanted ads in the local paper when I travel anywhere, just to get a better idea of the community. Much to my surprise, there was an ad for a reference librarian at the Brooks Memorial Library in Brattleboro. The next day, we visited Brattleboro, and I stopped in at the library and picked up the application form.

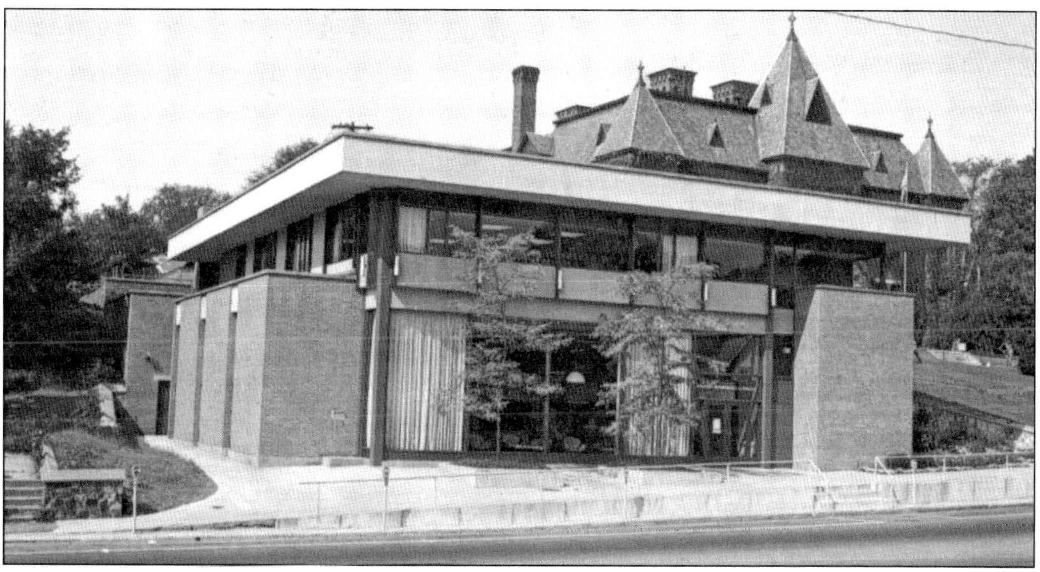

The George J. Brooks Memorial Library, located on Main Street, opened in 1967, replacing an older structure that was torn down to create a parking lot for the post office. The roofline of Brattleboro's Municipal Center, formerly the Brattleboro High School, is visible in the background.

I never expected to hear from them and had put the idea out of my mind when I received a telephone call from Jerry Carbone, the library's director, asking me if I would like to come up to Brattleboro for an interview. The interview went well, and I was offered the position.

Relocating to Vermont and giving up my job at the New York Public Library was something I had dreamed about but somehow never acted on it, and now I was being given the opportunity to do it. I had to think about all this. I did, but it was not for long. I accepted the position and started work on July 16, 1993, and have been at the library ever since. And, oh yes, I married Susan and we have bought a house in Brattleboro. So, one might say that we now have roots in the community.

—Richard Shuldiner

The Episcopal Church on the Move

When I moved to Brattleboro in 1949, St. Michael's Episcopal Church was on Main Street, about where Candle in the Night is located. The church membership was growing. There was not room for expansion, and moving the church to a new location was being considered. In 1953, a chain store looking for a downtown space made an offer to buy the land the church was on at a price the church governing body couldn't refuse. Then the preparation began! A location was found on the corner of Bradley Avenue and Putney Road, and soon the church was hoisted onto a huge trailer truck. Then, on May 26, the church was slowly moved out to the road on Main Street. What excitement! I remember watching teams of telephone company and electric company men lifting and sometimes removing

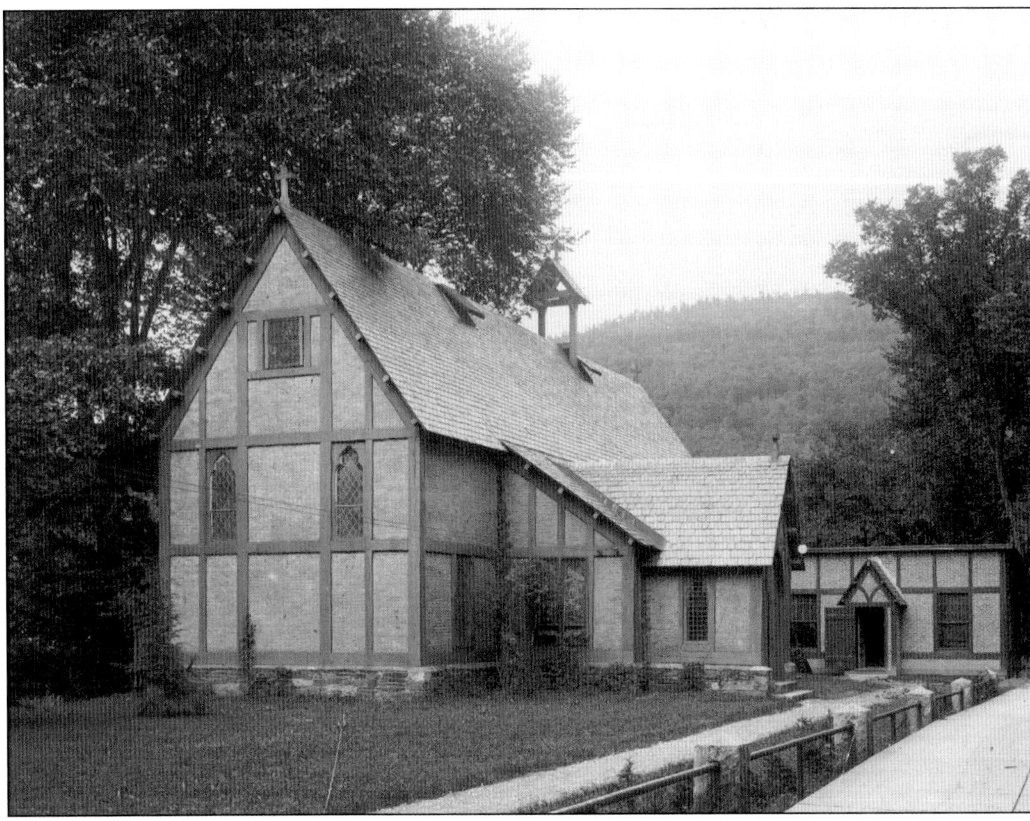

St. Michael's Episcopal Church is pictured at its former site, on Main Street.

wires and cables so the large structure could pass safely. For two days I was among the many people who left homes and jobs to watch the slow but steady progress up Main Street. There were all kinds of viewers along the sidewalks. There were town officials, retired people, employees on their lunch breaks, church members, and all sorts of "sidewalk superintendents." The schools allowed some teachers to take their classes to view the spectacular sight of a large church moving up the middle of Main Street. For two days, the church inched its way along until, on May 28, it reached the foundation upon which it was to rest. Brattleboro hadn't had so much excitement in years! However, there were many people, including town officials, police, utilities personnel, and members of St. Michael's, who heaved a collective sigh of relief when the church was safely placed on the foundation prepared for it.

For a month or two, the Episcopal church services were held in the Masonic Hall, then located on Main Street. I, among many, was happy when we finally resumed services in our beautiful church in its wonderful new location.

—Evelyn Walker

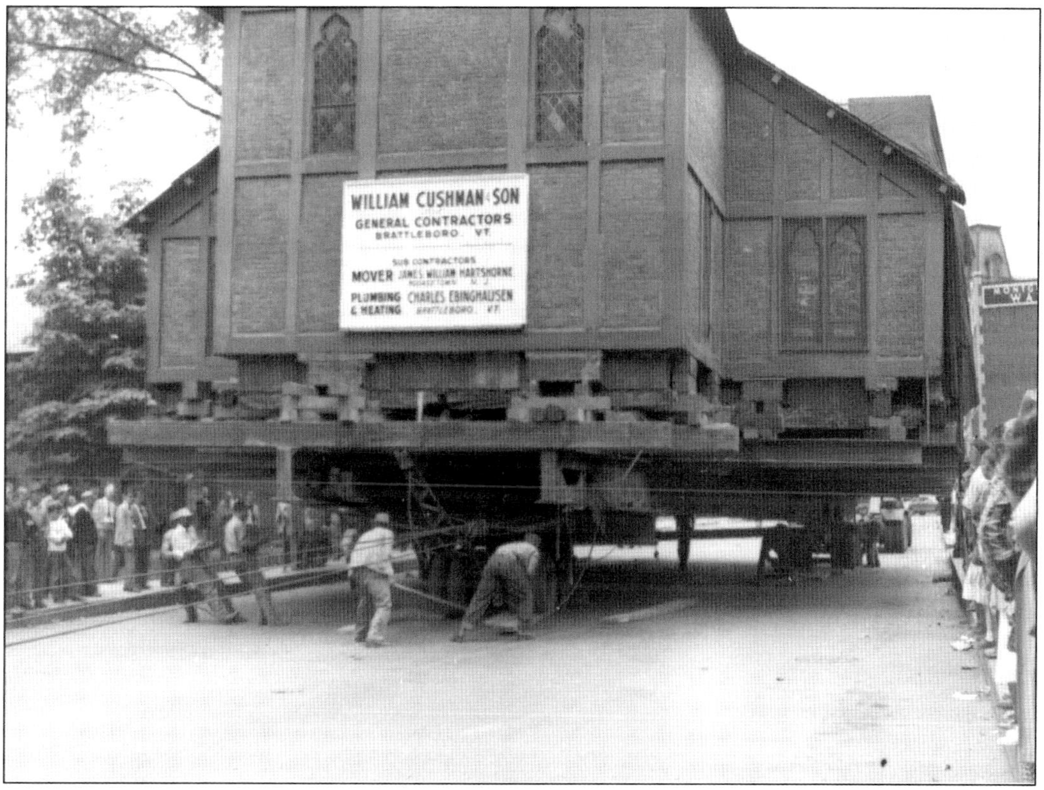

St. Michael's Episcopal Church is being moved from its foundation on Main Street on May 26, 1953.

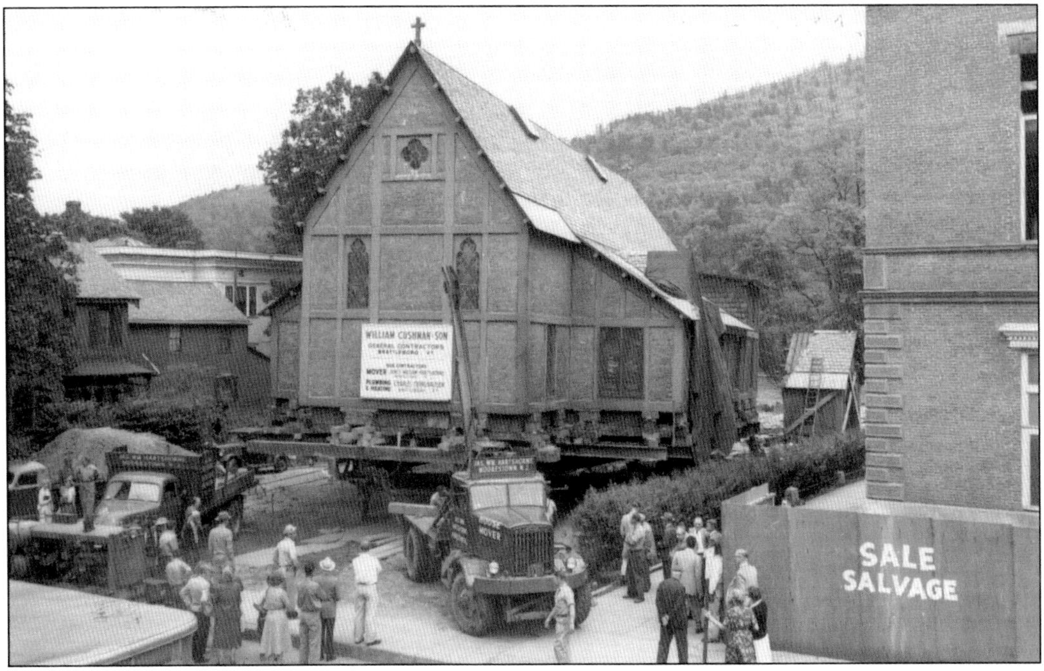

These May 27, 1953 views look south as St. Michael's Episcopal Church inches its way onto Main Street and moves slowly north.

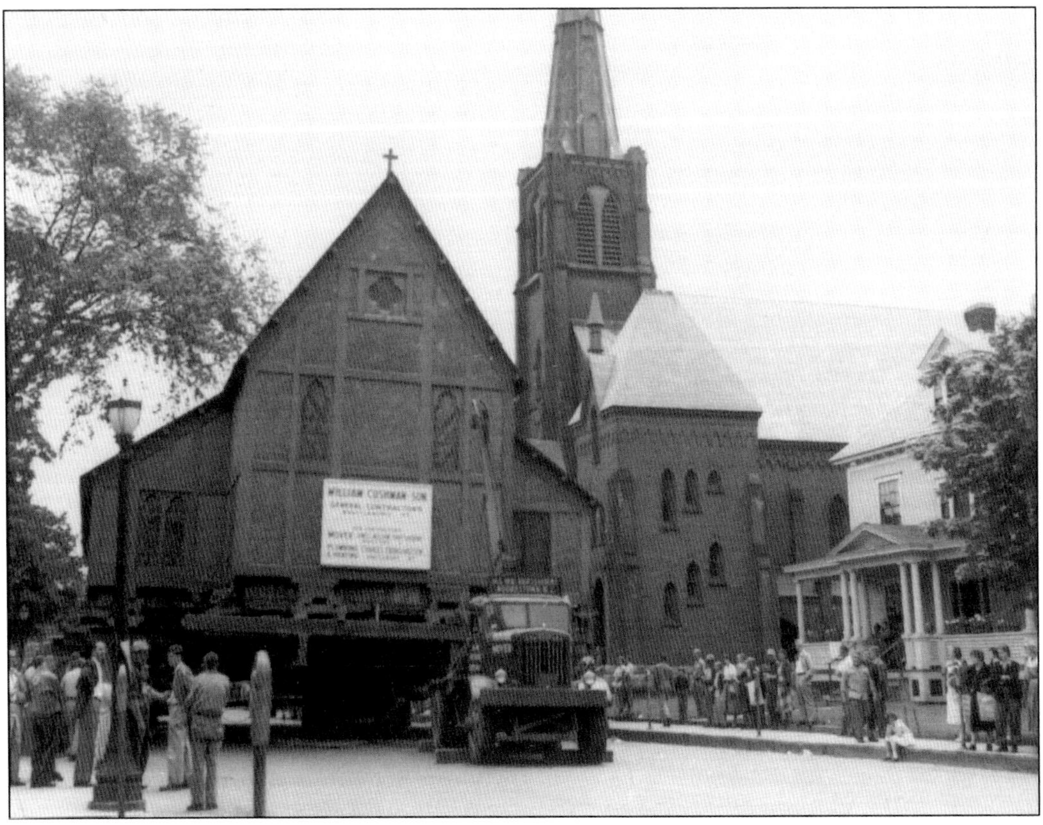

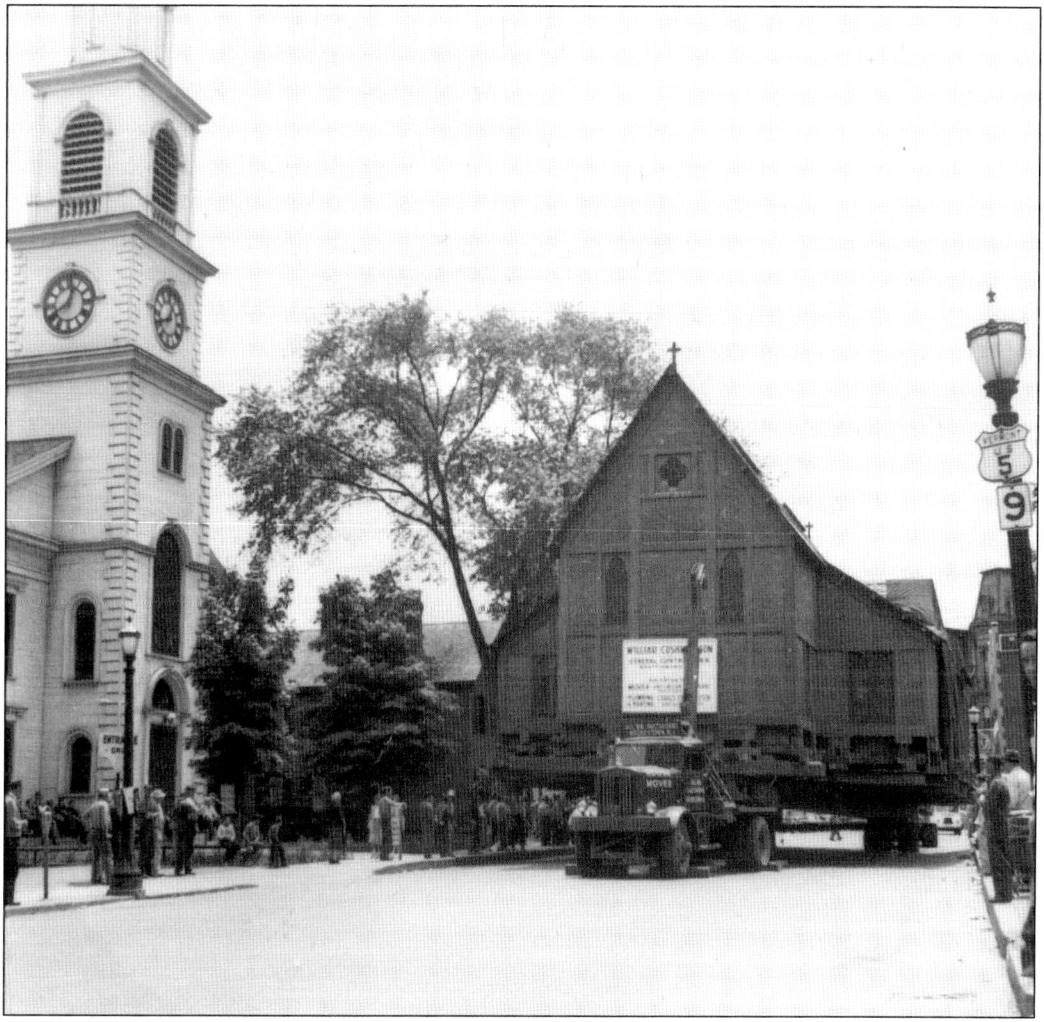

This May 27, 1953 view looks south at Saint Michael's Episcopal Church heading along Main Street toward its new foundation on the corner of Bradley Avenue and Putney Road.

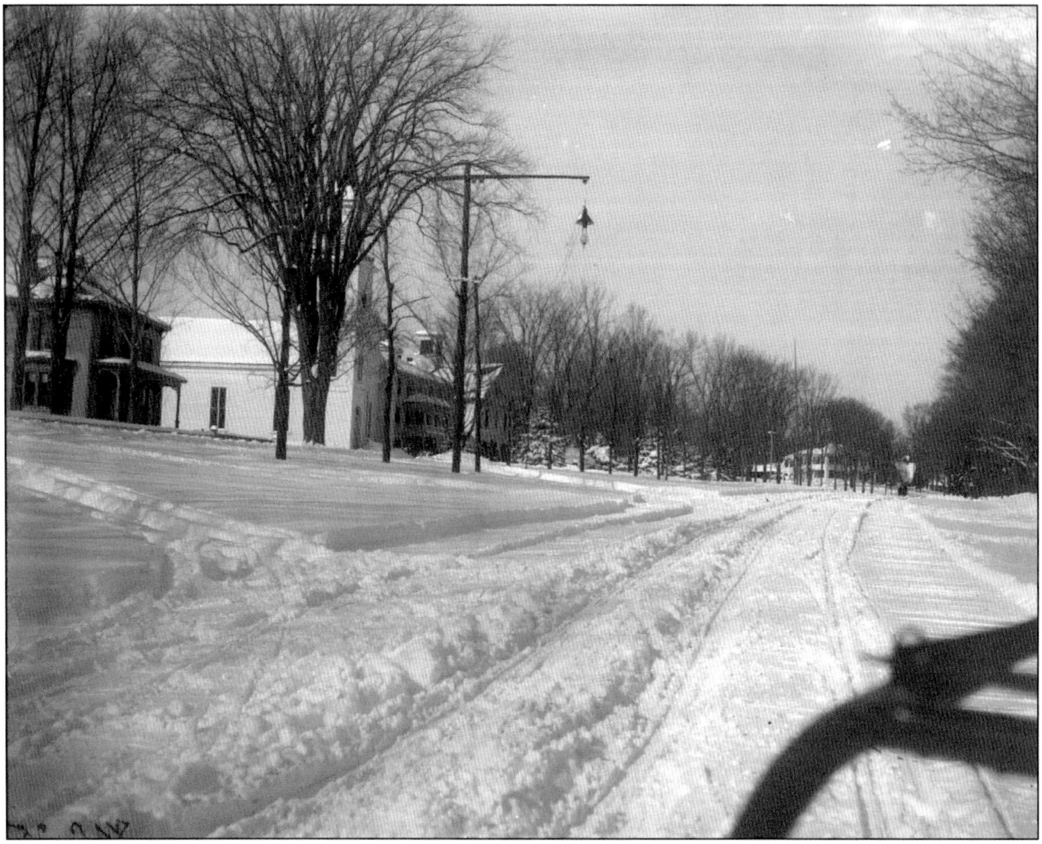

This winter scene was taken looking west from the trolley in West Brattleboro c. *1900. Notice the arc streetlight and the Congregational church on the left.*

A Walk into the Past

My daily walk takes me from Melrose Terrace to the West Brattleboro post office and then back east on the north side of Western Avenue to the Route 91 overpass and then back to Melrose Terrace.

Taking that walk a century ago, I'd leave Melrose Terrace, which was a chicken farm and before that strawberry fields, and I'd walk to the Hayes Tavern, at the present location of the post office. Noting an octagonal house and the end of the trolley line at that same location, I'd proceed east noting the Beal House (the Brattleboro Historical Society's present home) and then the Melrose Hospital (now the Village Green apartments) opposite the present firehouse. Then came the Stockwell building and the Glenwood Seminary across the road from it. Then I'd go past George Miller Drive (present entrance to Melrose Terrace) where sat another octagonal house in the middle of Miller Drive. Proceeding east, I'd pass by the gristmill on the Whetstone Brook, behind Ziter's deli, and then cross the Whetstone through a covered bridge. Continuing on, I'd pass the Creamery Bridge and adjacent creamery. At the upcoming completion of my walk, I'd pass through Centerville with its Centerville School opposite today's Country Deli. I would stop just beyond

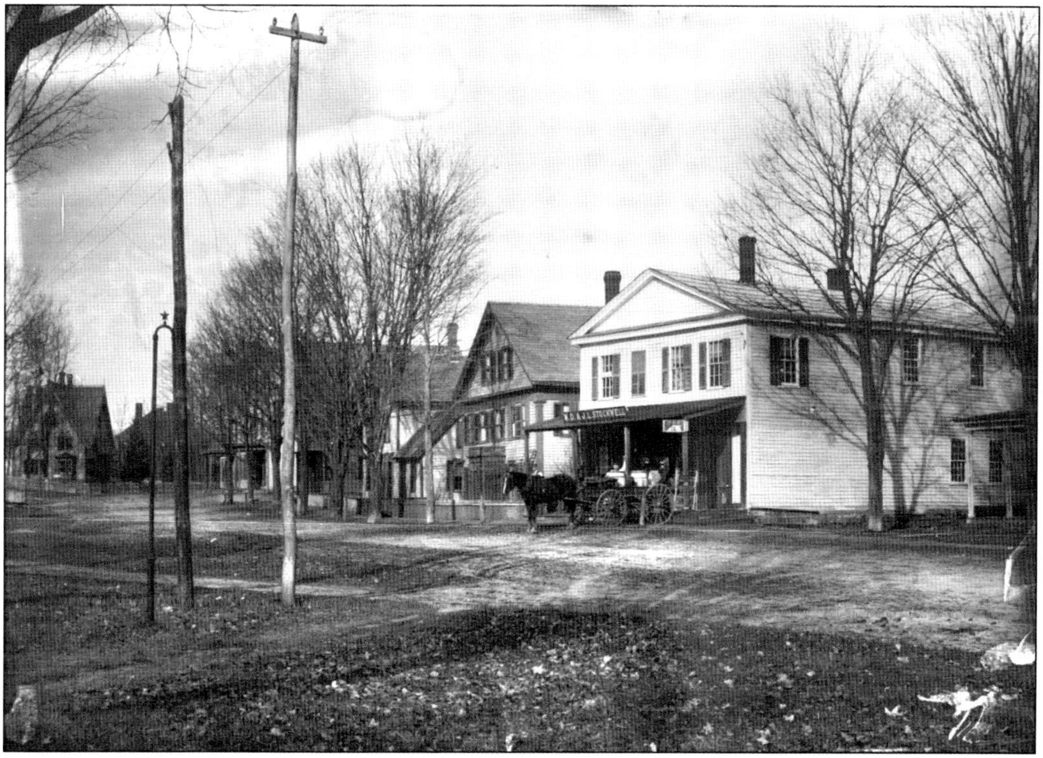

This c. 1890 view shows the W.D. & J.L. Stockwell store, in West Brattleboro.

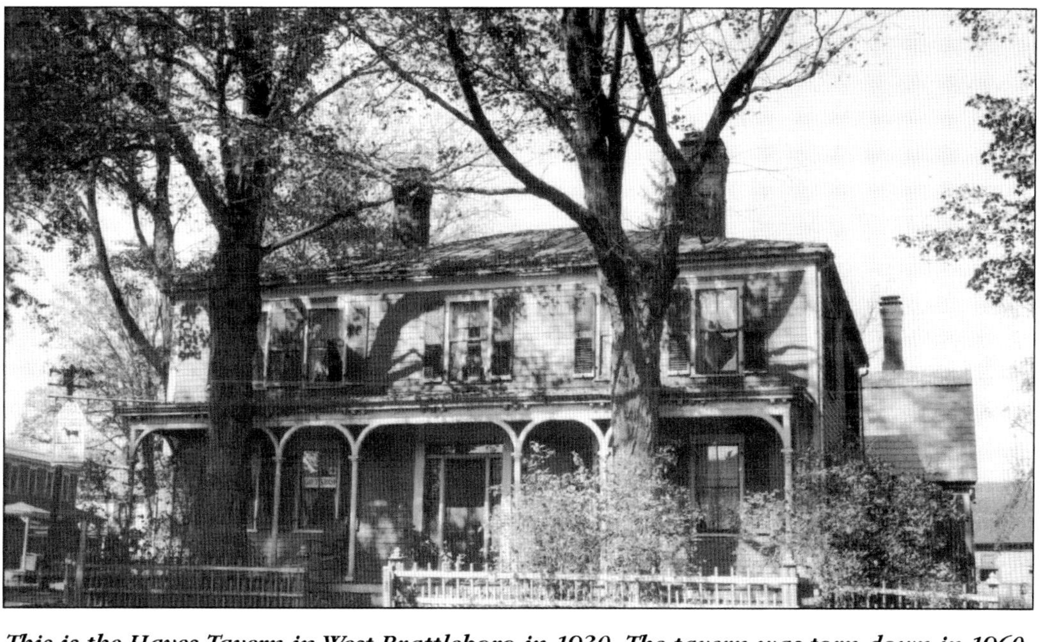

This is the Hayes Tavern in West Brattleboro in 1930. The tavern was torn down in 1960. It is now the site of commercial buildings.

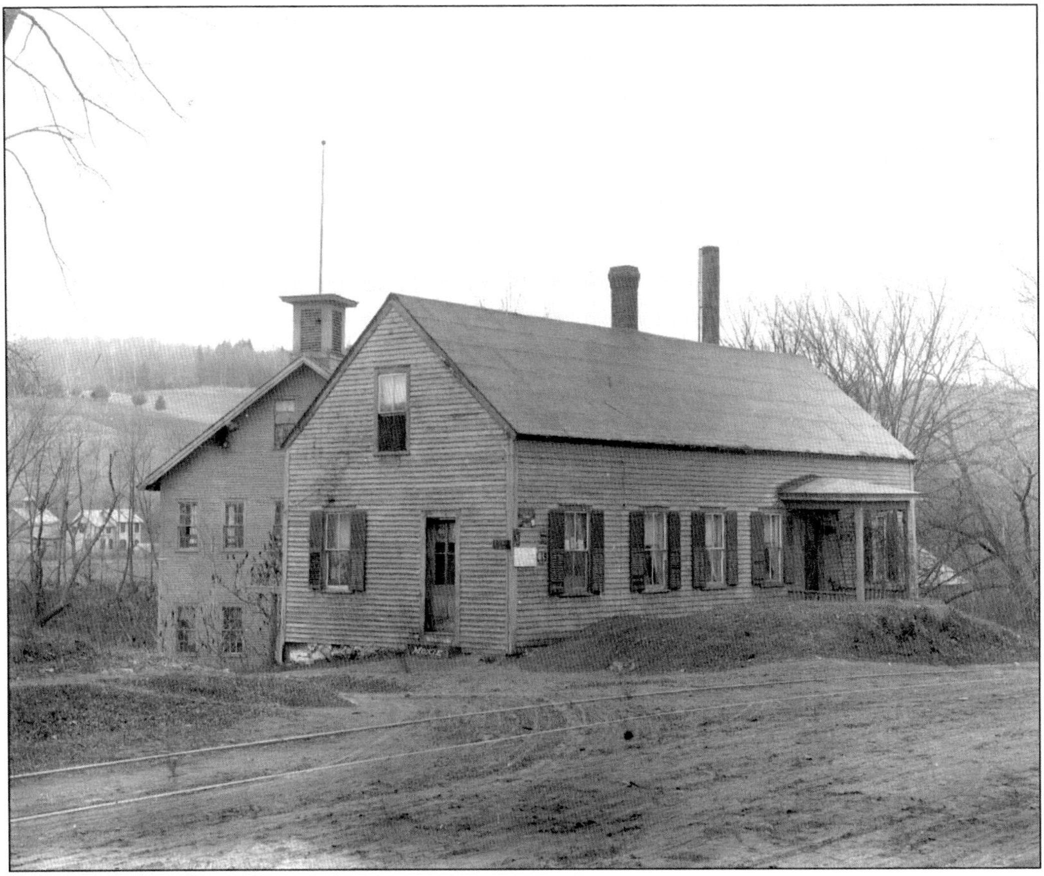

The Centerville Mill, on the left, was owned by the New England Furniture Company and was located at the intersection of Williams Street and Western Avenue. The building in the foreground is now the Vermont Country Deli.

Brattle Street, noting that many years later, there would be a U.S. 91 throughway that would cross the avenue at that point. On this early walk though, the trolley line would continue east on the avenue toward its destination in downtown Brattleboro. The Beal House, the Melrose Hospital, Stockwell's, the Creamery Bridge, the creamery, and the Centerville School buildings remain today.

—*C.L. Billings*

CHAPTER SEVEN
BAD TIMES

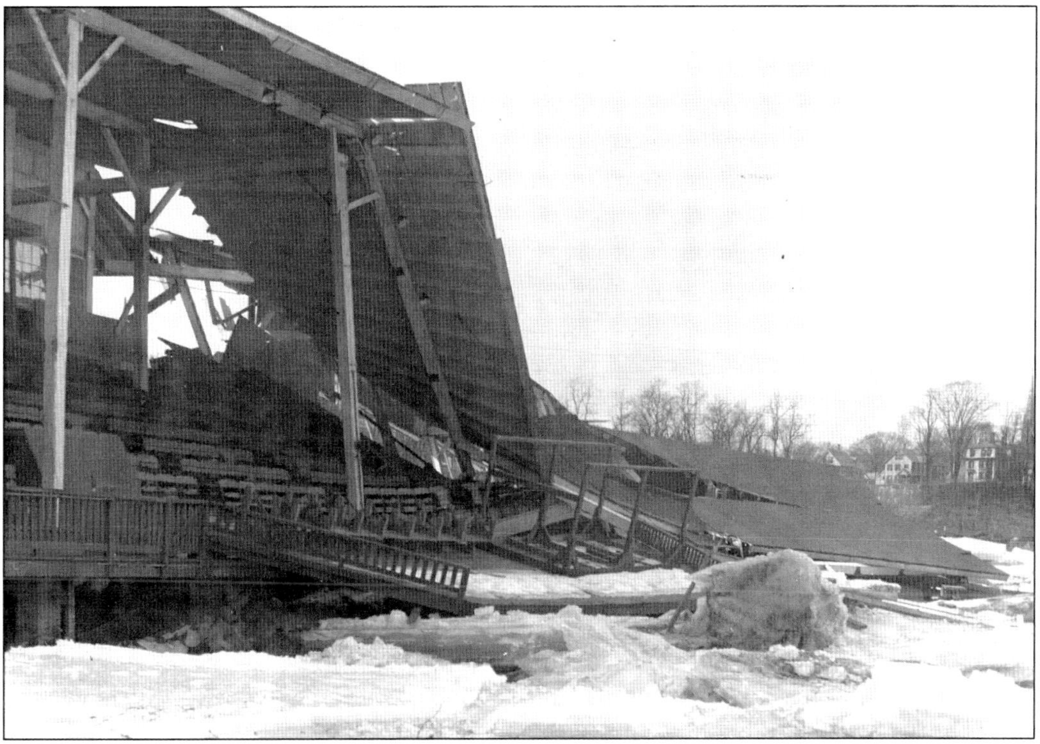

Bad times befell the Island Park pavilion and grandstand more than once during their existence on the island between Brattleboro and Hinsdale, New Hampshire. From acreage large enough to support a farm, water and ice eroded the land, crushed structures, and reduced the popular entertainment spot to a meager area of land that supports the abutment of the bridges. The construction of the dam downriver contributed to the high water problem. Finally, after the 1927 flood, the promoters of island activities decided they could no longer endure the bad times.

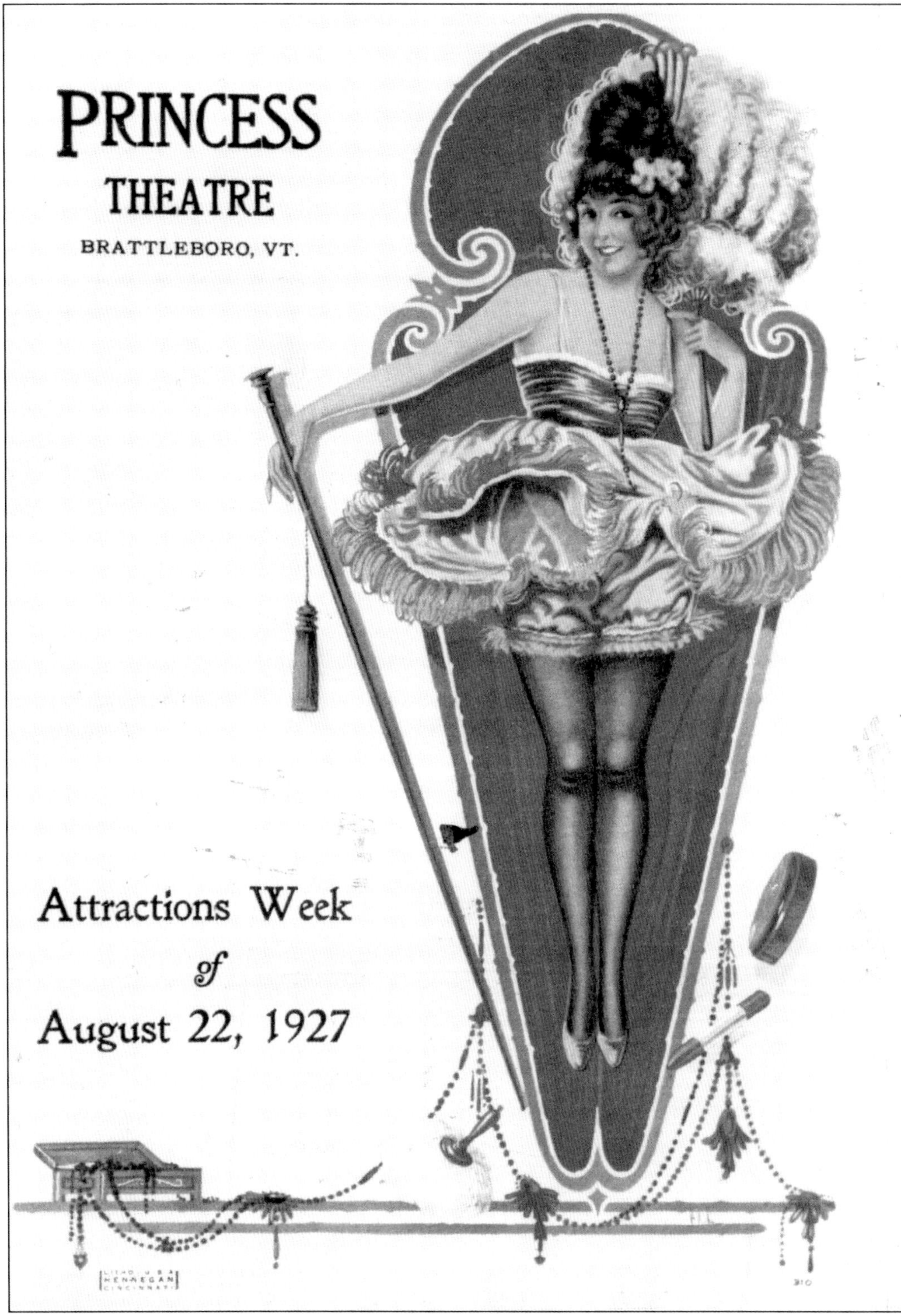

This was the cover of the program for the Princess Theatre for the week of August 22, 1927, before the building was struck by fire once again.

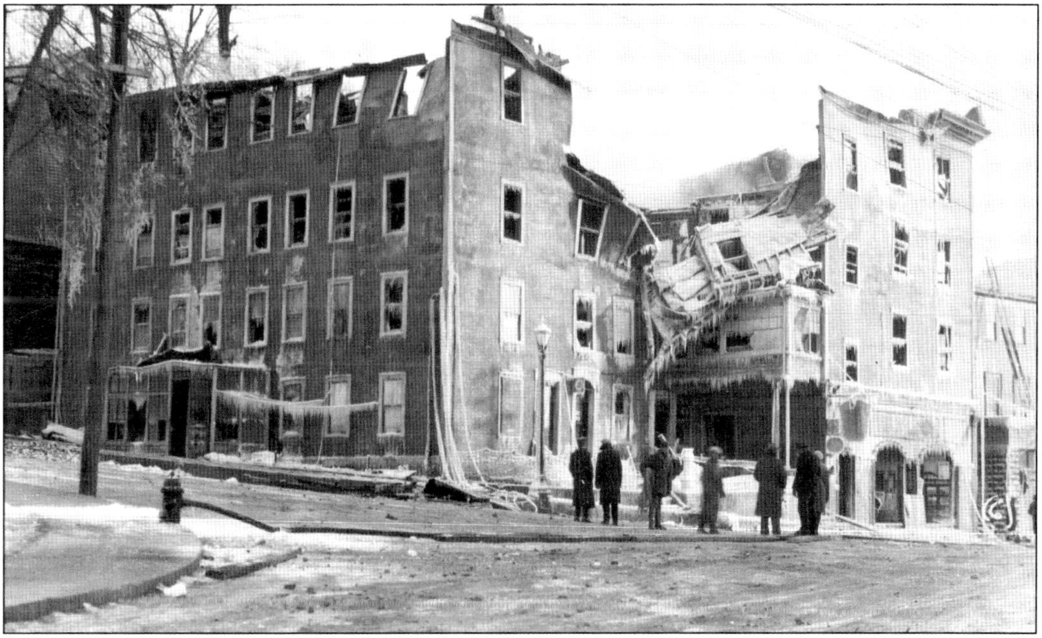

The Princess Hotel and Theatre fell victim to fire several times over the years. Several people survey the extensive damage after the 1929 fire was extinguished. The building was rebuilt but was destroyed by fire for the final time in 1937.

THE PRINCESS FIRE

Seeing the photo of the old fire station on Elliot Street reminded me of an incident that touched on my family's personal life.

On Tuesday, February 12, 1929, at about 6:20 p.m., the fire alarm rang from an alarm box on Elliot Street. In those days the entire town could hear the alarm and count the number of rings, which told everyone the approximate location of the fire.

My father threw on his coat and hat and dashed to the station. He was a "call," or volunteer, member of the department. A little later a second alarm sounded. I'm sure my mother put on her "worry cap" and prayed.

Hours later my father came home, cold, tired, unhurt, almost pleased with his efforts and adventure. The final climax, provoking a hearty laugh, came when he took his wet, frozen pants off. They stood upright on the floor all by themselves.

The fire had been in the Princess Hotel. The building was composed of a four-story wood-frame covered with sheet metal. It contained 125 rooms, including a few suites. Many rooms had steel ceilings. There were approximately 150 tenants.

During the first few hours, Miss Theodore Chase, 68 years old, was taken from the second floor but was already dead. Firemen tried unsuccessfully to revive her. Cause of death was unknown. Miss Chase had been warned to leave the building but had returned to collect some belongings. (Too bad she didn't obey the time-honored instructions: "When a building is on fire—Get Out and Stay Out!")

Mrs. Miner, the aged wife of Charles Miner, owner, was carried by firemen on ladders from the fourth floor. Also on the top floor, two young men were going to make a rope ladder out of sheets. Town manager Plattner warned them that the sheets would not hold their weight and they would go tumbling down. So they waited for help.

Several firemen were injured, some from falling on ice-covered stairs.

The damage to the property was estimated at $60,000. It had been rented to Charles Morgan, who managed it. He had $6,000 worth of insurance; Charles Miner, owner, had none. The ground-floor theater was operated by Arthur Sharby. It contained $10,000 worth of equipment, covered by $4,000 of insurance.

Mr. Sharby, in a later interview, said that his contract contained a clause saying that in case of catastrophe the theater would be returned to its original condition.

It was refurbished, as in later years I attended the showing of the film *Great Expectations.*

—Marion Deaett

The Hurricane of 1938

In September 1938, I was 10 years old and attending Canal Street School in the sixth grade. At about 2:00 p.m., we were all excused from classes and sent home, as there were reports of high winds and more rain. It had been raining for several days just prior to this day. At this time weathermen did not worry about hurricanes in our local area.

As I left school, making my way home by way of Prospect, Central, and Blakeslee Streets, I had to dodge flying branches and debris. When we arrived home, my mother couldn't understand why we had been released so early. To her it was only a rainy day. At about 3:30 p.m., with the wind and rain increasing, my mother sent me out to close doors on our garage on the back street. As I got to our driveway, the doors came flying through the air and crashed onto our shop building. I went in and told my mother what had happened. She didn't believe me until she looked for herself.

For the next two to four hours I watched trees on South Main Street being blown over. Two huge pines on the upper part of our neighbor's land, three to four feet at the butt section and over 90 feet tall, finally succumbed to the wind and toppled into our driveway where my father usually parked the car.

Winds in the Connecticut River Valley were unofficially estimated to have been over 100 to 125 miles per hour, doing extensive damage. The next day, after the storm had passed, we drove over to Spofford Lake to see how our cottage had fared. It took over five and a half hours to walk approximately a mile and three-quarters over and around downed trees and electrical wires. We did find on our arrival at the cottage on the North Shore that no damage had been done, even though others had not been so lucky.

This was my first encounter with a hurricane and hope to never experience one like this again. In later years I did go through several storms but a lot different than this one in 1938.

—Harry A. Pike

Hurricane Memories

September of 1938 was the year of the great hurricane. We had moved to Brattleboro early in June. It had been raining for several days and my mother had done the usual family laundry on Monday. The lines were full of sheets and personal wash, which had soured due to the high humidity. My brother, myself, and a cousin who was living with us were trying to open and close the door as my mother was carrying in the soggy, wet laundry. It took the strength of all three of us to do this, as my brother was only seven, and my cousin and I were 11 years old.

In the meantime, my father had got out of work at the Holden and Martin's cabinet shop on Frost Street and had to get me a

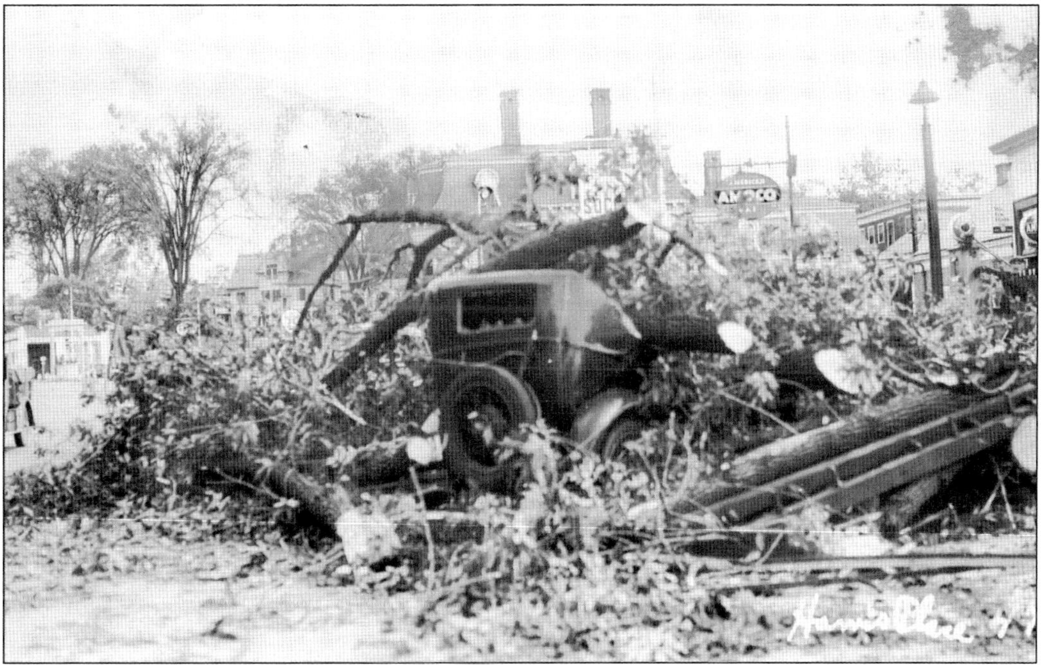

The 1938 hurricane wreaked havoc throughout the town. The owner of this car moved it to the corner of Harris Place and Main Street because he thought it would be safer. Had he left it where it was originally, it would not have been badly damaged.

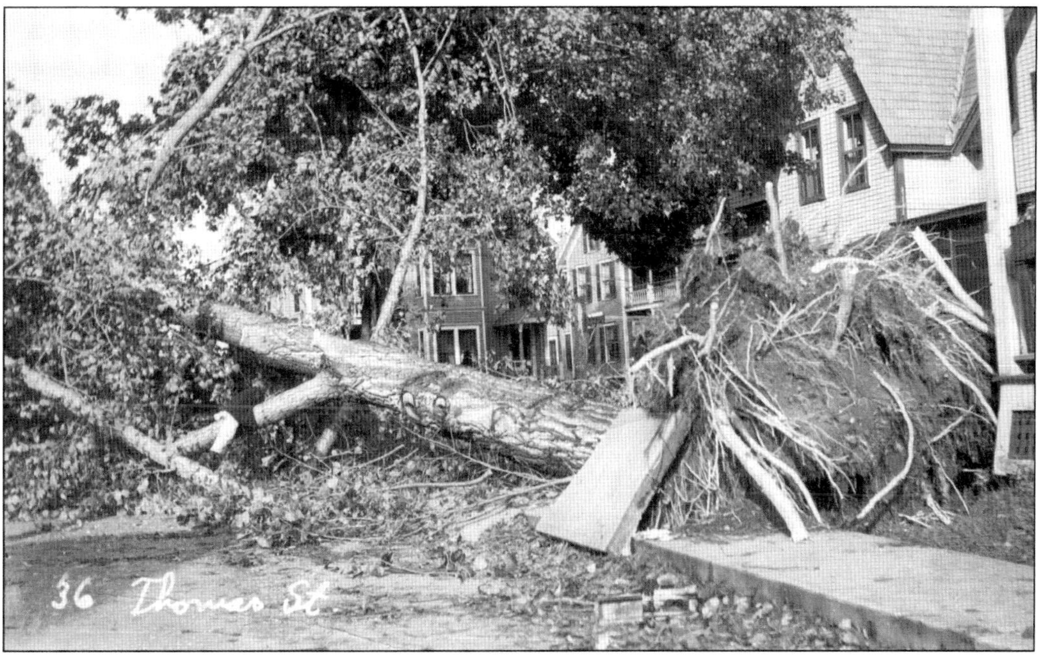

Many residential streets were blocked by uprooted trees and fallen power lines during the 1938 hurricane. Thomas Street, in the Prospect Hill section of town, was a good example of the devastation. An observer climbs among the tree branches to check damage or to find an alternative path since the sidewalk had disappeared.

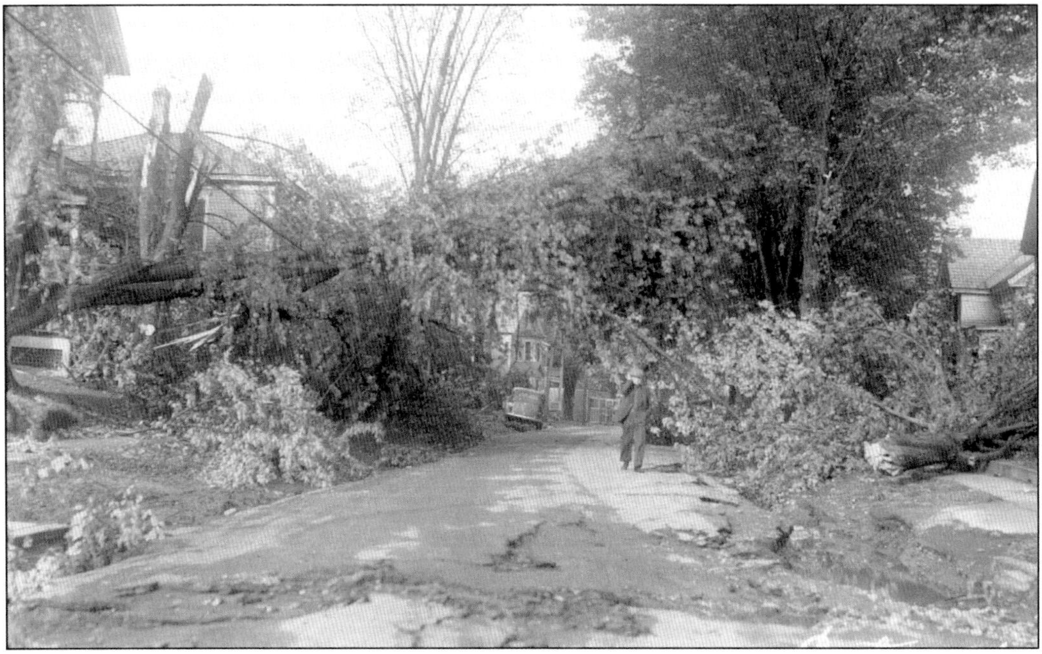

A sole pedestrian makes his way along Frost Street to check the damage in the aftermath of the hurricane. Treetops littered the roadway and splintered trunks reached skyward on one side of the street while the trees on the opposite side emerged unscathed.

pair of new rubbers to put over my shoes because of the inclement weather. We lived on the corner of Estey and Organ Streets. As he made his way up Estey Street Hill to our home, he had to pass the row of garages that housed the automobiles of some of the organ company employees. He rested there for a short time, as he was fighting the wind and rain. When he arrived home, he went into the dining room and sat in his rocking chair, which was in the bay window facing the route he had just traveled. To his great surprise, the roofs of many garages were on the sidewalk that he had barely climbed.

We sat in great wonderment of the severity of this storm. The Lord above was with him. A lot of damage had been done to the town of Brattleboro in a very short time.

—*Elfleda Pike*

DOUBLE-CLUTCHING

The Elks Club in Brattleboro sponsors an Elks Youth Day that enables high school students to be assigned to various government and related jobs in the community. This program was in existence when I was a high school senior, and I was made chief of the Brattleboro Fire Department for one day. After graduation, I applied for a temporary firefighter's job with the department and planned to leave after the summer. This did not happen, because a permanent firefighters job became available and I applied and got it.

The first fire I responded to was on Stark Road, and I had to drive the department's 1957 Mack fire truck. It was a pumper and held 500 gallons of water but did not have any baffles in the tank to keep the water from sloshing around, which made the truck unstable on turns. It had a capacity to pump 750 gallons per minute, compared to today's trucks that not only have baffles but have a pumping capacity of 1,500 to 2,000 gallons per minute.

The most memorable part of that ride was that it was a first-time experience. While I had practiced driving that old Mack, this was the real thing, and I did not want to screw up. It had no mufflers and made one heck of a racket, which I could sure hear sitting behind the wheel in its open cab. The steering wheel was huge because the truck had no power-assisted steering, and the large wheel gave the driver the leverage needed to turn the front wheels on this heavy vehicle. I had to keep in mind that if I took a turn too fast, the weight of the water would shift and might cause the truck to roll over. It did not have syncromesh transmission, which meant that when I shifted the gears, I had to depress the clutch pedal another time as I shifted from one gear to neutral and then to the next gear, hence the term double-clutching. When I didn't do this just right, everyone riding the truck heard those gears grinding. Fortunately, the fire was extinguished quickly and there were no injuries. But I sure remember how I was trembling after we got there, and how hard I tried not to show it by getting involved with fighting the fire.

As Brattleboro's fire chief, I see today's kids in the Elks Youth Day program, and I can't help but remember how it got me involved with firefighting and that great old Mack pumper.

—David Emery

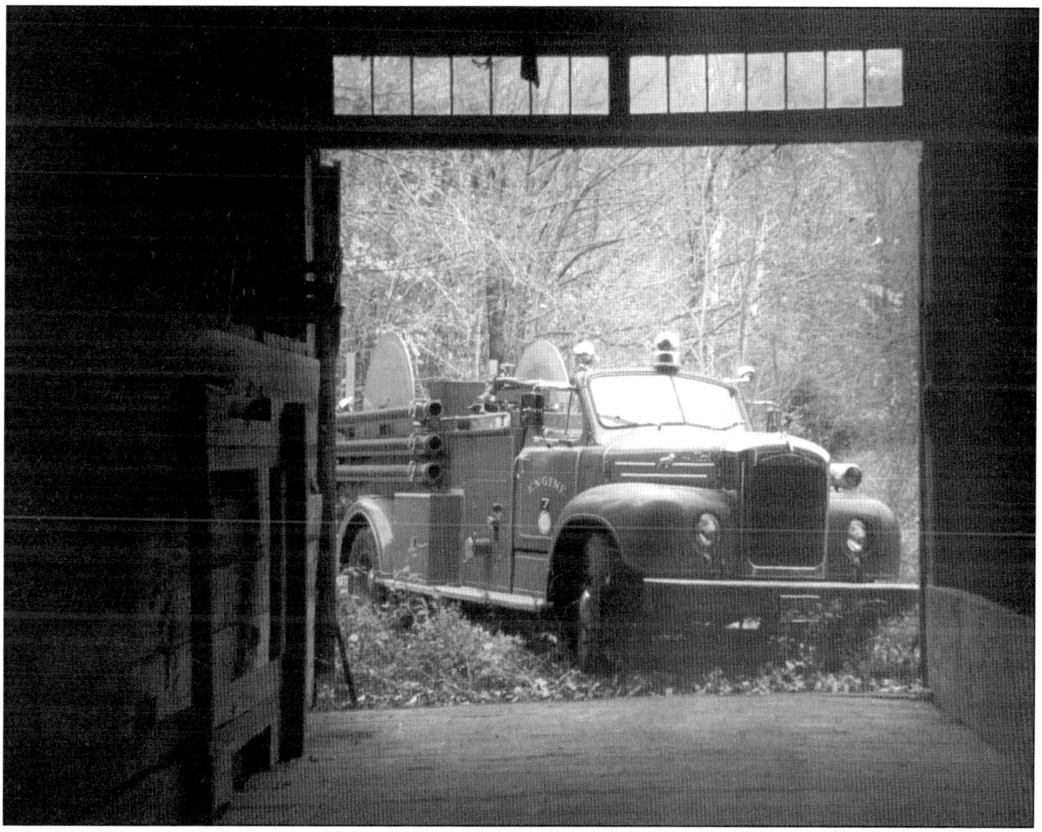

A former piece of the Brattleboro Fire Department's equipment, a 1957 Mack B model pumper, rests in retirement, no longer answering the call.

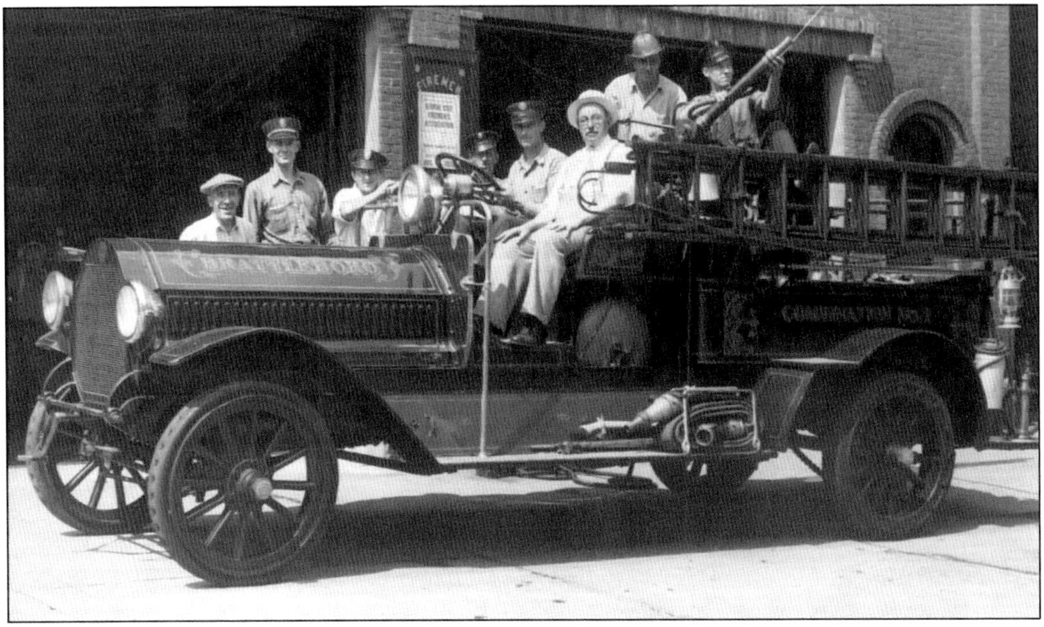

Prior to 1949, the Brattleboro Fire Department's central station was located on Elliot Street near the Harmony Lot entrance. Identified firefighters in the photograph, from left to right, are Dick Goodell (second), Tony Roitero (fourth), Phillip L. White (seventh), and Lawrence Thomas (eighth).

Waiting for the Dispatcher's Call

Firefighting has changed a lot over the years. We called the old guys smoke-eaters. John Wheelden was such a firefighter. You'd be dying, and he'd walk in a burning building without a pack on, cool as a cucumber and always with a cigar in his mouth. Today we are expected to have formal training and pass proficiency examinations before we can join the department. Technology has helped a lot; thermal imaging cameras, reflective markings on the gear, and radio communication are used today. No one would even think of entering a burning building without a pack on.

We still have to deal with the unexpected, like the fire at the Renaud building at the Estey Organ complex on the first day of deer season. We thought we were jinxed for a while because for three or four years we had a fire every New Year's Eve or Day. In the winter we are used to working under a turtle shell of ice. The water mist just freezes on everything. And then we get a real surprise and have to deliver a baby. Mark "Sparky" Robinson, Chris Pollica, Mike Bucossi, Tom Barrows, and Marty Rancourt are some of the guys who have earned a Stork Pin for their efforts. We get 130-plus hours' emergency medical training, and delivering babies is part of that program.

Firefighting used to be a man's domain, but that has all changed, and here in Brattleboro we have two women firefighters, Lisa Barry and Lynette Hamilton. We have all passed the same test. They are good at their job and are considered an equal part of the team. We did have to make some accommodations, like putting a lock on the shower area and stop walking around in our underwear in the sleeping area, but that wasn't a problem.

—Capt. Peter Lynch, Lt. Mark Geno
—Firefighters Allyn Olney and John Hill

CHAPTER EIGHT
THREE R'S

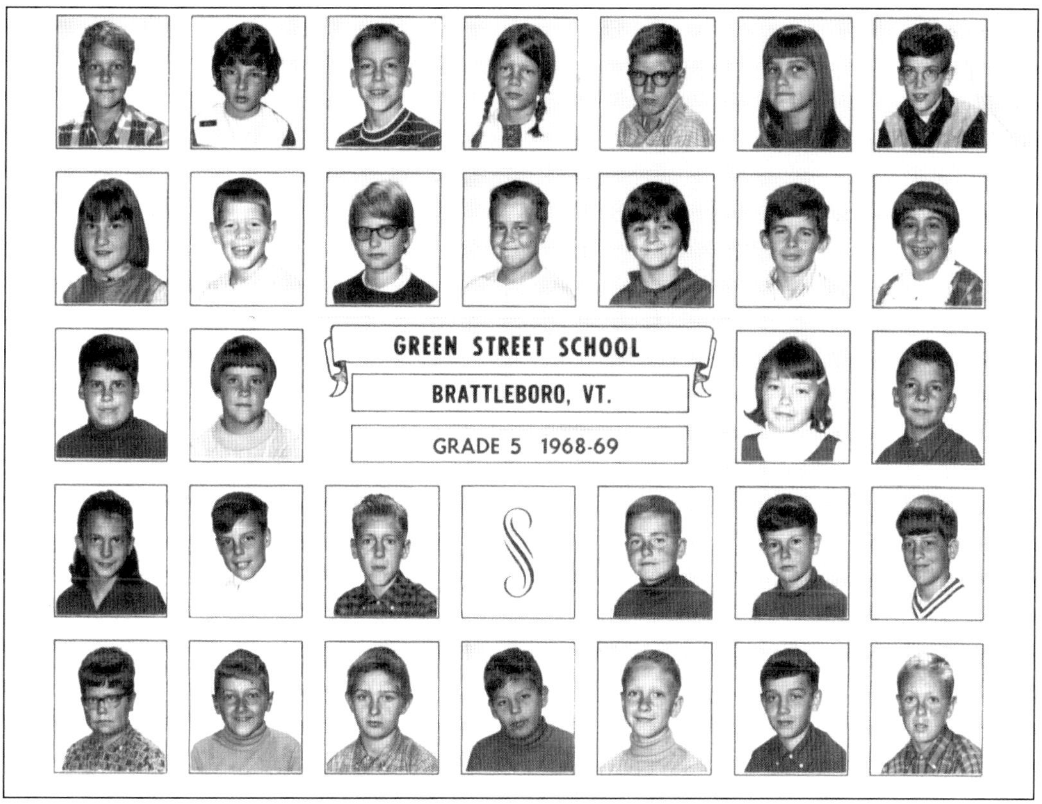

Smile for the camera and become part of the annual class picture. The students in this group have almost completed the elementary grades at Green Street School, with only one year left in their neighborhood school before heading off to the larger middle school. Hopefully, with mastery of the three R's and other subjects, these young people will go on to successful lives and careers.

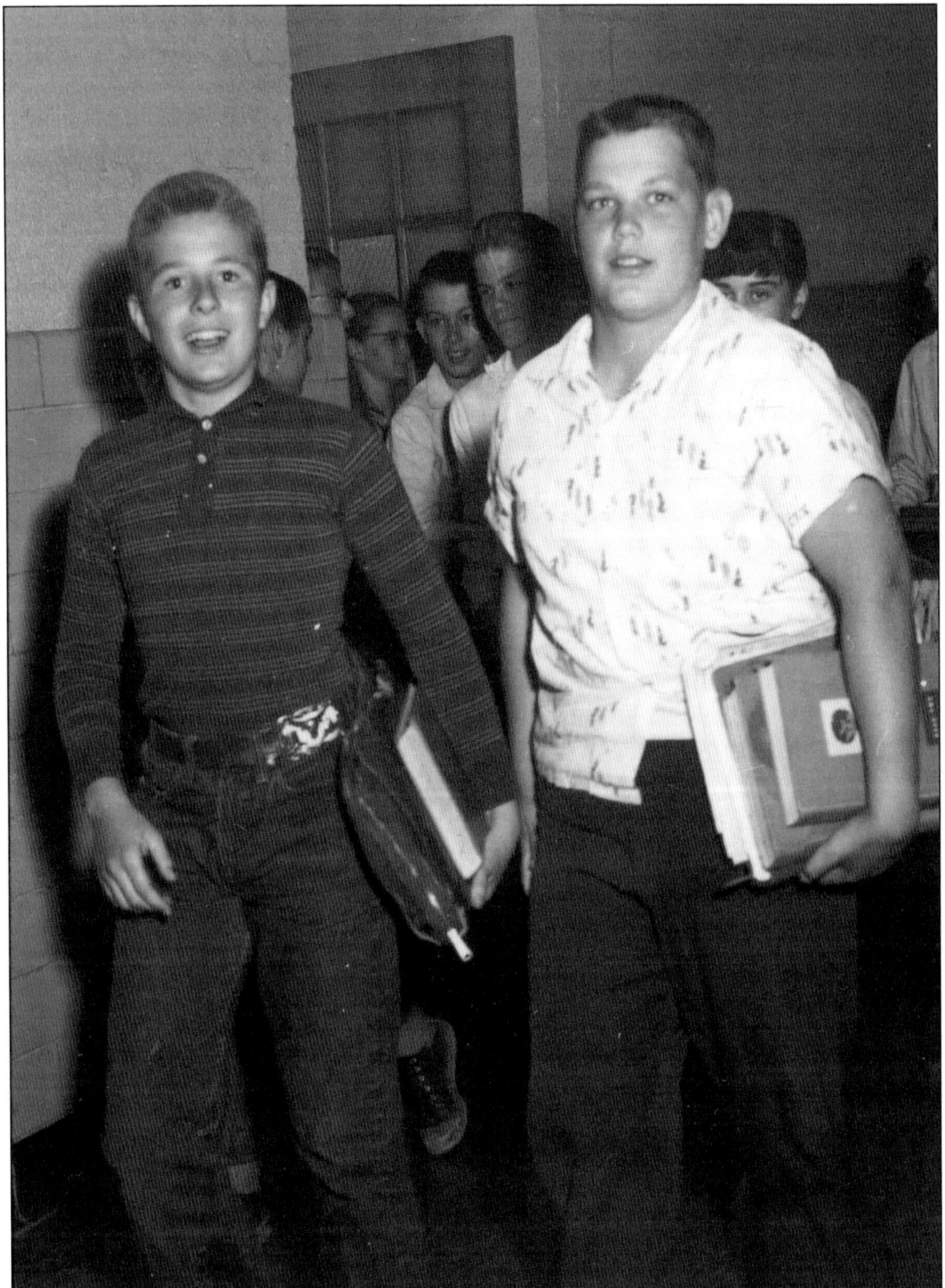

Brattleboro High School students moved into their new facility on Fairground Road in the fall of 1951. The modern structure, with increased space, new equipment, and close proximity to the athletic fields, generated smiles of appreciation as students and faculty anticipated the new school year.

School Mischief

Kids had more respect in those days. We never pulled fire alarms or bomb threats, and the school was never locked.

It was closed campus back then, meaning you were in the building 8:00 a.m. to 2:17 p.m., and you were either in class or in study hall.

Now, you can leave school if you don't have a class, and I think it makes it more confusing for everyone. If you see a student on the street, are they there because they don't have a class, or are they skipping school?

We had one of the last senior parties, and back then the drinking age was 18. It was tempting not being able to drink having friends in school who could, but being involved in athletics helped a lot. The people in my social circle had different commitments.

We weren't all goody-goody though; we had harmless fun. During homecoming there used to be a big pep rally every year. The junior class was in charge of stealing outhouses to put on top of the bonfire.

Everyone in town just kind of assumed this would happen, and most were OK with it just as long as kids didn't destroy any other property. It was all fun until someone came with a chemical toilet that was quite a bit more expensive than a wooden outhouse!

They don't have the homecoming bonfire anymore, after the trouble they had with gangs hanging around it a few years ago. It's a shame because it was a great thing to do in the fall. It was a tradition, a real coming together of the school. We would have a big car caravan through town down Main Street.

There was always a strong rivalry between Brattleboro and Keene [New Hampshire]. The game would alternate locations each year. Inevitably, a group of kids from Brattleboro would go over to Keene and spray-paint the fields or the buildings purple and white, or kids from Keene would come over and spray-paint Brattleboro black and orange.

—Barbara Vinci

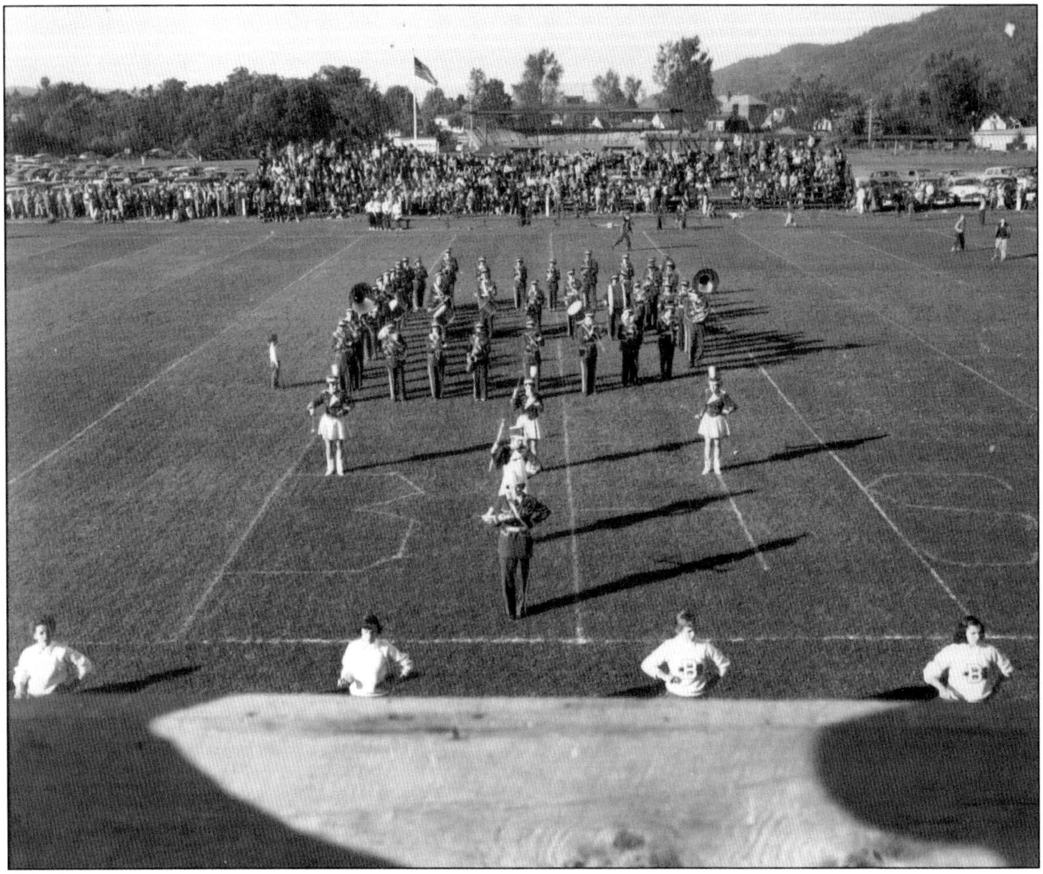

Members of the Brattleboro Union High School band and cheerleaders practice their marching routines on the football field prior to a big game.

PLAYING IN THE BAND

My folks, especially my mom, who played the piano, wanted all four of us kids to play a musical instrument. My dad wanted me to play the accordion in addition to the clarinet. I think my brother played a trumpet or a baritone saxophone, I am not sure, but it was sure a loud instrument. I remember my first accordion recital was a major bust. I was about 13 years old, and when I got on the stage, I just stood there. I was never so frightened in my life. After that I stayed with the clarinet.

When I entered high school, I was asked by "Doc" Forbes, the music teacher, if I wanted to play the bass clarinet. It wasn't all that different from the B-flat clarinet that I had been playing at the time, so I agreed.

All the band members were given wool uniforms that were OK except when they got wet, which they did at some of the football games when the heavens opened up. Boy, could they smell. We played at halftime and impressed ourselves perhaps more than we did the crowd by forming a large letter B in the middle of the field. We also played at basketball games and pep rallies.

Another memory that stands out during my time at the Brattleboro High School was when my girlfriend pierced my ears during homeroom. We accomplished this by sitting in the back of the room. She had

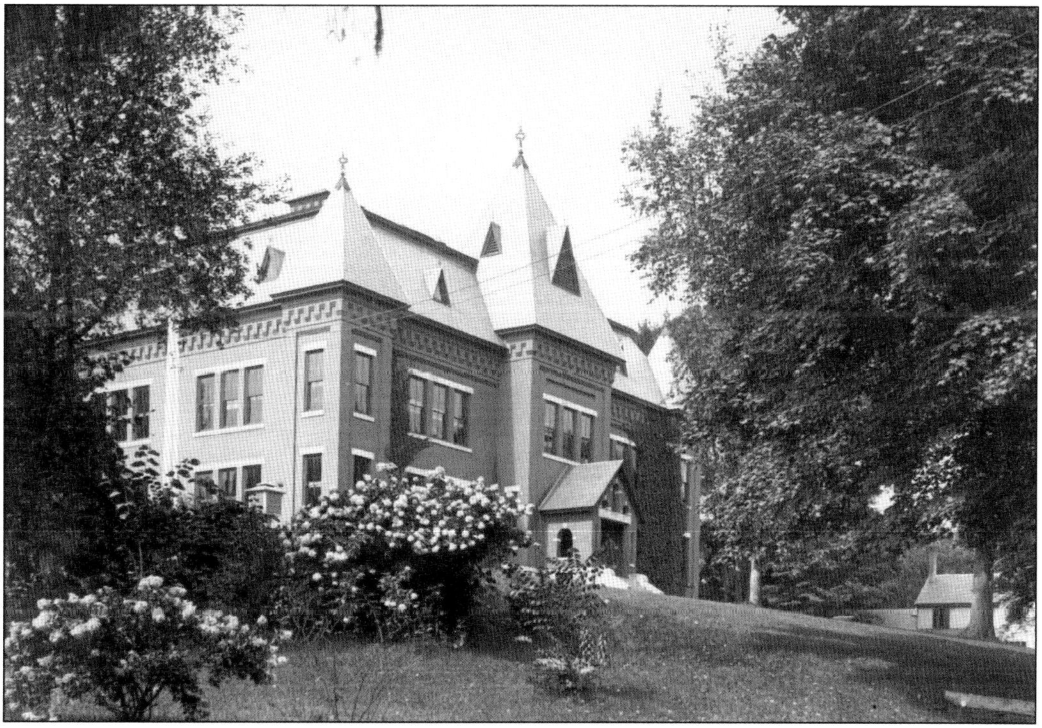

Until 1951, Brattleboro High School students attended classes in the building constructed in 1883 at the north end of Main Street. No longer needed for education, the structure was converted to the Municipal Center.

brought some ice cubes in from home and placed a cube behind my earlobe and stuck a needle all the way through. Then she placed the earring in. I remember being careful to not cry out, for fear of being caught by the teacher.

—Cynthia Green

Passing Through

Between 1980 and 1982, when I was in fifth and sixth grades, I would walk to school every day from my house on High Street to Walnut Street. The Brattleboro school system rented the third floor space from St. Michael's and used it as the overflow for the Green Street School. On my trips to and from school, I would cut through the Municipal Center. The building was a nice break from the weather: cool in the late spring and warm in the winter. My mom's friends Andi and Emmy worked in the finance department (then on the first floor). I would always pop my head in to say hello to them. If I stayed longer and chatted, I would have to take my coat off. I would say to them, "How can you stand to work in this building? It is so hot in here."

In the afternoons, when there was no snow on the ground, I would continue straight out the back of the parking lot and sneak through Tim and Martha O'Connor's backyard. In the fall and spring, it was like an enchanted forest back there. Their house is big and castlelike to an 11-year-old. There were flowering trees and a pussy willow tree back there. I would very carefully (so no one would notice although they could have been watching me from the house for all I knew) break off one branch from the pussy willow to rub across my face for the rest of the walk home.
In August of 1988, the year I had graduated

from high school, I applied for and was hired as a floater clerk for the town of Brattleboro. It never occurred to me that the building might not be any cooler then as it was six years prior to that. It was only after I worked here for a while that I remembered how terribly hot it was in here. Thirteen years later I am now assistant town clerk, and I have a fan on my desk to combat the heat.

—Melissa Snow Murphy

Green Street School

I attended Green Street School grades one through six. Some of my favorite teachers, I realized in later years, were those I had while attending Green Street. There was Mrs. Averill, who taught science, and Mrs. Marion, who taught sixth grade. It was Jeannie Marion who taught me about penmanship and cursive writing. Today, whenever I do any of my calligraphy work, I think about how I learned to form basic cursive letters from Mrs. Marion.

The playground behind the school was much smaller than what it is now, but being of grade-school age, it seemed to be immense then, with so many places to explore.

I had attended Power's House Kindergarten, next door to Green Street but located up on the hill. There, I learned about all the wonderful different toppings one could dream up to put on baked potatoes—peanut butter and raisins were a favorite!

I had my first serious crush on a boy while in fifth grade at Green Street; his name was Stuart, and he was a dream. It wasn't until we had been out of high school for about 15 years that I admitted this to him when we met at a reunion! How shy I was!

The auditorium at Green Street School served as not only cafeteria space, while I attended school there, but also as our indoor playground when weather was too foul outside.

For a period of time, Mr. Ross was principal of Green Street. I had never heard of nor seen a Nehru-cut jacket before I met Mr. Ross. He wore this jacket style regularly. On rainy days, he would collect the entire

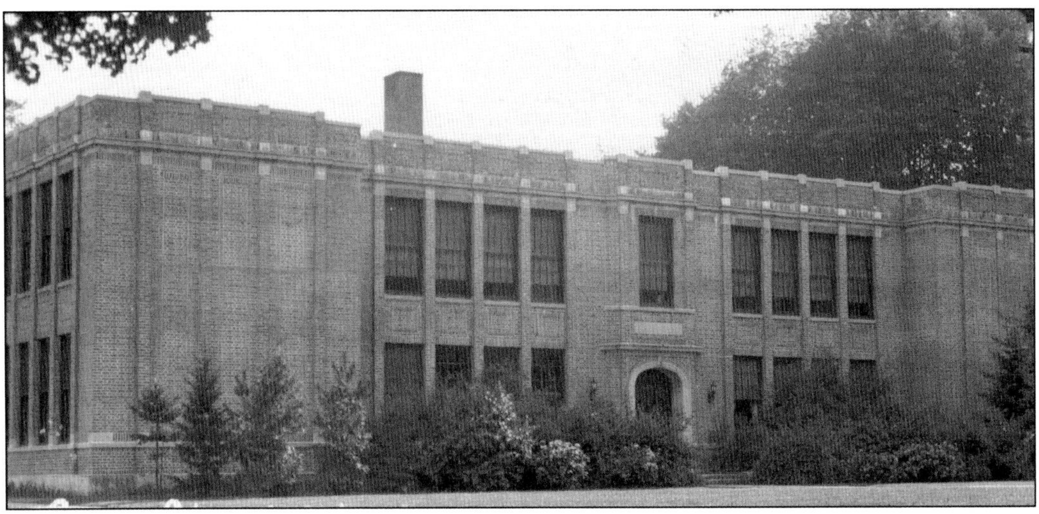

The Green Street School, located on land once owned by Alonzo Hines, was dedicated in the fall of 1925. Before the advent of middle schools, classes for kindergarten through eighth grade were housed in the building. In more recent times, the grade levels were limited to kindergarten through sixth.

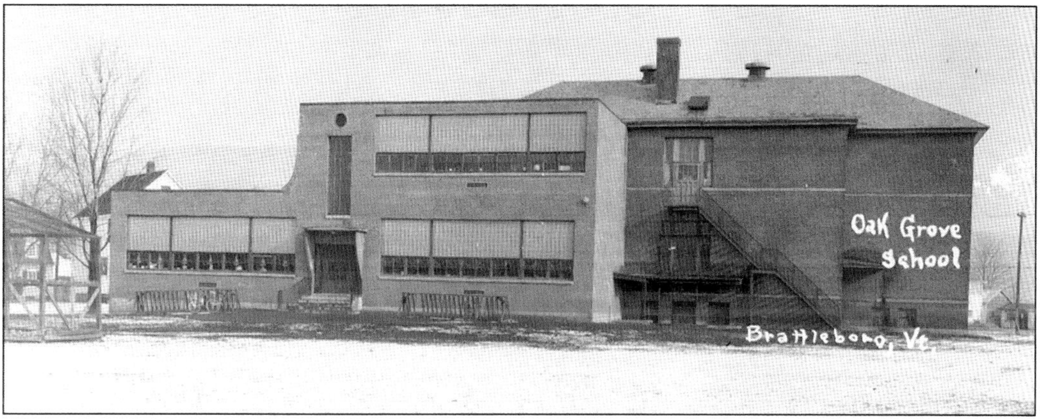

Since 1912, the Oak Grove School, on Moreland Avenue, has served the educational needs of children in the southern section of town. There have been several additions to the original building to accommodate the changing requirements of education.

school, or so it seemed then, into the auditorium space, and he'd teach us songs. One of the tunes I remember us learning was "There's a Hole in My Bucket, Dear Lila." Mr. Ross's musical talent and artistic flair made recess exciting, and we often hoped it would rain just so we could join in on a song we'd already learned or have fun learning a new one. Ah, the innocence of youth!

—*Darlene Gladke Bialowski*

Oak Grove School

This picture is more recent than when we were there. In 1937, there were four rooms and five grades with about 150 kids. In the lower left room was the first grade with Mrs. Lilian Dodge. The lower right was the third grade with Mrs. Edith Douglas. The upper right was the second grade with Miss Elinore Holden, and the upper left were the fourth and fifth grades with Mrs. Frances Mack. To get to the auditorium, you entered the building and went straight back. We had music once a week with Mrs. Eastman, and Mrs. Marsh, the nurse, also came once a week.

Our second-grade teacher was Elinore Holden. She had a Ford with a rumble seat. She was a soft-spoken, sweet teacher. She lived with her mother and two sisters. Her fiancé was in the air force. One day she told us all to go outside because he was going to fly over. At 1:00, we went out into the yard and over he flew and tipped his wings. She had her wedding gown made out of his parachute.

Mrs. Frances Mack taught fourth and fifth grades in one room. She was stern but soft. You never heard a peep out of anyone, even though there were 45 to 60 kids in the class. Milk was available for lunch for 5 cents. Mrs. Mack would always give leftover cartons to the children who couldn't afford it. It was delicious.

We remember that we were not allowed to step on the front lawn. One day after school, some kids went out and played on it. Mrs. Florence Wellman, the principal, found out, and she gave us all a lecture.

Another thing I remember is the bathroom, which was in the basement. It was like a dungeon, but we weren't scared.

At Christmastime, we were always given a box of animal crackers and an orange. We don't know who gave them to us, but they were much appreciated by everyone.

—*Regina Witalis* and *Margaret O'Connell*

AUTHOR INDEX